The Romans: An Introduction

The Romans: An Introduction 2nd edition is a concise, readable, and comprehensive survey of the civilization of ancient Rome. It covers more than 1,200 years of political and military history, including many of the famous, and infamous, personalities who featured in them, and describes the religions, society, and daily life of the Romans, and their literature, art, architecture, and technology, illustrated by extracts in new translations from Latin and Greek authors of the times.

This new edition contains extensive additional and revised material designed to enhance the value of the book to students especially of classical or Roman civilization, Roman history, or elementary Latin, as well as to general readers and students of other disciplines for whom an understanding of the civilization and literature of Rome is desirable. In particular, the chapter on religions has been expanded, as have the sections on the role of women and on Roman social divisions and cultural traditions. There is more, too, on the diversity and administration of the empire at different periods, on changes in the army, and on significant figures of the middle and later imperial eras.

New features include a glossary of Latin terms and timelines. Maps have been redrawn and new ones included along with extra illustrations, and reading lists have been revised and updated. The book now has its own dedicated website packed full of additional resources: www.the-romans.co.uk.

Antony Kamm is a former lecturer in publishing studies at the University of Stirling. His other publications include *Collins Biographical Dictionary of English Literature* (1993), *The Israelites: An Introduction* (Routledge 1999), and *Julius Caesar: A Life* (Routledge 2006).

Also by Antony Kamm

THE ISRAELITES: AN INTRODUCTION

JULIUS CAESAR: A LIFE

THE ROMANS:
An Introduction

Second Edition

Antony Kamm

Routledge
Taylor & Francis Group

LONDON AND NEW YORK

First published in 1995
by Routledge

Second edition published in 2008
by Routledge
2 Park Square, Milton Park, Abingdon, Oxon OX14 4RN

Simultaneously published in the USA and Canada
by Routledge
270 Madison Ave., New York, NY 10016

Reprinted 2009 three times, 2010 (with corrections)

Routledge is an imprint of the Taylor & Francis Group, an informa business

© 1995 and 2008 Antony Kamm

Typeset in Avenir and Amasis by
Keystroke, 28 High Street, Tettenhall, Wolverhampton
Printed and bound in Great Britain by TJ International Ltd, Padstow, Cornwall.

British Library Cataloguing in Publication Data
A catalogue record for this book is available from the British Library

Library of Congress Cataloging in Publication Data
A catalog record for this book has been requested

ISBN10: 0–415–45824–2 (hbk)
ISBN10: 0–415–45825–2 (pbk)
ISBN10: 0–203–89508–8 (ebk)

ISBN13: 978–0–415–45824–5 (hbk)
ISBN13: 978–0–415–45825–2 (pbk)
ISBN13: 978–0–203–89508–5 (ebk)

For Eileen

CONTENTS

FIGURES AND TABLE

Table

MAPS

ACKNOWLEDGEMENTS

The original edition of this book was published in 1995, since when, through ten reprints, I have made small changes and corrections. The publication of this second edition has enabled me to expand or recast certain sections in the light of current teaching practices, and to reconsider the balance of the whole. I am especially grateful to the academics in the UK and USA who responded to my publisher's request for suggestions: notably Jeffrey Brodd, Garrett G. Fagan, Amanda Krauss, Richard LaFleur, Teresa Ramsby, Rebecca Resinski, and Alison Cooley, who also revised the reading lists.

The translation of Catullus (p. 156) was originally published by Rupert Hart-Davis; those of Horace (p. 157), Livy (p. 167), and Tacitus (p. 168) are published by Penguin, and of Virgil (p. 159) by Vintage.

In researching and obtaining new illustrations I have received outstanding help and generosity from Barbara McManus and Allan Kohl. Particular thanks are also due to Claus Grønne of Ny Carlsberg Glyptotek, to Robert Leacroft and Joanna Glaister for permission to reproduce their father's drawings, and to Todd Bolen. The chapter head image is reproduced with the kind permission of the Bibliothèque nationale de France.

My editor, Matthew Gibbons, drove all the way from Oxford to central Scotland to discuss with me the contents of the new edition and then, having done so, much like the Spaniard who travelled to Rome just to look at Livy, turned round and drove back home, all in one day. He has throughout been a positive fount of sensible suggestions. The production of the book has been eased by the contributions of his colleagues, Lalle Pursglove and Geraldine Martin, by the knowledgeable and sympathetic copy editing of Monica Kendall, and by the meticulous proof reading of Ian Critchley.

I have also benefited from the experience and classical knowledge of Andrew Wilson, whose generosity and technical skills have enabled the web-site version of this book to be available on line.

The publication of the sixth impression of this edition gave me the opportunity to incorporate additions and corrections suggested in print or in person by Salvador Bartera, Gisella Negrão Neto, and Ann R. Raia, to whom I am very grateful for their attention.

A.K.

A NOTE ON CLASSICAL LITERARY SOURCES

Readers will find that the text is interspersed with translations from classical sources, illustrating historical events or characters, legal and political issues, and aspects of social history. History is a branch of literature, a story constructed from a variety of historical (and archaeological) sources. Ancient historians and biographers were not too particular about the provenance of a piece of evidence, as long as it contributed to the vividness of the story they were telling or the slant they wished to put on it. Factual details were embellished for the same reasons, and speeches devised for dramatic purposes. Livy, Tacitus, and Suetonius are examples of such writers. Livy was writing over 500 years after some of the events he describes. Tacitus was much nearer; some events happened during his lifetime. The same is true of Suetonius, who had access to the imperial archives for his impressionistic studies of the early Caesars. Writers of history and biography such as these and others cited, were often, however, as concerned with transmitting a message to the reader as with strict accuracy, while representing ancient traditions as the bedrock of present society.

It should also be remembered that the earliest texts of these and other writers that we have are copies made several hundred years or more after their first publication, with attendant errors and emendations. Nor, in many cases, do we have anything approaching the complete writings of an author. Of Cassius Dio, for instance, a Roman historian writing in Greek, what survives are effectively twenty-five out of eighty books, together with medieval summaries of about forty further books.

Ancient historiographical sources should therefore be treated with caution; quotations are included here as examples also of how their authors thought, and wrote. We are on somewhat firmer ground, however, with poets, letter writers, and novelists whose works illuminate, or satirize, contemporary life. Their observations can enhance one's understanding of the Roman people and the times in which they lived.

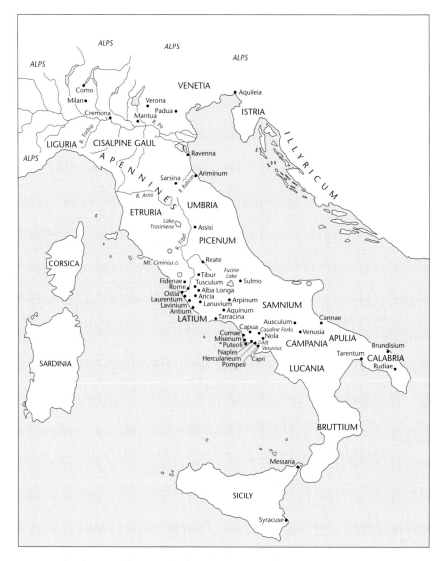

MAP 1 Italy: showing places and other geographical features mentioned in the book

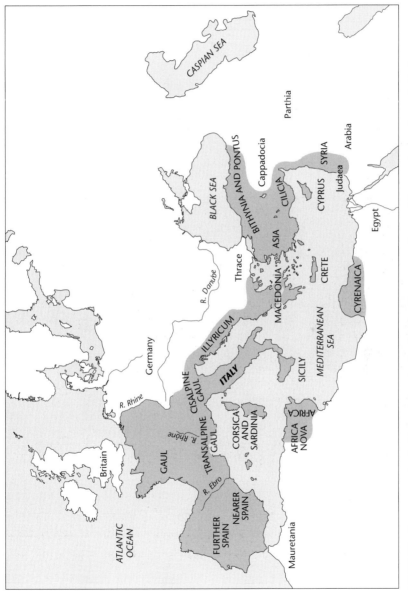

MAP 2 The Roman empire in 44 BC at the death of Julius Caesar: provinces of the empire are in capital letters

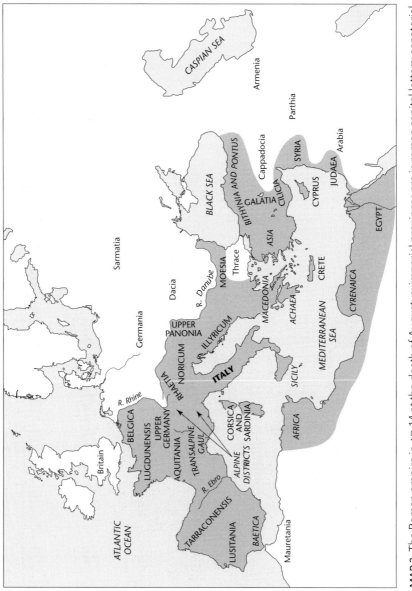

MAP 3 The Roman empire in AD 14 at the death of Augustus: imperial provinces are in roman capital letters; senatorial provinces are in italic capital letters

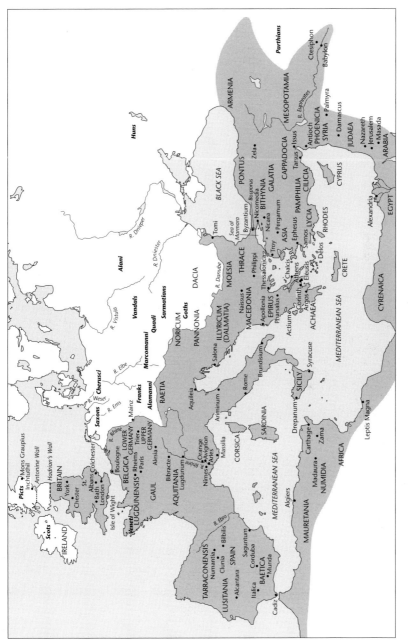

MAP 4 The extent of the Roman empire during the rule of Hadrian: including places and peoples outside Italy mentioned in the book

1 THE ORIGINS OF ROME

Whoever coined the epigram 'Rome was not built in a day' – and it was probably the sixteenth-century English dramatist John Heywood – established a permanent reminder that the Roman civilization was twelve hundred years developing, flourishing, and ultimately disintegrating. This is a considerable time in the history of thinking man: almost as long as from the Dark Ages in Britain and the establishment of Islam in Arabia to the present day, and over three times longer than the period since the foundation of the first English settlement in Jamestown, Virginia. It was, too, a thoroughly impressive epoch, which had, and still commands, a profound influence on western society.

The civilization of Rome owed most to ancient Greece, whose golden age is generally regarded as having lasted from about 490 BC to the death in 323 BC of Alexander the Great. The Romans were not great innovators. They learned what they could from others and then applied that knowledge to their own needs and purposes. They were dedicated and often ruthless in their pursuit of order and organization, and in the administration of their own brand of firm, but inherently benevolent, imperialism. The free-born Roman was not even a particularly hard worker. He did not need to be: there was an accepted convention in the ancient world that it was a mark of humanity to inflict slavery, rather than slaughter or maiming, as a penalty for those on the losing side in battle. Marcus Terentius Varro (116–27 BC), who is regarded as Rome's pre-eminent scholar, refers to slaves as a 'species of articulate farming stock', as opposed to 'inarticulate stock' (oxen) and 'dumb stock' (carts), in his agricultural treatise (I. 17). In the first century AD, it is probable that one in three of the population of Rome was a slave; this was also the proportion of black slaves to whites in the American South in the 1850s.

The Roman era can be divided into three parts. The years from the founding of the city of Rome until 510 BC, when the last of its kings was ejected, are known as the period of the kings. The republic of Rome effectively lasted from 509 until 27 BC, when

Augustus established legal precedents for absolute rule. This was the beginning of the age of imperial Rome, that is rule by emperors. In AD 476, the sitting emperor in Rome, Romulus Augustulus, was deposed by Odoacer, his German mercenary commander, who ruled Italy as king. That action brought to an end the Roman empire in the west. An eastern empire carried on into the Middle Ages, until it finally collapsed in 1453, when Constantinople was captured by the Turk, Mehmed II.

The Romans themselves were in no doubt when Rome was founded: 21 April 753 BC. Roman dates were calculated according to the number of years *ab urbe condita* (from the city's foundation, usually referred to as AUC). Annually, on 21 April, there was celebrated the traditional festival of the Parilia, in honour of Pales, the god (or goddess – the Romans sometimes expressed uncertainty about the gender of some of their deities) of shepherds and sheep. In 1948, traces of the huts of a settlement of shepherd folk dating from about 750 BC were found on the Palatine Hill, the central and most easily fortified of the seven hills of the ultimate city – the other six are the Capitoline, Aventine, Quirinal, Viminal, Esquiline, and the Caelian Mount. Later excavations have uncovered the remains of a ritual boundary wall of about the same period.

THE FOUNDING LEGENDS: ROMULUS AND AENEAS

The legend of the founding of Rome by Romulus was circulating at least by the beginning of the third century BC. It tells how a local king, Numitor of Alba Longa, was ejected by his younger brother, Amulius. To secure his position, Amulius then murdered Numitor's sons and forced Numitor's daughter, Rhea Silvia, to become a vestal virgin, thus, he thought, preventing her from having any children, at least for the time being. Vestal virgins normally served as priestesses in the temple of Vesta for thirty years from between 6 and 10 years old, and the penalty for failing to remain virginal was a singularly nasty death. Rhea Silvia, however, caught the lascivious eye of the god Mars, who had his way with her while she slept. The outcome of this unconscious but divine experience was twin sons, who were named Romulus and Remus.

There was a fine rumpus. Amulius had Rhea Silvia thrown into the river Tiber, where she sank conveniently into the arms of the god of the river, who married her. The twins were also consigned to the Tiber, but in a reed basket, which floated away until it was caught in the branches of a fig tree. They were suckled by a she-wolf (appropriately, for wolves were sacred to Mars) until the royal shepherd found them and rescued them. In another version of the story they were breastfed by his wife, a former prostitute, who had just lost a stillborn child – the Latin word *lupa* means both 'she-wolf' and 'prostitute'.

FIGURE 1 The bronze sculpture of the Capitoline wolf and twins is one of the most famous symbols of early Rome. The wolf (85 cm high) was believed until very recently to be Etruscan work from the end of the sixth or early fifth century BC. It was officially announced in July 2008 that carbon dating and other tests now gave an indication of a thirteenth-century date for the sculpture, with the suggestion that it was cast somewhere in the valley of the river Tiber. The figures of the boys were added in the fifteenth century.

Source: Deutsches Archäologisches Institut, Rome: Guidotti, Neg. D-DAI-Rom 1953.0434

The couple cared for Romulus and Remus and in due course revealed to them the circumstances of their birth. Amulius was killed in battle and their grandfather Numitor was restored to his throne. As a contribution to the ensuing celebrations, the brothers resolved to establish a new city near the spot where they had been washed ashore. They took auspices by watching the flight of birds, which indicated that the city should be built on the Palatine Hill, on which Romulus was standing, and that he should be its king. Romulus then set about marking the boundary with a plough drawn by a white cow and a white bull. Remus, either in fun or as a gesture of derision, committed the impropriety of jumping over the furrow. Romulus lost his temper and killed his twin.

The embryo city, still no more than a settlement, was rather short of women. Romulus invited the neighbouring Sabine tribe to a programme of games he was organizing to mark the harvest festival. When the guests were comfortably settled, the Romans, as they were now known, abducted at sword point 600 Sabine daughters, all but one of them, it is said, virgins. In an addition to the traditional story, they proved to be sterile until Juno, goddess, among other things, of child-birth, took a hand and sorted out the problem. Or it may be that the Sabine women, having suffered abduction, refused at first to co-operate with their self-styled husbands.

A further tradition, well known at least by 240 BC, traces the origins of Rome to the even earlier time of the legendary Trojan hero Aeneas, son of a mortal father and of the goddess Venus. He fought against the Greeks in the Trojan War, escaped from the sack of the city, and, after many wanderings, vicissitudes, and divine interventions, landed in Italy and founded the dynasty from which Romulus eventually came. This was the version of the story much favoured by the emperors of Rome, who liked to think of themselves as being nominally descended from the ancient heroes, and by the Romans themselves, who could thus see the early history of their city, which was one of continual struggle for survival, reflected in heroic legend. It was written up in verse by Virgil (70–19 BC), largely in response to the encouragement of Augustus, in the *Aeneid*, which was published posthumously. It is the national epic of the Roman empire, and the most famous poem of the Roman era.

According to the legend, and to Virgil, Aeneas cast anchor at the mouth of the Tiber.

> Now, Aeneas, looking out from the glassy ocean, sees a vast stretch of forest. The river Tiber's pleasant stream flows through it before bursting into the sea in swirling eddies made yellow by the copious sandy sediment. Above and all around, different kinds of birds indigenous to the river banks and reaches sweeten the air with song as they dart among the trees. Having ordered his companions to change course and steer for land, Aeneas is elated as he makes the river's shade.
>
> **(Aeneid, VII. 29–36)**

The Tiber flowed through Latium, whose king, Latinus, has divine intimation that he should hand over his daughter in marriage to a stranger. So he offers her to Aeneas, much to the discomfort of another local king, Turnus of the Rutuli, who fancies her for himself. Reluctantly drawn into war, Aeneas obtains the support of Tarchon, king of the Etruscans, and finally triumphs.

The historical sack of Troy was in about 1220 BC. To cover the period between the presumed arrival of Aeneas and the traditional date for the founding of Rome, the Romans invented a string of monarchs from Ascanius, son of Aeneas by his first (Trojan) wife, to Numitor. Though there is no firm tradition about Aeneas' death, there is an intriguing reference to a tomb by the Greek historian Dionysius of Halicarnassus, who lived in Rome at the very end of the first century BC:

The Latins built a hero-shrine to Aeneas, inscribing it to him as 'The god and father of this place, who guides the waters of the Numicius [a river in Latium]' . . . It is an earth mound, not very big, with trees set around it in regular rows – well worth seeing.

(Roman Antiquities, I. 64)

The shrine that Dionysius visited at Lavinium is almost certainly the seventh-century BC tumulus excavated in 1968. Originally it contained a burial chest, which was rifled about a hundred years later. The tomb was restored at the end of the fourth century BC.

So much for the legend. Historically, Latium and Etruria (land of the Etruscans) were crucial in the development of Rome into an autonomous and then an independent city state, though it is not known for certain where the original Latins and Etruscans came from. The Latins who first settled on the Palatine Hill, however, had been in the region since about 1000 BC. They herded sheep, goats, and cattle, and kept pigs. In the manner of such people, they lived in small scattered communities, in round or oblong huts made of wooden poles interwoven with twigs and branches and then covered with clay.

THE SITE OF ROME

The summit of the hill itself was roughly trapezoidal in shape, the longest side being about 400 metres long. On three sides, the rock sloped steeply down into valleys which were often full of floodwater. On the other, north-eastern, side, a narrow saddle of rock led to the adjoining hill. The cluster of hills, each between 60 and 100 metres high, stood on a plateau above the surrounding plain, the soil of which was continually enriched by deposits of volcanic silt from the Tiber and its tributaries. We may imagine, then, the summit of the Palatine Hill covered with clusters of small thatched huts of wood and clay, and somewhere a flat, open meeting space, the forerunner of the Roman forum. The burial place was in the marshy ground at the foot of the hill, where years later would stand the great forum of republican and imperial Rome. Only infants, and sometimes young children, appear to have been buried within the community.

The site was an inspired one for other reasons, too. The sea, with its potential for foreign trade, was only a few miles down stream. The hill overlooked the shallows which constituted the most convenient point for crossing the river as it neared the sea, and thus commanded the main route along western Italy. The city lay midway between the north and south of Italy, that natural formation of land enclosed by the Alps to the north, and by the sea everywhere else. Furthermore, Italy itself lay centrally in the Mediterranean, with ready access to the rest of Europe, to Africa, and to the east. Thus the fourteenth-century proverb, 'All roads lead to Rome,' was true from the start. At much the same time as the first settlement on the Palatine Hill, the Greeks were establishing seaports along the south and west coasts, and in Sicily. The port farthest north, and one of the first to be built, was Cumae on the Bay of Naples, within comparatively easy reach of Rome. Through these ports Rome had access to the Greek world; from the Greeks at Cumae, the Latins learned the Greek alphabet, which they adapted for their own use and language.

ETRUSCAN INFLUENCE

Etruria was immediately across the Tiber to the north. It was, unusually for the times, predominantly an urban society; its wealth came from trade and its supremacy through sea power. The Etruscans were given to extravagant but extraordinarily varied decoration and artistic display, and to the worship of gloomy gods, from which the Romans derived some of the more repulsive features of their religious observances and public entertainment. In much the same way as their culture, the Etruscans' political philosophy took its origins from the east and its direction from the Greeks, while developing on lines distinctive to Italy.

At some time between 650 and 600 BC, the Etruscans crossed the Tiber in force and occupied Latium. It would have been now that the villagers on the Palatine Hill joined up with settlers on the other hills to form one united community, either in an attempt to fend off the Etruscan invaders, or to be brought in line with the Etruscan policy of imperial government by means of autonomous city states. From this point until the establishment of the republic in Rome (assuming Romulus to have been as mythical as his origins lead us to suppose), we have the names of six kings: Numa Pompilius, Tullus Hostilius, Ancus Marcius, Tarquinius Priscus (Tarquin the Elder), Servius Tullius, and Tarquinius Superbus (Tarquin the Proud). While there is little doubt that all six existed – though the rule of six kings is not enough to fill the time-gap between the historical founding of Rome and the republic – the main events of the period are so entwined with folklore that it is difficult to assign many of them accurately to a particular reign.

UNDER THE KINGS

The Roman talent for empire building first emerged in the period of the kings, even though the original intention may have been to survive by aggression and by dominating the local scene. Territory gained provided additional fighting power, and the kings of Rome succeeded in subjugating a fair slice of land south of the Tiber. The most significant advance to a position of supremacy among Latin states came with the defeat of Alba Longa; destruction would be a better term, for nothing has been found of that city of a date later than the sixth century BC. With that victory, the Romans assumed precedence in religious affairs in Latium, for they then took over the administration of the sacred festivals which had for years been celebrated on the Alban Mount. Servius Tullius transferred the regional festival of Diana from Aricia to the Aventine Hill of Rome, where he built a shrine to her.

In this period, too, the roots of the later Roman constitution are to be found. The king was nominally appointed by the senate, an advisory body of patricians, members of a closed group of families of noble origins. He wielded much the same power over his subjects as that of a Roman head of family over his household, which included the right to inflict capital punishment. The king was also responsible for foreign relations and for war, for security, public works, justice, and the maintenance of religion. Wherever he went in public, he was accompanied by a band of attendants, or lictors, each carrying the *fasces*, a bundle of rods with an axe in the middle, signifying the punishments that could be meted out to criminals.

The concept of the father (Latin *pater*) was extended into the community at large. Each patrician family had its clients (from the Latin word meaning 'listener'), an extended body of hereditary hangers-on, who depended on the patricians for patronage and for economic support. In return for these favours they gave their labour and, in time of war, military service, in the same way as the villeins in medieval times. There was a sharp distinction between the patricians and their clients on the one hand, and the plebs, the common people, on the other. The community was divided, probably territorially, into three tribes, Ramnes, Luceres, and Tities, each responsible for providing 1,000 infantry and 100 cavalry in time of war, which occurred frequently. Each tribe was further divided into ten *curiae*, whose representatives were responsible for civil affairs, and met together as required by the king to discuss, but not to decide upon, matters of national importance. Servius Tullius is credited with reforming the army, to which he also gave the status of a political assembly, the *comitia centuriata*.

We are a far cry from the notion of a primitive people scratching the soil and herding rudimentary flocks. Not only were craftsmen plying their various trades from the start, but, under Numa Pompilius, they were properly represented by guilds, according to the first-century AD historian and biographer Plutarch: 'Numa divided the craftsmen according to their trades – flute-players, goldsmiths, carpenters, dyers, shoemakers, leather-dressers, potters, and workers in copper and brass. He created a further guild of all the other trades grouped together' (*Lives: Numa*, XVII). This diversity of crafts served a society which, unlike the Greeks, did not use money. Trade was conducted by barter (wood or wool for bronze, salt for pottery, grain for shoes, and so on) or, in cases where the system was inadequate, by expressing value in terms

FIGURE 2 The earliest Roman denomination of money was the *as*, a piece or bar of copper weighing one Roman pound. This bronze *decussis* (= 10 *asses*) of the third century BC reflects the stamped copper design of the period of the kings, and also the ox as the original monetary unit.

of head of cattle. A head of cattle (*pecus*) was the first Roman unit of value, from which came the Latin word for money (*pecunia*); one head of cattle was equal to ten sheep. Latterly during the period of the kings, a primitive monetary system evolved based on ingots of raw copper, weighed on a clumsy balance which probably measured only a single standard unit, the Roman pound (*libra*) of 327 grams. An ingot could then be broken up into lumps of different sizes and values. According to the historian and scientist Pliny the Elder (AD 23–79), 'King Servius first put a stamp on the copper; up until then, Timaeus [*c.* 346–*c.* 250 BC] says, they used raw metal. The stamped design was that of an ox or a sheep' (*Natural History*, XXXIII. 13).

The Etruscans had considerable skill in three aspects of building and civil engineering at which the Romans were to excel: road construction, hydraulics, and the use of the arch to bridge space – examples of Etruscan arches still survive at Volterra and Perugia. The idea for and planning of the great temple to Jupiter on the Capitoline Hill, 60 metres long and 55 metres wide, are attributed to Tarquinius Priscus, but his grandson Tarquinius Superbus supervised most of the building, calling up labour from Etruria as well as from Latium to get the job done. His zeal appears to have matched his pride.

> Having selected from the plebs those who were loyal to him and fit for military service, he put the rest to forced labour on public works. For he believed that kings were most vulnerable when the poor and needy were idle. He was also keen to

complete during his reign the projects left unfinished by his grandfather. These included extending the drainage system, on which digging had begun, and adding a colonnade all round the amphitheatre race-track, of which only the foundations had been built. The poor were set to work in return for a miserable ration of grain: quarrying stone, cutting timber, leading the wagons filled with these materials, or even themselves carrying the materials on their backs. Others were put to digging underground conduits, constructing arches and supporting walls for them, and assisting the various craftsmen, copper-smiths, carpenters, and stonemasons, all forcibly removed from their private businesses to labour for the public good.

(Dionysius of Halicarnassus, *Roman Antiquities*, IV. 44)

Pliny describes the dimensions of some of the underground sewers constructed at this time as 'large enough for a loaded hay-wagon to pass through' (*Natural History*, XXXVI. 24). The Cloaca Maxima (Great Sewer) of republican and imperial Rome was originally an open ditch, designed to drain the water from the valleys between the hills of Rome, including the ancient forum, and to collect the streams of other drains before discharging itself into the Tiber, where its arched exit can still be seen under the Ponte Palatino.

The Etruscans were also past masters at the art of delicate sculpture in terra-cotta. Tarquinius commissioned some Etruscan sculptors from Veii to fashion a chariot to stand on top of the new temple. According to Plutarch, when it was put into the furnace the clay, instead of contracting as the moisture evaporated, swelled up to such a size that the furnace had to be dismantled before the finished piece could be removed.

By the time the temple was finally completed, however, the period of the kings was over for good. Their fall, as told by Livy (59 BC–AD 17), is a rattling good story idealizing in Greek terms the removal of a tyrant and promoting Roman female virtues in a patriarchal society. Sextus, son of Tarquinius Superbus, inflamed by the chastity, beauty, and dedication to her domestic duties of Lucretia, wife of Collatinus, calls on her while her husband is away. Courtesy dictates that she should offer him a bed for the night, which he accepts. When all is quiet, he enters her bedroom, sword in hand. When she refuses his advances, he threatens to kill her, and to lay beside her corpse the naked body of a slave with his throat slit. Sextus will then tell the world that he caught them at it, and that he duly exacted the penalty. For Lucretia, to be reckoned to have committed adultery with a slave was a thought worse than death itself. She submits to Sextus who, having enjoyed her, rides away triumphant.

Lucretia is still technically guilty of adultery, which was during Livy's lifetime officially designated a crime for a woman of the upper class. She sends for Collatinus and for her father, whose authority, in Roman tradition, exceeded that of the husband.

In front of them, and witnesses, she confesses her guilt, demands reparation for Sextus' invasion of her body, and kills herself with a knife that she has hidden in her clothing. The challenge is immediately taken up not by her family, but by one of the witnesses, Lucius Junius Brutus. In Latin *brutus* means stupid, which, again according to Livy, Lucius Junius has pretended until now to be, in order to avoid the attentions of the tyrannical Tarquinius Superbus, who is his uncle.

The rape of Lucretia has proved a popular subject for art, literature, and even the stage, ever since, but, if it ever took place, there is no evidence that it was the cause of the fall of Tarquinius. It is more likely that the rebellion by a band of nobles, perhaps led by Lucius Junius Brutus, was the natural reaction of a society which, on the Greek model, was verging towards democratic government, against a monarch who had exceeded his constitutional brief and made himself even more unpopular by his imposition of forced labour. It is possible, too, that the conspiracy was part of a wider revolt by several Latin cities, including Antium, Aricia, and Tusculum, against a king of Etruscan origin.

Rome was not yet entirely free. Tarquinius escaped and naturally commanded the support of the Etruscans, one of whose chiefs, known as Porsena, occupied Rome for some time by force. To this campaign belong the legends of Horatius, who held the bridge against the advancing Etruscans, and of Mucius Scaevola, who plunged his right hand into the flames rather than reveal details of a plot to kill Porsena. The Etruscan leader, having previously survived one assassination attempt, was so unnerved by the thought of further ones, that he withdrew his garrison from the city in return for hostages.

> Now the women too were inspired to emulate Scaevola's example. When the Etruscans, purely by chance, camped close to the banks of the Tiber, the girl Cloelia, one of the hostages, tricked the guards and swam the river under a hail of missiles and javelins at the head of a group of other girls, all of whom she restored safely to their dear ones in Rome.
>
> When this was reported to Porsena, his first reaction was one of fury. He sent a deputation to Rome demanding that Cloelia be handed over; he said he didn't care about the others. Then, in admiration of a feat which he reckoned was more impressive even than Scaevola's, he announced that he would regard the treaty as having been broken if she were not handed over; if she were surrendered, however, he would send her back safe and sound.
>
> Both sides behaved honourably. The Romans returned their surety of peace according to the terms of the treaty: Porsena gave her not only his personal protection but also further recognition. He offered to send back with her a certain number of hostages of her choice. The story goes that when they were all paraded, she picked out only young boys, as being more appropriate to her maidenly

modesty. In the opinion of the other hostages this was sensible also in that it removed from the hostile environment those least able to look out for themselves.

(Livy, *History of Rome*, II. 13)

Whether this, and other romantic episodes, are truth or fiction, several sources state that Cloelia was subsequently granted the unprecedented honour, for a woman, of an equestrian statue, which used to stand at the head of the via Sacra in Rome. There are also, in the *Histories* of Tacitus (*c.* AD 56–after 117) and Pliny's *Natural History*, passing references to Rome, after the expulsion of the kings, capitulating to Porsena and then being forced to sign a treaty agreeing that they would not use iron implements except for agricultural purposes, not even for writing.

It would appear, however, that the war against other cities smouldered on until 505 BC, when Porsena's attempts to extend the hostilities were finally extinguished before Aricia by a force of Greek auxiliaries from Cumae, called up to bolster the Latin army.

In the meantime, Rome had become a republic.

FURTHER READING

Barker, G. and Rasmussen, T., *The Etruscans*, Blackwell, new edn 2000.

Cornell, T., *The Beginnings of Rome: Italy and Rome from the Bronze Age to the Punic Wars (c. 1000–264 BC)*, Routledge, 1995.

2 THE REPUBLIC

The Latin term *respublica* (from which comes the word 'republic') is usually translated as 'state' or 'commonwealth'. At no time was Rome a democracy (that is rule by the people) in the Greek, or true, sense. Its society was rigidly divided by legal status (free or enslaved) and by class. Free men or women were further classified, for example, according to whether they were so by birth or by release from slavery, were Roman citizens or Latins, or were independent or answerable to a guardian or other person in authority. The republic began, and finished, as a state largely dominated by the two upper ranks in the social hierarchy, the senators, who originally qualified by birth and wealth, and the equestrians or knights (*equites*), those in the second of the five categories to which people were allocated according to their means; until the second century BC, the latter were, by reason of their property holding, provided at public expense with a horse, with which they were required to report for military duty.

OFFICERS OF STATE AND ASSEMBLIES

The constitutional change from monarchy to republic was gradual. The main functions of the king, including full military command, were undertaken by two consuls with equal powers, elected for one year only. '[Lucius Valerius] Publicola [one of the original consuls] instituted the rule that the lictors should march in front of each consul on alternate months, so that the insignia of office should not be more numerous in the republic than under the kings' (Cicero, *On the Republic*, II. 31).

The *fasces* borne by the lictors symbolized the authority with which consuls or other very senior state officials were invested. The Latin word for this authority is *imperium*, of which a literal translation is 'power' or 'command': a more accurate modern rendering would fall somewhere between the two.

From 367 BC, one consulship was normally held by a plebeian. According to the scholarly Varro, the 'consul was so named because he "consults" the people and the senate' (*On the Latin Language*, V. 14). The consuls presided over the senate and over those assemblies which they were eligible to attend as members; they also could propose laws for consideration by the people. Their authority within the city was subject to *provocatio* (literally, a 'calling out'), whereby the people could formally appeal against a decision. In time of war, however, right up to the beginning of the first century BC, the consuls, by tradition, led the troops. When both consuls were on a campaign together, sole command alternated on a daily basis.

If the politics of the republic were about power, to achieve the consulship was also about prestige. To be, and to have been, consul was a privilege which was jealously guarded by leading families, on whom it conferred *nobilitas*, which can mean 'nobility', but also 'fame' or 'recognition'. The first of a family to achieve the highest office was referred to sneeringly as *novus homo*, 'new man' or 'upstart'.

The constitution allowed, however, that in time of crisis, and particularly in war, a single 'dictator' could be nominated who would exercise complete control for not more than six months. This was an ancient office whose origins lay in the appointment of one commander over the armies of several Latin city states. He was called 'master of the infantry', and even in republican times his second-in-command was known as 'master of the cavalry'.

In 356 BC, Gaius Marcius Rutilus became the first plebeian dictator, in charge of operations against a combined Etruscan force which had advanced into Roman territory as far as the ancient salt-works on the coast. The patricians put all sorts of difficulties in his way, but he marched his army out of the city, put it across the Tiber on rafts, captured the enemy camp by surprise, took 8,000 prisoners, and killed or drove away the rest. On his return the patrician-dominated senate denied him the statutory triumphal procession which he had earned, but the people took no notice and gave him his triumph all the same.

Matters of state religion were in the hands of the *pontifex maximus* (chief priest) – the literal meaning of *pontifex* is 'bridge builder'. This was an elected office, in the same way as those of other state officials, but with it in his case went an official residence in the middle of the forum. The *pontifex maximus* was responsible for the calendar, for presiding at state ceremonies, and for the nomination of vestal virgins and some priests. He also had disciplinary powers over the priestly classes.

As the tasks of government of state and empire grew, so other political offices were created.

Censor (Two): chief registrar, financial and tax officer, inspector of public works, and arbiter of public morality:

> Censors shall list all citizens, recording their age, antecedents, families, and
> means. They shall supervise the city's temples, roads, water system, treasury, and
> revenues. They shall divide citizens into tribes, and list them also according to
> wealth, age, and rank. They shall assign young men to the cavalry and infantry.
> They shall discourage the unmarried state, guard public morality, and suspend
> from the senate anyone guilty of improper conduct.
>
> **(Cicero, *On the Laws*, III. 3)**

The office was instituted in 444 BC; the first plebeian to hold it was Gaius Marcius
Rutilus in 351 BC. The post was usually restricted to those who had climbed the *cursus
honorum* (ladder of honour) from quaestor to consul. From the second century BC
elections took place every five years, to coincide with the taking of the census of
the people. A censor held office for only eighteen months, though his acts remained
in force until the next election. He had wide disciplinary powers. Aulus Gellius
(*c.* AD 123–*c.* 165), lawyer and antiquarian, describes some of these in a series of
wide-ranging essays, originally composed on a visit to Attica and completed some
years later for the edification and amusement of his children.

> Anyone who let his land grow wild and was not giving it enough attention, or had
> not ploughed it or weeded it, or had neglected his orchard or vineyard, did not
> go unpunished. It became a matter for the censors, who would reduce him to the
> lowest rank of citizen. In the same way, a knight whose horse looked skinny or was
> badly turned out was charged with negligence.
>
> **(*Attic Nights*, IV. 12)**

Praetor (Six after 197 BC): chief law officer and judge, and understudy to the consuls,
particularly in the administration of provinces (provincial governors were normally
drawn from the ranks of former consuls and serving or former praetors). The first
praetor was in 366 BC; about a century later a second was appointed, the two dividing
their responsibility for justice according to whether a suit was between citizens or
outsiders. The first plebeian praetor was in 337 BC. A praetor, in the same way as
consuls, dictators, and masters of the cavalry, was automatically invested with
imperium, and was preceded in public by six lictors.

Aedile (Four after 366 BC): supervisor of public works, temples, markets, and games.
Two at least were always plebeians.

Quaestor (Four after 421 BC, eight after 267 BC, and twenty from about 80 BC, during
the dictatorship of Sulla): assistant to the consuls, particularly as controller of the
military or the civic treasury, and as keeper of records. The minimum age was 25,

FIGURE 3 The early Roman coinage in certain respects still followed the principle established under the kings of currency being linked to weight. This *aes grave* (heavy bronze) *dupondius* (*c.* 265 BC) was worth 2 *asses* (represented by the two bars) and carries the head of Roma, the personification of the city. Actual size.

Source: Photograph © copyright Hunterian Museum and Art Gallery, University of Glasgow

to allow for the completion of military service. The first plebeian quaestor was in 409 BC.

While the existence of the various assemblies gives the Roman constitution an air of democracy, the senate was officially an advisory body, and in none of the other assemblies did members vote as individuals. Voting was by group or category according to the assembly's composition; the majority voice of a group represented a single vote. State officials (*magistri*) were elected by this means.

Senate: about 300 members up to the reforms in 82–79 of Sulla, who doubled the number. Nominations were originally automatic and by birth or rank; later they were made by the consuls and, after about 350 BC, by the censors. Plebeians were admitted during the fourth century BC, after which the senate became a body predominantly of men who had served as government officials. It did not pass laws so much as refer its advice (*senatus consultum*) to the popular assemblies. It had, however, complete control over finance, administration of the state and its empire, and relations with foreign powers. It also adjudicated on religious matters and acted as an intermediary between the Roman people and the gods.

Comitia curiata: an assembly of representatives of wards, comprising a tenth part of each of the three original tribes of Rome; it was the original people's council at the time of the kings. It formally ratified the election of consuls and acted as a court of appeal. In the fourth century BC its functions were largely assumed by the *comitia centuriata*.

Comitia centuriata: originally the assembly of representatives of military units (centuries). It was reconstituted into 193 centuries, to which eligible voters (all Roman citizens) were allocated according to their means. Each century comprised an indefinite and variable number of members. Ninety-eight of the votes (that is, a majority) were in the hands of the eighteen centuries of equestrians and the eighty representing the top of the five property bands. The assembly elected senior state officials, declared war, instituted peace treaties, approved legislation, and, until the function was completely transferred to the courts, had the final say in cases of execution or exile.

Concilium plebis (meeting of the people): the original plebeian parliament, sitting and voting in thirty-five tribal or district divisions. It elected its own officers and formulated decrees (*plebiscita*) for observance by its own kind which, after 287 BC, could be made binding on the whole community.

Comitia tributa (tribal assembly): organized in tribes in the same way as the *concilium plebis* but open to all citizens. It elected minor officials and was a means of approving legislation on a different voting basis to that of the *comitia centuriata*.

THE CONFLICT OF ORDERS

At the outset of the republic, the aristocrats by birth who were known as patricians had not only the means and inclination to exercise government, but all the power as well. The bid by the plebs for rights with which to improve their lot was accompanied neither by revolution nor violence, but by passive resistance and collective bargaining. One major concession was the creation in about 494 BC of the office of *tribunus plebis* (tribune of the people), to be a convenor of the popular assemblies and to present the people's grievances to the consuls or senate. A tribune had extraordinary powers. Whereas a government official could quash an act of a colleague of equal status, a tribune of the people could hold up almost any business of state, including actions of officials and resolutions of the senate, merely by pronouncing a veto (Latin, 'I forbid'). He was required to be on call day and night, to any citizen who required help. Cicero, who was an equestrian by birth, describes the initial process of change in one of his political dialogues:

> Quite soon, in the sixteenth year of the republic, something happened which by the nature of things was inevitable: the people, freed from the rule of kings, claimed rather more rights for themselves. There was perhaps some justification for this, yet often it is in the very nature of a republic to contradict the justifiable. Remember what I said at the beginning: unless a state maintains a balance of rights, duties, and functions, so that state officials possess enough power, deliberations of the leading citizens enough authority, and the people enough freedom, it is not possible for it to remain stable. At a time when the community was in financial difficulties, the plebs occupied first the Sacred Mount [5 km outside the city], and then the Aventine Hill itself. Just as the disciplinary measures of Lycurgus could not keep even Greek citizens in check, and in Sparta in the reign of Theopompus five officers called ephors and in Crete ten *cosmoi* were appointed to act as opposition to the monarchy, so the plebs elected its own tribunes to represent its rights in the face of the power of the consuls.
>
> **(*On the Republic*, II. 33)**

As the plebeians achieved political and military prestige which entitled them to be classed as aristocracy, some of the great patrician families began to fall behind. A new ruling class emerged, distinguished by families, in addition to the patricians, whose members had acquired *nobilitas*. Nobles bred nobility, and by the third century BC the lists of consuls and priests are dominated by similar names from the same families. Members of the nobility exercised their power through wealth, intrigue, and the system, which appears to have gone back to the period of the kings, whereby armies of dependent clients were collected, and protected, by patrons. The nobility effectively controlled the senate and, through patronage, influenced the election of officers of state, who included the holders of religious posts.

THE TWELVE TABLES

Another significant development in breaking down the class conflict between patricians and plebs was the appointment in 451 BC of the *decemviri*, a committee of ten, to refine, standardize, and record a statutory code of law. Until then the law had been the prerogative of the patricians, who administered judgements on the basis of what was customary, or manipulated it to suit themselves. The result of the deliberations, known as the Twelve Tables, was engraved in copper and permanently displayed to public view. Infuriatingly enough, and perhaps largely because these laws became so well known that three centuries later schoolboys were required to chant them in class by rote, only a few fragments and references survive. They clearly constituted, however, a condensed set of rules for public, private, and political behaviour, covering in each case a variety of circumstances within a precise format.

Thus, if a defendant in a civil case refused to appear in court, the plaintiff could apply physical force to get him there; if the defendant was too old or ill to attend, the plaintiff must provide transport. Anyone caught stealing at night could lawfully be killed by the owner of the property. By day, other regulations applied. If the thief was a free man, he was to be flogged and bound over to the injured party; if a slave, flogged and thrown over the Tarpeian Rock; if under the age of puberty, flogged and required to make reparation.

There were laws governing hygiene and fire-risk (no burials or cremations within the city limits), and the upkeep of roads (the responsibility of those on whose property they bordered). There was a statutory maximum rate of interest on loans. Anyone confessing or adjudged to be a debtor had thirty days in which to pay; after that he could be sold into slavery by his creditors or, according to Aulus Gellius, carved up into proportionate pieces. There was a fixed penalty for assault (with a reduction if the victim was a slave). Stealing crops was a capital offence: so was slander (by clubbing to death). We do not know what penalty was prescribed for murder, only that according to Pliny the Elder it was lighter than for stealing crops. There was a distinction between intentional and accidental homicide: Cicero illustrated it by comparing a javelin which has been aimed to one which has simply 'slipped from the hand' (*Topica*, XVII. 64). It was a criminal offence to cast a spell on anyone by incantation or to demonstrate in the streets against an individual. You could remove any parts of your neighbour's tree which overhung your property. And a father had the right to kill his badly disabled child.

Even more important than the actual details – and the laws contained in the Twelve Tables were never formally repealed in Roman times – was the fact that now everyone, patrician, plebeian, consul, senator, state official, ordinary citizen, was subject to the same written code, professionally drafted and precisely stated in terms which demonstrate the Roman aptitude for legal expression and constitute the starting point of European as well as of Roman law.

According to the historian Livy, the *decemviri* themselves came to sticky ends. The committee's chairman, Appius Claudius, lusted after Virginia, the daughter of a centurion. When she resisted his advances, he got one of his lackeys to claim she was his slave. When the matter came to court, Appius was the judge who pronounced against her; whereupon Virginia's father, preferring her death to her dishonour, killed her with his sword. At this point the tribune of the people took a hand, and Appius himself was remanded in custody, where he committed suicide rather than face trial. Another *decemvir* also killed himself, and the rest, who had refused to give up their offices at the end of their statutory year's appointment and were alleged to have used their self-assumed judicial authority to commit crimes, were exiled and their property was confiscated.

Corruption in high places, and the corruption that is fostered by power itself, was neither a Roman prerogative nor a Roman invention. The system did, however, allow some dedicated idealists and radicals genuinely to make felt their attempts to reform aspects of the constitution and to break down the prevailing dichotomy between rich and poor.

FROM CITY STATE TO ITALIAN EMPIRE

The empire began as an exercise in security and tactical aggression. By 265 BC the Romans had conquered the whole of the Italian peninsula below the river Arno, by a process that was more like explosion than expansion. They also successfully resisted several incursions into their territory by the Gauls who occupied the Po valley, and in 275 BC had finally seen off the hired army under Pyrrhus (318–272 BC), king of Epirus, who had been called in by Tarentum to protect its own interests and those of other Greek city states in the south. This was a fine achievement, over a Greek army which was organized and which fought in the style and tradition of Alexander the Great, and against the foremost general of the time. To him we owe the term 'Pyrrhic victory'. After defeating the Romans at Ausculum in 279 BC by the ingenious deployment of his elephant corps but otherwise at considerable cost to his own forces, he is reported as remarking that one more victory like that against the Romans and he would be finished! According to Plutarch, he died during an assault on Argos, after an old woman, seeing him engaged in hand-to-hand combat with her son, hurled a roof tile at him, and scored a direct hit.

The attitude of the Romans to the peoples they defeated was enlightened and tactically sound. They refused to deal with conglomerates of states, such as the league of Latin cities to which Rome had originally belonged, or with the Etruscan empire as a whole. They insisted on treating each conquest on its individual merits, and imposed restrictions or awarded privileges according to the circumstances. Some were granted Roman citizenship without voting rights, and some a kind of probationary citizenship; others had to give up part of their territory, which became public land or was carved up into lots for the use of Roman citizens, or employed as the site for a new colony. Defeated states were sometimes allowed the right of trade and intermarriage with Rome, but never with each other – it was a case of applying in practical terms the Roman proverb 'divide and rule'. All were required regularly to provide manpower for the armies of Rome. This continuous supply of recruits was a factor in the determination to extend the power of Rome. It was not until the second century BC that soldiers received any formal pay, though from 406 BC they were reimbursed for their field expenses, less the cost of rations and other items from the military stores. A soldier's reward was in spoils and land: the Roman empire grew as a means of providing these.

A crucial date in the Romanization of Italy was 338 BC. This marked the final capitulation and dissolution of the Latin league of states, and the establishment of Roman colonies along the coast of Latium which were out of bounds to settlers from other Latin towns. Shortly afterwards, treaties were made with the important Campanian towns of Cumae and Capua, originally of Greek foundation but more recently under Etruscan domination, whereby these, and certain other communities in the region, accepted a form of Roman citizenship and the duty of supplying soldiers in return for a promise of military protection.

It was not long before the call for protection came, against the Samnite invasions of Campania. The Samnites were a different proposition from any enemy of Rome so far. They could be contained quite easily on the plains of central Italy, but once they retired to their mountainous homelands new military tactics were required to dislodge them. The war lasted with few interruptions for thirty-seven years until 290 BC. It culminated in predictable victory for the Romans, but not before they had, in 321 BC, suffered the most shameful defeat in their history. Trapped in the Caudine Forks, a series of narrow mountain passes, the whole Roman army, with its consuls and officers, was forced to surrender. Six hundred equestrians were demanded and handed over as hostages. Then the real humiliation began.

> The lictors were ordered to stand aside from the consuls, who were stripped of their cloaks of office. This so affected the ranks, who only a short time before had cursed them and called for them to be tortured, that each man, ignoring his own situation, averted his eyes from the degradation of such high office as though from an unspeakable horror.
>
> First the consuls, half naked, suffered the ignominious ordeal of being sent under the yoke. They were followed by their officers, in descending order of rank, then, one after the other, by the legions themselves, while the enemy, fully armed, stood round, hurling insults and cracking jokes. Many had swords brandished in their faces, and some, whose attitude of indignation at their treatment offended their captors, were maimed or killed.

So they went under the yoke: almost the worst thing about it was being watched by their enemies. When they emerged from the pass, though their appearance was of men back from the grave first seeing the light of day, as they looked around at the ghastly procession the light itself seemed grimmer than any death.

(Livy, *History of Rome*, IX. 5, 6)

The last-remaining Etruscan footholds in Campania had been swept away in the latter part of the fifth century during incursions by Oscan-speaking tribes from the southern Apennines. The disintegration of the rest of the Etruscan empire was begun in 310 BC when a Roman army not only penetrated as far as the wooded slopes of Mount Ciminius, but by a forced march through the forest got behind the opposing confederate army and crushed it. Three major Etruscan cities immediately sued for peace. The rest followed suit by degrees until 283 BC, when the capitulation was complete.

The Gallic tribes who had spilled over into the fertile valley of the Po as a result of Celtic migrations in the fifth century BC resisted Roman attempts to annex their territory until 191 BC, and though Ligurian tribes on the east coast offered pockets of resistance for a further twenty years, the whole region now recognized as Italy was soon in Roman hands.

CATO THE CENSOR (234–149 BC)

The progress from quaestor to consul via the offices of aedile and praetor was a natural one, and came more quickly to those who had proved themselves able soldiers in time of war. On the other hand, as under normal circumstances no-one could hold the same office twice in ten years, unless there was a suitable provincial governorship available, some very accomplished men could be left without full-time employment at the height of their powers. Such a one was Marcus Porcius Cato, also known as Cato the Elder to distinguish him from his great-grandson, Marcus Porcius Cato 'of Utica' (95–46 BC), a political leader of the utmost integrity and single-mindedness. Cato senior was born at Tusculum and brought up there on his father's farm. He first saw army service when he was 17. He was consul in 195 BC – he led his forces to a great victory in Spain – and retired from the army in 191 BC after a distinguished military career. As a senator he participated enthusiastically in debates on civil affairs, notably to support restrictions on the rights of women. Having failed to become censor in 189 BC, he stood again in 184 BC, and was elected.

Cato took his duties as guardian of public morals very seriously:

He expelled Manilius, a prospective candidate for the consulship, from the senate for embracing his wife during the day in front of their daughter. For himself, he said that he never embraced his own wife except when it thundered loudly, adding jocularly that he was delighted when it did happen to thunder.

(Plutarch, *Lives: Cato*, XVII. 7)

He could be ruthless and implacable with his enemies, especially when they were members of the urban aristocracy, which he was not, and strenuous in his pursuit of those who misused public property. He cut off the pipes by which people were in the habit of siphoning off the municipal water supply into their own houses and gardens, and knocked down private buildings which encroached upon public land. He imposed taxes on the rich, and even heavier taxes on the very rich, and introduced police regulations to restrict luxurious living and entertaining. He was hated for his rural ways, his harshness, his outspokenness, and his parsimony, but he was respected as a skilled politician and a persuasive public speaker. Thus it was that in his last political act, as a senator of 85, he was able to initiate a war that ultimately resulted in the destruction of a whole civilization, as we shall see.

He never properly retired from active life. He compiled the earliest Roman encyclopaedia, and wrote a medical work, a history of Rome, and a treatise on agriculture. The latter, the only book of his that we have, is the oldest surviving complete prose work in Latin. It is revealing of its author and the times in that it extols not so much the glories and virtues of drawing on the bounties of the land, as the pursuit of cash-farming as a less perilous investment than commerce. Its approach is practical, traditional, and often picturesque.

When it rains: Look for what can be done under cover. Don't stop work, clean up. Remember, even if there is nothing to do, expenses still mount up . . .

To make green olive oil: Collect windfalls as soon as possible; if they are soiled, wash them and remove any leaves and dirt. Pick olives when they are black. Oil made from sourest olives is the best. The most profitable oil is from ripe olives. If they have been touched by frost, press the oil three or four days after picking; if you want, add salt to them . . .

For snake bite: If an ox or any other animal has been bitten by a snake, mix a cup of ground fennel (doctors call it camomile) into a pint of old wine. Administer through the nostrils and apply pig's dung to the bite itself. Treat a person in the same way, if the situation arises . . .

The properties of cabbage: Cabbage is a marvellous digestive and an excellent laxative; after you have eaten it, your urine will relieve all complaints. If you want to gorge yourself at a party and imbibe freely, before you go eat as much pickled cabbage as you need, and when you get home chew about five raw leaves of the stuff. You will feel as though you have eaten nothing, and you can drink as much as you like.

(On Agriculture, XXXIX, LXV, CII, CLVI)

A fervent nationalist, Cato was ambivalent towards Greek culture. He professed himself averse to Greek philosophers and doctors, and claimed that Greek literature was worth only a passing glance – in 155 BC, worried by the effect their lectures might be having on the youth of Rome, he proposed that an embassy of Greek philosophers should be sent home. From what we know of his speeches and writings, however, and from the observations of his contemporary, the Greek historian Polybius (c. 200– c. 118 BC), it is clear that he was steeped in Greek rhetorical theory and literary tradition.

THE PUNIC WARS (264–146 BC)

The spark which ignited the metamorphosis of Rome from an Italian to a Mediterranean power was a small enough incident. The Greek city of Messana, on the north-eastern tip of Sicily, had in 289 BC been seized and occupied by a notorious gang of retired Campanian mercenaries. They were still there in 264 BC, when the king of Syracuse, the famous Greek stronghold lower down the coast, decided to winkle them out. The mercenaries asked the Carthaginians, who occupied parts of the west coast of Sicily, to send a fleet and raise the siege. The Carthaginians duly obliged, but their fleet stayed on in the harbour. The mercenaries then appealed to Rome to rid them of the Carthaginians, on the somewhat specious grounds that their Campanian blood entitled them to the same protection as the Campanian allies of Rome on the mainland. The senate havered and passed the buck to the *comitia tributa*, which voted if not actually for war, then at least for the dispatch of an expedition against the interfering Carthaginians to restore Messana to its criminal element. The arrival of the expedition so surprised or unnerved the Carthaginian commander at Messana that he embarked and took his ships home. The Carthaginian government, however, humiliated by what they saw as a defeat, resolved to recapture Messana.

Thus was started, by accident, a war contested on principles. It was fought to the finish, and to the death. It lasted, in three periods totalling forty-two years, for well over a century. When it ended, Carthage, which at one time had, according to the Greek geographer Strabo (c. 64 BC–c. AD 24), '300 cities in Libya and 700,000 people in its own city' (*Geography*, XVII. 3), was a smoking heap of rubble.

Carthage was originally a Phoenician colony: hence the Latin name for a Carthaginian, Poenus, from which comes the adjective 'Punic'. The language of the Carthaginians was Semitic, and their gods, too, were those of the Phoenicians, notably

Ba'al-Hammon, god of the sky and of fertility, and Tanit, the moon-goddess. Their literature has not come down to us. The Punic wars went on for so long and were fought with such intensity on both sides that within a hundred years the word *punicus* had an accepted literary meaning of 'treacherous', though, while hostilities were conducted with the utmost passion and brutality, there is no evidence that either side acted more dishonestly than the other.

The Carthaginians can justly be called one of the most successful peoples of the ancient world. Virgil refers to their city as 'opposite Italy and the mouths of the Tiber, rich in resources and especially severe in the pursuit of war' (*Aeneid*, I. 13–14). It was this key strategic position in the Mediterranean which governed their military tactics and, in turn, their economic policy. Carthage was a sea-going nation, using its fleet, which was manned by its citizens, virtually to close the western Mediterranean to other nations, to wage war, and to trade in goods all round the Mediterranean and down the west coast of Africa as far as Guinea – gold, ivory, bronze, tin, pottery, grain, perfume, dyes, and, of course, slaves. It founded colonies along the north African coast as far as Cyrenaica, in southern Spain, in Corsica, in Sardinia, and on the western tip of Sicily. Carthaginian citizens did not normally fight in the army, which was composed mainly of African conscripts and mercenaries from all parts of the Mediterranean – and Carthage could afford to employ the best. This multi-racial army still had to be forged into a coherent fighting force, which was the responsibility of its commanders, who were Carthaginians and professional career soldiers.

The First Punic War (264–241 BC) was largely fought at sea. The Romans purpose-built a series of fleets to match the Carthaginian numbers and manned them with marine commandos trained in hand-to-hand fighting – in an age of rudimentary artillery, the standard naval tactic was to attach grapples to an enemy ship and then overwhelm its crew by superior numbers. The losses on both sides were enormous, but the Romans were better at unearthing and deploying ever more resources, and finally the Carthaginians sued for peace and agreed to withdraw all claims to Sicily. Shortly after hostilities ceased, however, the Romans took advantage of the temporary preoccupation of the Carthaginians with a revolt of their mercenaries to annex Corsica and Sardinia, an act which was undeniably foul play.

Carthage retaliated by increasing its empire in another quarter: the whole of central and southern Spain, with its potential wealth and manpower, was overrun, partly to pay war reparations to Rome. This Spanish campaign was led successively by a brilliant family trio of generals: Hamilcar (d. 229 BC), his son-in-law Hasdrubal (d. 221 BC), and Hamilcar's son Hannibal (247–182 BC). It was so successful that in order to prevent Carthage extending its influence still farther north, the Romans were forced into a diplomatic manoeuvre. The river Ebro was to be regarded as the boundary between the interests of the two sides, but the east-coast town of Saguntum, an ally of Rome, would remain under Roman protection. When in 221 BC Hasdrubal was murdered by a slave whose master he had put to death, Hannibal succeeded to the command. He started the Second Punic War (218–202 BC) by attacking and capturing Saguntum. This was clearly a deliberate ploy. The Carthaginians were motivated to set up this new confrontation by a desire for revenge and by their fear of Roman incursions into their newly won territory.

The Romans began by assuming that tactically this war would be a continuation of the first, and prepared a fleet in which they could cross to Carthage and this time take the city itself. Hannibal confounded them (and the rest of the world then and since) by doing not just the unexpected, but the impossible. He marched his army – infantry, cavalry, baggage train, and heavy tanks in the form of his famous elephants – out of Spain and across the river Rhône in a flotilla of boats and rafts, against continual opposition from native Gallic tribes. He invaded Italy by a route which took him over, and through, the Alps; at one point he had to blast away a wall of solid rock by heating it with fires and then dashing onto it quantities of raw wine. According to Polybius, who is regarded as the most reliable authority, Hannibal entered Italy with 20,000 foot and 6,000 cavalry, having lost 18,000 infantry and 2,000 horsemen since crossing the Rhône. With these, and the surviving elephants, he soon gained control of northern Italy, having outflanked one Roman army before the river Trebia, and trapped another by Lake Trasimene. Rome itself was too tough a nut to crack, so Hannibal bypassed the city and went on into the south, where at Cannae he outmanoeuvred a numerically much stronger Roman force and virtually annihilated it. Then for fourteen years he and his army rampaged around southern Italy before being lured back to Carthage, and to defeat at Zama in 202 BC, by a splendid African campaign conducted by Cornelius Scipio (234–183 BC), who had already driven the Carthaginians out of Spain and was afterwards awarded the honorific surname of Africanus. In particular, he managed at Zama to neutralize Hannibal's tactics of opening the battle with a frontal charge of his eighty elephants. Hannibal survived the battle, only to end his life in exile in Asia, having failed in his attempt to rebuild his country's fortunes by political means.

As a man, Hannibal was 'notorious in Carthaginian circles for his love of money, and among the Romans for his cruelty' (Polybius, *Histories*, IX. 26). As a soldier, Hannibal is just one of a line of gallant and spectacular commanders whose efforts finally ended in failure but whose exploits are remembered better than, or at least as well as, those of the men who ultimately defeated them: Leonidas of Sparta, Spartacus the gladiator, Saladin, Montrose, Napoleon, Custer, and Rommel are others. Scipio Africanus was the equal in the field of that most renowned of Roman generals, Julius Caesar. Livy has a neat story of how Scipio and Hannibal met again in Ephesus in 193 BC. He claims it originated with Acilius, a senator who was writing in Greek not long after the meeting was supposed to have taken place. The conversation went like this:

SCIPIO: Who do you think was the greatest army commander of all?

HANNIBAL: Alexander, because time and again he overwhelmed armies with a tiny force of his own, and marched right through regions of the world farther away than anyone had ever expected even to see.

SCIPIO: And after him?

HANNIBAL: Pyrrhus, for being the first to teach the art of making a proper camp, for choosing his ground and arranging his defences better than anyone else, and for his quality of leadership, which enabled him to persuade Italian races to accept his command, that of a foreign king, rather than Rome's, which had been predominant for so long.

SCIPIO: And third?

HANNIBAL: Why, myself!

SCIPIO (*Laughing*): What would you have said if you had beaten me?

HANNIBAL: Then without question I'd put myself ahead of Alexander and Pyrrhus and all other generals.

(*History of Rome*, XXXV. 14)

After the Second Punic War, Rome confiscated Spain, leaving Carthage with just its north African colonies, and promptly waded into local Spanish conflicts to keep the tribes there in order, besides being involved in full-scale wars in Macedonia, Asia Minor, and Syria. In spite of the sanctions and conditions of peace that had been imposed on Carthage at the end of the war, there was the possibility that it might rise again and try to take revenge on its conquerors. Old Cato, who in 157 BC had been a member of a diplomatic mission to Africa to mediate between Carthage and neighbouring Numidia, saw this more clearly than anyone else.

It is said that he even contrived to drop a Libyan fig on the floor of the senate as he rearranged his toga. Then, as the rest admired its size and lusciousness, he warned them that the land where it grew was only three days away from Rome by sea. In another respect, he was even more uncompromising. Whatever question was being addressed in the senate, he incorporated into his speech the words, 'In my opinion, Carthage must be destroyed.'

(Plutarch, *Lives: Cato*, XXVII)

The Carthaginians were finally manoeuvred into the position of having to defend themselves against Numidian invasions of their territory. This was technically a breach of the treaty of 201 BC, under which they were forbidden to take up arms without Rome's permission. The senate, which, egged on by Cato, had made plans for just such an eventuality, voted for war once again. They sent out a trained army comprising, according to the Alexandrian Greek historian Appian (*c.* AD 95–*c.* 165),

80,000 infantry and 4,000 cavalry, under the command of the consuls, 'to whom they gave secret orders not to discontinue the war until Carthage had been razed to the ground' (*Punic Wars*, VIII. 11). The Third Punic War lasted for just three years (149–146 BC). That it continued so long was due to a heroic Carthaginian defence of their city. It was hastily mounted, since the messenger who brought the news of the senate's declaration of war also carried the announcement that the expeditionary force had sailed. It was, too, frenziedly maintained, since as part of the conditions of the surrender of the city at the end of the previous war the Carthaginians had handed over '200,000 full suits of armour and 3,000 anti-siege engines as sureties against their going to war again' (Strabo, *Geography*, XVII. 3).

Carthage was duly destroyed. The 50,000 survivors of the siege were sold into slavery.

THE GROWTH OF EMPIRE AND THE EARLY PROVINCIAL SYSTEM

Security demanded the actions against Carthage, in the course of which Rome acquired Sicily (241 BC), Sardinia and Corsica (administered as one province from 231 BC), and Spain (197 BC), which was divided into two provinces. A province came to be defined as a territory outside Italy with its own borders, belonging to the Roman people, governed by a Roman officer of state, and subject to Roman taxation. The inhabitants of provinces annexed by conquest, however, had few rights, and the fruits of their labours were even more likely to be diverted to Rome.

Profit and imperialism (whether motivated by national aggrandizement or international Romanization) also came into play in the programme of aggression. Though the liberty of peoples was not a usual Roman concern, between 197 and 146 BC the expansion of Roman influence was curbed by political considerations which favoured giving support to client kingdoms, especially in the east. A client kingdom was a convenient device for keeping the peace in outposts of the empire where local knowledge and local methods of warfare were likely to be the most effective means. Officially, client kings were known as *socii et amici* (allies and friends), but the reality was somewhat different. Client kings paid no taxes as such, but provided troops as required to fight Rome's wars. In return, Rome would in theory supply diplomatic assistance and even troops to maintain a kingdom's sovereignty against internal or external pressures, though the mere threat of interference by the legions was usually enough. Inherent in what was no more than a gentlemen's agreement was an understanding that if there was no obvious heir to the kingdom, it would, on the monarch's death, be bequeathed to Rome.

Annexation became the policy again in the middle of the second century. As merchants in particular grew richer, new sources of wealth and new entrepreneurial opportunities needed to be found overseas. In 146 BC, on the destruction of Carthage, the territory of the Carthaginians became the province of Africa. That same year, the Achaean city of Corinth was destroyed as an example to the Greeks, who, since being given their freedom at the end of the Second Macedonian War (200–196 BC), had failed to govern themselves in harmony. Achaea was now incorporated into the new Roman province of Macedonia. By this time also, Illyricum had been fully annexed to Rome. In 133 BC, Attalus III, who left no heirs, bequeathed his kingdom of Pergamum to the Roman people. The wealthy province of Asia was now established by force, with the city of Pergamum as its capital.

To meet the need for a regular supply of responsible governors, with appropriate *imperium*, a system of *prorogatio* (prorogation) was now introduced. After their year of office in Rome consuls and praetors would be liable to serve a further term as provincial governors *pro consule* or *pro praetore* as the case might be. The senate chose who would go where, and there was often enthusiastic lobbying by candidates for the provinces which offered the richest pickings or the greatest military glory.

TIBERIUS GRACCHUS (168–133 BC) AND GAIUS GRACCHUS (c. 159–121 BC)

To have as father a famous consul and military leader, and as mother a Scipio (one of the most distinguished of all the patrician families) who, when widowed and faced with bringing up her surviving children, turned down an offer of marriage from the king of Egypt, are unusual antecedents of two men whose political reforms and championship of the poor and needy did most to upset the established order in republican Rome. Yet, if there may have been no precedent for such a response to an aristocratic upbringing, there have been many examples since.

In the same way as all young men of his social class, Tiberius Sempronius Gracchus served in the army. This he did with considerable distinction, and was elected quaestor. In a campaign against Numantia in Spain, his instinctive political bent involved him in negotiations with the enemy to prevent the Roman army from being annihilated. His efforts were successful, for he saved the lives of 20,000 Romans and countless auxiliaries and camp followers (and had his accounts' books returned to him by the enemy), but the surrender did not go down well at home. Largely thanks to the intervention of his brother-in-law, yet another notable member of the Scipio clan, Tiberius and his fellow officers avoided any further indignity, but their commanding officer was stripped, put in irons, and returned to the enemy who had originally spared him.

Tiberius then turned to politics and was elected a tribune of the people for 133

BC. The main reform he proposed was the reclamation of large tracts of land which had been acquired by the state in its conquest of Italy, and its redistribution among smallholders with guaranteed tenure in return for a nominal rent. Those currently occupying the land, who were in fact merely tenants of the state, would be restricted to what had for some time been the legal limit of ownership (500 acres plus a further 250 acres for each of up to two sons), and would be compensated by being granted a hereditary rent-free lease.

> He did not draft his law on his own, but consulted leading citizens who were noted for their uprightness, among them Crassus the *pontifex maximus*, Mucius Scaevola the legal expert, who was consul at the time, and Appius Claudius, his own father-in-law. And it is considered that a law against injustice and greed has never been expressed in such mild and diplomatic terms. For men who should have submitted to the process of law for disobeying it, and been fined and deprived of the land which they occupied illegally, were instead merely required to give up their unjust holdings in return for fair recompense, and to allow them to be taken over by needy citizens.

> **(Plutarch, *Lives: Tiberius Gracchus*, V)**

It was a significant political package at a time of general unrest and of expansion abroad in that it also restored to the list of those eligible for military service (for which a tradition of qualification was the possession of land) a section of society which had fallen out of the reckoning. Recruits were normally enlisted by a process known as *dilectus* (choosing). The selection was done from citizens of military age (17 to 46), who were required each year to report on the Capitoline Hill in Rome. As citizenship was extended, troops were raised also in centres outside Rome. In the later years of the republic, levies such as these were held when not enough volunteers had come forward.

Though Tiberius' bill had the backing of several prominent members of the senate as well as of one of the consuls, his tactics in trying to make it law were questionable. Instead of submitting it first for discussion in the senate, he proposed it straight to the *concilium plebis*, where it was bound to succeed. This inevitably annoyed the senate, which persuaded one of the other tribunes to veto the bill as it was being read out. Tiberius retaliated by invoking his right to suspend all business. He then refused to listen to attempts to get him to refer the bill to the senate, and took the unprecedented step of asking the *concilium plebis* to vote his refractory colleague out of office, which it promptly did. The bill was then passed to acclamation, and three commissioners were appointed to administer the scheme: Tiberius himself, his younger brother Gaius Sempronius Gracchus, and Appius Claudius Pulcher, 'leader' of the senate as well as being Tiberius' father-in-law.

The commission immediately began work, and in all about 75,000 smallholdings may have been created and farmed as a result. When it began to look as though the commission would run short of funds, Tiberius coolly proposed to the *concilium plebis* that the revenue confiscated from the newly acquired kingdom of Pergamum should be diverted to its use. The senate, rather than risk being outflanked again, and this time in the area of finance, which it regarded as its prerogative, capitulated, but Tiberius was a marked man. State officials could not be brought to task while in office, but they could be prosecuted afterwards for acts committed during their term. Tiberius Gracchus now took the unprecedented and arguably unconstitutional step of announcing himself as a candidate for a tribuneship for a second year running. A group of senators, failing in an attempt to have him disqualified from standing, charged out of the senate, broke up an electioneering meeting which Tiberius was addressing, and clubbed him to death with stools and cudgels.

They had not by any means heard the last of the Gracchus family. Nine years after his brother's assassination, Gaius Sempronius Gracchus was elected a tribune of the people. He was elected again, unopposed, the following year – there is some suggestion that one of his first acts in office was to have the law repealed whereby a man could not hold office for two years running. Gaius was a different and more formidable proposition than Tiberius. He was more flamboyant and passionate, and a skilled and powerful demagogue. His programme of reforms passed by the *concilium plebis* was wide ranging and designed to benefit all interests, except of course those of the senate. He reaffirmed and reactivated his brother's land laws and established smallholdings in Roman territory abroad. For city-dwellers who could not be persuaded to leave the teeming streets of Rome for the hazards of country life, he enacted grain laws which entitled every citizen on demand to a monthly ration at a fixed price. While the nobility still dominated the senate, the wealth and business acumen lay largely with the equestrian class. Gaius Gracchus gave them greater power, and riches, by awarding them the right to contract for gathering the enormous taxes which accrued from the newly created province of Asia, and by substituting equestrians for senators as jurors in cases of extortion brought by the state against provincial governors. He also forced through massive measures for expenditure on public works, particularly roads and harbours, which again benefited the business community. His most enlightened piece of legislation, however, fell foul even of the *concilium plebis*. This was a proposal to extend full Roman citizenship, and thus voting rights, to the population of the surrounding area of Latium, and to give all allied states in Italy the rights enjoyed by the Latins, such as trade with Rome and intermarriage with Romans.

When Gaius Gracchus offered himself in 121 BC for a third term of office as tribune, the senate resorted to terrorism once again, though this time with quasi-constitutional overtones. They put up against him a straw candidate with an entirely fallacious programme of reforms which would be even more acceptable to the people, who was duly elected. The supporters of Gaius Gracchus held a mass rally on the Aventine Hill, but made the mistake of carrying weapons. The consul, Lucius Opimius, armed with a *senatus consultum ultimum*, a decree invented for the purpose which gave moral backing to a senior official to take action against those who were endangering the stability of the state, raised a levy of citizens, augmented by a company of soldiers and archers, to disperse the demonstrators. Gaius escaped the first wave of violence, but then, recognizing that the cause was hopeless, ordered his personal slave to stab him to death. It is said that 3,000 of his supporters were rounded up and thrown into jail, and there strangled.

The actions and ultimate fates of the brothers Gracchus constituted a watershed in Roman politics. Their legislation highlighted the links between the problems of property holding, poverty, the army, and the extension and retention of the empire. Their use of a popular assembly to initiate legislation gave it powers rivalling those of the senate. That political conflict could lead twice to violence established a precedent which affected the equilibrium of Roman society and instigated periods of anarchy and civil war.

GAIUS MARIUS (157–86 BC) AND THE REFORM OF THE ROMAN ARMY

For an inherently agricultural society to be a perpetual war machine is to attempt to mix two incompatibles. The soil and climate of the Italian peninsula offered its inhabitants means of personal survival and economic development which were not available on a similar scale to any other society of the ancient world. The geographical situation, however, of early Rome, hemmed in by inimical or potentially inimical tribes, meant that its survival depended not so much on defence as on aggression. What Tiberius Gracchus tried to halt when he was tribune in 133 BC was a trend which had begun centuries earlier and which, by the very success with which Rome had conducted its military operations, had become a vicious circle. Ancient armies were manned by peasant farmers. A society continually at war required a constant supply of conscripts. Smallholdings fell into disuse because there was no-one to tend them. As Roman conquests spread through the Mediterranean lands, even more men were required, and wealth and cheap grain poured back into Rome, much of it into the hands of entrepreneurs, who became even richer, and invested in land out of which they carved vast areas for vegetables, vines, olives, and sheep farming, all managed by slave labour. The dispossessed rural poor became the urban poor, thus also becoming ineligible for military service as no longer being nominal property holders. Not only was there a shortage of recruits, but the soldier had nothing to return to between campaigns or at the end of his service.

A working solution to the problem of recruitment was devised by Gaius Marius, a man of humble origins who was born near Arpinum, a town in Latium about 100 km from Rome but not far off the main road to Capua, the via Latina. He first saw military service in Spain, and did not hold any public office until he was 38, when he was elected tribune of the people. Four years later, in 115 BC, he managed to achieve a praetorship and made a good marriage, to Julia of the family of that name; he was thus to become an uncle by marriage of Julius Caesar. He then served in the African wars against Jugurtha, who in the wake of the destruction of Carthage had usurped the whole of Numidia after being granted half of it. Marius returned to Rome in 108 BC to stand successfully for consul, in which capacity the *comitia tributa* elected him to assume military command in Africa, an infringement of the traditional prerogative of the senate to make military appointments. Abandoning the usual methods of enlisting servicemen, Marius openly recruited volunteers from the ranks of the urban poor, promising them victory, booty, glory, and, of course, permanent jobs. He introduced new training methods and, with the first professional army the Romans ever had, brought the fighting to a speedy end; though the final negotiations, which resulted in the kidnap of Jugurtha and his being handed over to Rome for execution, were conducted by a young quaestor called Cornelius Sulla.

Sallust (86–35 BC), a former member of the senate and the first governor of Africa Nova (eastern Numidia), who in his retirement became a commentator on recent and contemporary political issues, summed up the situation prevailing in 106–105 BC:

> At about this time, our generals Q. Caepio and M. Manlius fought a disastrous battle against the Gauls, which caused general consternation throughout Italy. From that time to this, the Romans have been convinced that other wars were no problem, but when you fought the Gauls, it was for survival, not glory. When the war in Numidia was over, and it was announced that the defeated Jugurtha was being brought back to Rome in chains, Marius was elected consul in his absence and assigned the province of Gaul: as consul he celebrated a magnificent triumph on 1 January. From that time onwards the hopes and prosperity of the state depended on him.

> **(The War against Jugurtha, CXIV)**

The Gauls to whom he refers were two displaced Celtic tribes from the north, the Cimbri and Teutones, who in 105 BC, near Arausio (modern Orange), inflicted the greatest defeat on the Romans since Cannae – Caepio and Manlius were later exiled for their incompetence. Marius, having been elected consul for a second term for the year 104 BC, was re-elected for the three successive years 103–101 BC, during which he destroyed the menace of both the Cimbri and the Teutones.

As a professional soldier, at the head of a now professional army, he needed to establish the means for his soldiers to receive allotments of land on discharge and to continue his own career by getting a new command. He threw in his lot with the tribune Lucius Appuleius Saturninus, a man not above using street violence to achieve political ends, with whose help he was elected consul for a sixth time for the year 100 BC. Saturninus now put forward on Marius' behalf a number of legislative proposals in the Gracchus mould, including the usual controversial measures for land allotments to be made to army veterans from the Italian states and full franchise for some of them. The whole programme was accepted, but not without predictable opposition from both the nobility and the people of Rome which culminated in violent demonstrations. These were put down by Marius' soldiers, who, of course, had a vested interest in the outcome of the debate. This appearance on the streets of Rome of armed military, and their use, without an act of the senate, was a precedent of profound significance. From that time onwards, the rule of Rome was always in the hands of whoever had the support of the army.

The rest of the story of Marius is sheer melodrama. Saturninus instigated the tragic sequence of events by organizing the assassination of an inconvenient political opponent. The senate issued a *senatus consultum ultimum* obliging Marius to take action against his principal supporter, which he did by arresting him with an armed force. An enraged mob then broke into the prison, and lynched Saturninus and several of his cronies. The senate now repealed all Saturninus' laws on the grounds that they had been implemented by force, which was technically true. Marius, left high and dry, with no legislation to back his plans for his soldiers and no political support, went into temporary exile at the end of his year of office.

When he returned, it was to take an active part in the 'Social War' (91–89 BC). A confederacy of Italian states in the south, fed up with having to fight for Rome without being treated as equals, and not even being allowed to participate in the decisions for which they were fighting, rebelled. They lost the war but eventually gained their objective, most of them being granted full citizenship. In 88 BC all Roman eyes were turned to the east, where Mithridates (*c.* 132–63 BC), king of Pontus, had invaded the Roman province of Asia and massacred 80,000 Roman and Italian citizens. The senate appointed Sulla, who was consul that year, to lead a force against Mithridates. The tribune Sulpicius Rufus (124–88 BC) passed through the *concilium plebis* a package of laws, one of which called for the transfer of this command to Marius. Sulla marched on Rome with his six legions and had the decision reversed. This was the first time that a Roman army had been used against Rome itself.

Sulpicius went into hiding, but was discovered and killed. Marius, now in his seventieth year, fled, accompanied by his adopted son. According to Plutarch, Marius was picked up near the coast of Latium while hiding in a marsh and was sentenced to death by the local magistrates, but was hustled aboard a ship when no-one could be found to perform the execution. He ended up in Carthage, but was ordered by the Roman governor in Africa to move on. To the governor's messenger, he replied, 'Go tell your master that you have seen Gaius Marius, a fugitive, sitting in the rubble of Carthage' (Plutarch, *Lives: Marius*, XL).

In the meantime Sulla was carrying out his orders in Asia with some distinction. Cornelius Cinna (d. 84 BC), one of the two consuls for 87 BC, took the opportunity to reintroduce another of the proposals of Sulpicius, the enrolment of the newly enfranchised Italians and also freedmen as members of the traditional thirty-five tribes; he was promptly ejected from the city by his consular colleague. Cinna raised an army of Italian volunteers. He was joined by Marius, now back in Italy with a small force of cavalry, which he augmented by breaking into the quarters in which slaves who worked the farms were held at night and enlisting them as fighting men.

Together Marius and Cinna marched on Rome with their motley army. After a dreadful siege in which thousands died of plague, the city capitulated, having extracted from Cinna a promise that there would be no bloodshed. Marius, who had kept silent during this exchange, obviously did not regard himself as a party to the agreement. The moment the gates were opened, the killing began. It went on for five days. Marius and Cinna then proposed themselves as consuls for the next year, 86 BC. No-one dared oppose them. On 13 January, however, Marius died, according to Plutarch of drink and delirium, but possibly simply of old age. He had reformed the army and had been consul an unprecedented seven times, but his ambition, combined with his political naïveté, had caused the stability of authority in Rome to be permanently upset.

SULLA (138–78 BC) AND HIS CONSTITUTIONAL REFORMS

Lucius Cornelius Sulla (surnamed Felix) came of a good family of moderate means. When he returned in 83 BC from his successful eastern campaign, he had no political power beyond that which a man at the head of a trained army of veterans could command. This, however, gave him a more than adequate means of capturing Rome in the face of the nominally more constitutional opposition raised by the consuls, Gnaeus Papirius Carbo (d. 81 BC) and Marius junior (110–82 BC), but not without unnecessary butchery. This accomplished, Sulla then had himself appointed not consul, but dictator. In this capacity his first act was to rid himself of all political and personal opposition, using the novel device of proscription – the posting up of lists of undesirable characters whom anyone was now at liberty to assassinate, and for a reward.

Sulla himself called the Roman people to assemble, and harangued them with an outburst of self-aggrandizement mixed with menaces intended to put fear into them . . . He then pronounced sentence of death on forty senators and about 1,600 equestrians. He seems to have been the first to proscribe those whom he wished murdered, to reward the executioners and informers, and to punish any found hiding the victims. Very soon he added other senators to the list. Some of them, caught unawares, were killed where they were found, at home, in the street, or in the temple. Others were bodily heaved up from where they were and taken and thrown at Sulla's feet. Others were dragged through the streets and kicked to death, the spectators being too frightened to utter a word of protest at the horrors they witnessed. Others were expelled from Rome or had their property and belongings confiscated. Spies were abroad, looking everywhere for those who had fled the city, and killing any that they caught.

(Appian, *Civil Wars*, I. 11)

Sulla then reorganized the constitution to put power effectively back into the hands of the upper classes. He virtually nullified the traditional influence of the tribunes of the people. He doubled the membership of the senate by admitting some 300 equestrians and selected Italian holders of office in outlying municipalities. He also made the holding of a quaestorship an automatic qualification for membership of the senate, and raised the number of quaestors to twenty. This, together with the reapplication of the statutory ten-year gap between holding the same office, and the introduction of a new regulation that two years had to elapse between the holding of an office and election to the one above it, meant that there were now more junior state officials seeking fewer senior posts, and having to wait longer for them. As the competition grew, the ambitious were prepared to resort to unconstitutional means to achieve their aims.

Sulla's reforms of the legal system were less contentious. He established new courts to deal with specific offences, and crystallized the distinctions between civil and criminal law, though he removed the right of anyone except senior senators to adjudicate in lawsuits.

After three years of a reversion to what constituted an absolute monarchy, Sulla retired in 79 BC to his estate at Puteoli, and, like many politicians since, wrote his memoirs. He died not much more than a year later, probably from an ulcerous condition. Even though technically the Roman republic had some fifty years to run, it was the end of an era which had seen the deployment of two opposing factions. The *optimates* (best men), of whom Sulla was representative, stood for the rule by right of those of high birth, high social standing, and moral rectitude. The *populares*, such as were the Gracchus brothers and Marius, supported the people. Thereafter, though the designations survived, the distinction between them became blurred.

FURTHER READING

* indicates sourcebook

Beard, M. and Crawford, M., *Rome in the Late Republic*, Duckworth, new edn 2002.

Crawford, M., *The Roman Republic*, Fontana, 2nd rev. edn 1992; Harvard University Press, 2nd edn 1993.

Flower, H.I. (ed.), *The Cambridge Companion to the Roman Republic*, Cambridge University Press, 2004.

Goldsworthy, A., *The Fall of Carthage: The Punic Wars, 265–146 BC*, Cassell, 2003.

Holland, T., *Rubicon: The Triumph and Tragedy of the Roman Republic*, Abacus, new edn 2004; as *Rubicon: The Last Years of the Roman Republic*, Doubleday, new edn 2005.

Keaveney, A., *Sulla: The Last Republican*, Routledge, revised edn 2005.

Patterson, J.R., *Political Life in the City of Rome*, Bristol University Press, 2000.

Rosenstein, N. and Morstein-Marx, R. (eds), *A Companion to the Roman Republic*, Blackwell, 2006.

*Sherk, R. (ed.), *Rome and the Greek East to the Death of Augustus*, Cambridge University Press, 1984.

Syme, R., *The Roman Revolution*, Oxford University Press, reissue 2002.

Wiseman, T.P., *Roman Political Life, 90 BC–AD 69*, Exeter University Press, 1985.

3 TWELVE CAESARS

The twenty years that followed Sulla's death saw the rise of three men of particular ambition and power, and the flowering of the political and forensic skills of a fourth. Marcus Licinius Crassus (*c.* 115–53 BC) acquired prodigious wealth; Gnaeus Pompeius Magnus (106–48 BC), Pompey the 'Great', was a born military leader and organizer; Gaius Julius Caesar (100–44 BC) was both a military genius and an astute politician. Together they took advantage of Caesar's election as consul for 59 BC to form a political pact, known as the 'First Triumvirate', which ruled unconstitutionally for several years. Marcus Tullius Cicero (106–43 BC) lived through these times and left to posterity many examples of his oratorical and prose styles in the form of speeches and letters. All four were stabbed to death within ten years of each other.

Cicero, like Marius, was born near Arpinum, but of an upper middle-class family. He and his brother were sent to Rome to complete their education, which was interrupted by military service in 89 BC. Cicero's first significant speech in the courts was in defence of Roscius, charged with murdering his father, the penalty for which under Roman law was to be tied up in a sack with a dog, a cock, a viper, and an ape, and then thrown into the nearest river. It was a brave case to take on, for the charge had been brought by one of Sulla's favourite freedmen, who had an interest in a conviction. In Cicero's speech for the defence is the first recorded reference to the legal maxim, *cui bono*: 'His honour Lucius Cassius [consul 127 BC, censor 125 BC], whom the Roman people regarded as the most responsible and wisest of judges, was in the habit of asking repeatedly during the course of a trial, "Who stood to gain?"' (*Pro Roscio Amerino*, XXX).

In the event, Roscius was acquitted, though shortly afterwards Cicero went abroad for what he claimed were reasons of health and study. On his return to Rome after Sulla's death, he ascended the political ladder, helped by his oratory, which led the Sicilians to retain him as prosecutor in Rome of their former governor, Verres (d. 43 BC), a notorious embezzler and extortionist. Cicero's courtroom tactics, as well as his eloquence, were such that the defence counsel, up till then the leader of the Roman 'bar', threw up his brief while the evidence was still being called. Cicero, a *novus homo*, was elected consul for 63 BC, when he distinguished himself by dealing firmly with an alleged conspiracy against the state led by Lucius Sergius Catilina. Having, by means of a speech in the senate, shamed Catiline into leaving Rome, he arrested his fellow conspirators and had them summarily executed on the recommendation of the senate. Catiline was killed in battle the following year. The watershed in Cicero's career, however, came in 61 BC, when he appeared in court, this time as a witness, and destroyed the alibi of Publius Clodius (*c.* 92–52 BC), accused of attending in drag a 'ladies only' religious ceremony in honour of the Bona Dea. Clodius became an instrument of Caesar's will when, as tribune of the people for 58 BC, he secured the means of driving Cicero into exile. For Cicero had refused to enter into a political alliance with the triumvirate, and had gone even further and criticized its right to govern. Caesar only reluctantly acquiesced to Cicero's return in 57 BC.

Crassus had begun his trail to wealth and fame by buying cheap, from the state, the estates of those who had been proscribed by Sulla. He also had on call a team of 500 slaves who were skilled builders. He would wait for a fire in the city, which was never long in coming, as fire-risks were high, houses were crammed together, and there was then no fire service. At the first alarm, he rushed out and made a nominal offer not just for the burning house but for all the houses in the neighbourhood. In this way, and by rebuilding the damaged properties, he is said to have owned at one time or another most of Rome. He used much of his wealth to gain popular favour, both essential assets for an aspiring politician. As the supreme commander appointed by the senate in 72 BC against the slave revolt of Spartacus the gladiator, he is remembered for two acts. After his second-in-command had disobeyed orders and engaged the enemy with disastrous results, he revived the ancient punishment of decimation, dividing the 500 men he felt were most culpable for the actual defeat into fifty tens, and then choosing by lot one out of each ten to be publicly executed before the whole army. When, as praetor in 71 BC, he finally defeated Spartacus, he crucified the 6,000 survivors of the battle, leaving them to hang at regular intervals along the main road from Rome to Capua, where the rising had started.

Crassus and Pompey were consuls in 70 BC, and again in 55 BC, after which Crassus solicited for and obtained the governorship of the province of Syria, with its promise of rich pickings. There, in a misguided attempt to add military laurels to his wealth, he determined to resolve the problem of the Parthians, who, having settled in the region in about 250 BC, were now gradually making inroads into surrounding territories. Crassus was ignominiously defeated, and then murdered while trying to negotiate terms of surrender. It is said that his head was then cut off and molten gold poured into his mouth, as a symbol of his greed.

Pompey, the consular colleague of Crassus on two occasions, was first elected in 70 BC while under the statutory age limit and without having held any government office. He had, however, already served the state well as a soldier, having raised his own army in support of Sulla and won famous victories in Africa over the party of Marius and in Spain over Quintus Sertorius, a former praetor who had rebelled against Rome. His next command, in 67 BC, was an unusual one – to rid the Mediterranean of its infestation of pirates, who were making things intolerable for the ships, trade, and peoples of all the surrounding coasts. These pirates held important captives for ransom, while victims of lesser status, who hoped their Roman citizenship would give them protection, were treated to a bizarre charade. The pirates would profess awe and fear, and then fetch Roman clothes and footwear for them to wear, in order, so they said, that others would not make the same mistake. This done, the unfortunate prisoners were, one by one, hoisted out onto a ship's ladder and made to climb down, rung by rung, into the sea. Any who resisted were simply tossed overboard. The ceremony of 'walking the plank' is thus an ancient one.

The resources and powers put at Pompey's disposal were vast, and included 250 ships, 100,000 marines, and 4,000 cavalry from Rome alone, which he reinforced with what was volunteered by other interested nations. He divided the Mediterranean and the Black Sea, with the adjacent coastlands, into sectors, each the responsibility of a deputy with his own forces. By a concerted sweep against the pirates and their strongholds, he forced them out of business in three months, taking 20,000 prisoners, most of whom he spared and offered employment as farmers.

The following year Pompey was transferred to a more conventional command, against Mithridates, the king of Pontus who had been a sore trial to the Romans, and to everyone else, in Asia Minor for over twenty years. Pompey succeeded completely where others had failed, and in the process considerably enlarged the Roman empire. Unwilling at that time to assume sole power in Rome, but anxious to keep it within his sights, he threw in his lot with Crassus and Caesar, whose daughter Julia he married in 59 BC, as his fourth wife. Though it was no doubt originally intended as a marriage of political convenience such as Pompey had contracted before with Sulla's stepdaughter, who was forced to divorce her husband by whom she was at the time pregnant, it seems to have been a successful and loving partnership while it lasted. So much so that Julia's death in childbirth in 54 BC gives plausible substance to the account of the origins of the subsequent civil war offered by the young literary prodigy Lucan (AD 39–65) in his epic poem:

Julia alone, if granted by the fates a longer life, could have restrained her resentful husband, and her father, too; could have pushed aside their swords and joined the hands that held the weapons, just as the Sabine brides stood between their fathers and their men, who were then reconciled. Her death shattered family ties and released the enmity between the two. Ambition spurred them both. Pompey feared the exploits of his rival would obscure his own less recent triumphs; that the hammer of the pirates would take second place in people's esteem to the conqueror of Gaul. Caesar was driven by his craving for continuous activity and by a nature which would not let him give way. Caesar could not stand any longer someone above him, nor could Pompey abide anyone being his equal.

(Pharsalia, I. 114–26)

What is equally probable is that Caesar, at the end of a nine-year campaign in Gaul, needing a further consulship and command, and fearing prosecution for irregularities during his consulship in 59 BC if he did not get them, deliberately provoked the confrontation. He returned at the head of his army, had himself appointed dictator, and pushed Pompey, his army, and his senatorial supporters out of Italy and to final defeat in 48 BC at Pharsalus in Greece. Pompey himself escaped, but was assassinated, before the eyes of his fifth wife, by officials of the Egyptian government, with whom he was seeking asylum, as he stepped ashore.

Caesar, in hot pursuit of Pompey, was then persuaded by Cleopatra VII (68–30 BC), under her father's will joint ruler of Egypt with her brother, to stay a while as her personal guest, the pretext being that he should adjudicate between her and her brother, who were at loggerheads. Caesar accepted her invitation with such pleasure that a son, known as Caesarion, was born the following year. Whether or not Caesar was the father is open to question, but Cleopatra claimed he was, Caesar is reported to have admitted paternity, and Caesar's heir, his great-nephew Octavian, certainly believed Caesarion was Caesar's son, and had him murdered in 30 BC. Cleopatra, sometimes portrayed as an empty-headed temptress with a weakness for powerful Romans, was, according to medieval Arab scholars, highly intelligent, widely read, linguistically gifted, and politically aware. Caesar, having adjudicated in her favour, then found himself embroiled on her side in a local war. This was only resolved with outside Jewish help and the arrival of the Twenty-Seventh Legion, which he had ordered to join him from Pharsalus.

While Caesar was in Egypt in 48–47 BC, he had been confirmed in his absence as dictator, an appointment which was regularly renewed thereafter. Thus began, with a few brief interregna, the rule in Rome by twelve men who, with one exception, held the name Caesar, by birth, by adoption, by descent through the female line, or by adding it to their official title. Gaius Suetonius Tranquillus (the historian Suetonius, c. AD 70–c. 140), who had access to imperial archives, wrote

FIGURE 4 Life-size bust of Pompey: a first-century copy of a contemporary likeness with stylized hair reflecting Alexander the Great.

Source: Ny Carlsberg Glyptotek, Copenhagen

a racy and anecdotal account of these twelve men entitled 'Lives of the Caesars', incorporating pen portraits from which extracts are quoted in the individual accounts below. Subsequent emperors also assumed the title of Caesar, while adopting the surname of Augustus, thus maintaining the illusion of their descent, by birth or adoption, from the first emperor. From the end of the second century AD, it became customary for senior emperors to be addressed as Augustus, and their deputies as Caesar.

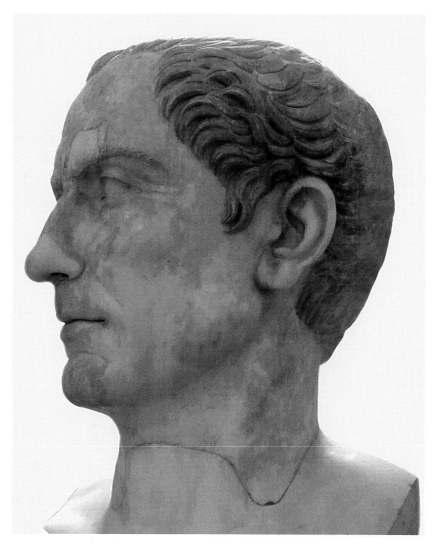

FIGURE 5 Bust of Julius Caesar (side view) of the era of Trajan.

Source: VRoma: Barbara McManus: National Archaeological Museum, Naples

JULIUS CAESAR

Gaius Julius Caesar: born on 12 July 100 BC in Rome, son of Gaius Julius Caesar (d. 85 BC) and Aurelia (d. 54 BC). First consulship 59 BC. Governor of Gaul 58–49 BC. Appointed dictator for ten years in 47 BC; for life, 14 February 44 BC. Married [1]

Cornelia (d. 69 BC), one daughter, Julia (*c.* 76–54 BC); [2] Pompeia (divorced 52 BC); [3] in 59 BC, Calpurnia, daughter of Lucius Calpurnius Piso, consul 58 BC. Assassinated on 15 March 44 BC. Deified in 42 BC.

> He was embarrassed by his baldness, which was a frequent subject of jokes on the part of his opponents; so much so that he used to comb his straggling locks forward from the back, and of all the honours heaped upon him by senate and people, the one he appreciated most was the privilege of being allowed to wear a laurel wreath at all times.
>
> **(Suetonius, *Julius Caesar*, XLV)**

At the age of 30, arguably the most famous Roman of them all was regarded as a dandy who had squandered his wife's fortune (they married when he was 17) as well as his own. He was, however, a fine public speaker and advocate, which served him well when campaigning successfully for the offices of quaestor (he served in Spain); aedile – his extravagance in providing gladiatorial shows and renovating public buildings and roads at his own expense to gain further popularity put him even deeper in debt; and praetor in 63 BC, when, according to Suetonius, baulked of his attempt to be appointed governor of Egypt, he resorted to massive bribery in order to be elected *pontifex maximus.* His duties as praetor took him to Spain, where he discovered a talent as a military commander and amassed enough by way of booty and tribute to pay off his debts.

The formation of the triumvirate with Crassus and Pompey was a mark also of Caesar's determination to push through genuine and innovative measures in the face of a senate which was suspicious of his motives, and to ensure that there was some continuity of progressive legislation after his year of office as consul. He then obtained for himself the governorship of Gaul, and Illyricum, for a period of five years, which was later extended for a second term. Gaul at that time comprised the sub-jugated region south of the Alps and to the east of the Apennines as far as the river Rubicon (Cisalpine Gaul), together with a small, but significant, portion of territory the other side of the Alps roughly corresponding to Provence and Languedoc (Gallia Narbonensis, or Transalpine Gaul). When Caesar had finished his series of brilliant but punitive campaigns, during which, according to Plutarch, his troops killed a million warriors and took prisoner as many more, he was master of the whole region to the west of the Rhine, which he crossed with his army over a purpose-built military bridge 400 metres long and 11 metres wide, to ensure that there would be no further trouble from the Germanic tribes.

The size of the operation was matched by its complexity. Even Lucius Annaeus Florus (*fl. c.* AD 130), who compiled his 'Abridgement of all the Wars for 700 Years' in the form of a selective panegyric, underestimates Caesar's real achievement in his subjugation in 51 BC of Alesia, the fortified hill-city in which Vercingetorix, the Arvernian chief who most successfully opposed Rome, made his final stand.

> This mighty city, garrisoned by 80,000 troops, was defended by its walls, its fortress, and sheer river banks [on both sides]. Caesar invested it with an earth wall, a fence of stakes, and a moat, into which he diverted water from the river. His wall was topped with a massive parapet and had eighteen towers built into it. First he starved the inhabitants out. Then, when they dared to sally forth, he cut them down at the wall and the fence, and finally forced them to surrender.
>
> **(Abridgement, I. 46)**

Florus fails to mention that at the same time, on his other front, Caesar had to cope with a Gallic relief force of 250,000 infantry and 8,000 cavalry, whom he forced back and finally routed.

The campaign was also in part a naval operation. In 56 BC, a fleet which Caesar had ordered to be built for the purpose destroyed, by employment of Roman ingenuity, the taller and more manoeuvrable ships of the Veneti, a sea-going nation which occupied territory in north-west Gaul. In 55 and 54 BC he mounted expeditions to Britain, which had up until then been virtually unknown to the Roman world. From his own account of his final departure:

> After taking delivery of hostages, Caesar took his army back to the coast, where he found that the ships had been repaired. When he had refloated them, he decided, since he had so many prisoners and some ships had been lost in a storm, to make two trips. And it was a fact that with all those ships and so many crossings, neither in that or the previous year did any sink while carrying troops. But of the ships that were returned empty from the continent – those which had disembarked the men from the first sailing and the reserve fleet of sixty ships which he had given Labienus [his second-in-command] orders from Britain to build – few made the crossing safely and of the rest almost all had to turn back. Caesar waited some time for them in vain, and then, lest he might be prevented from sailing altogether by the time of year, the equinox being imminent, he was forced to pack the troops more closely together on board. The sea went completely calm. He sailed at the beginning of the second watch, making land at dawn with the whole fleet intact.
>
> **(Gallic War, V. 23)**

The two expeditions to Britain gained nothing tangible for Rome, good public relations for Caesar, and for its Celtic inhabitants a breathing space of ninety-seven years before the next invasion. The annexation of the rest of Gaul, however, achieved a kind of peace within a traditionally volatile region, while adding to the empire a territory twice the size of Italy, with a population far greater than that of Spain. Caesar established guidelines whereby the tribes were economically able to continue as individual communities – in 27 BC, Caesar's new Gaul became three provinces under the control of the head of state: Aquitania, Lugdunensis, and Belgica. By making the river Rhine the eastern frontier of his acquisitions, Caesar effectively enabled a French nation, overlaid with Latin culture, to evolve from a predominantly Celtic society, while establishing a buffer zone between the hostile Germanic tribes and Italy. He enriched the Roman empire, while at the same time, of course, enriching himself.

When Caesar left Transalpine Gaul in 49 BC and crossed the Rubicon at the head of his troops, it signified that he came as an invader. After Pompey's hasty departure and ultimate defeat, and his own fruitful holiday in Egypt, Caesar returned to Rome with his army via Asia Minor, pausing at Zela to annihilate the forces of Pharnaces of Pontus (63–47 BC), son of Mithridates. This was the occasion of his celebrated message to the senate, '*Veni, vidi, vici* (I came, I saw, I conquered)!' Opposition from the Pompeian faction, however, was only stamped out after two more campaigns, in Africa and Spain, culminating at the battle of Munda on 17 March 45 BC. In October of that year Caesar was back in Rome. Five months later he was dead, at the hands of a band of senatorial conspirators, discontented officials, and former soldiers, led by Marcus Junius Brutus (c. 85–42 BC), latterly known as Quintus Caepio Brutus after his adoption by an uncle. Both he and his fellow conspirator, his brother-in-law Gaius Cassius Longinus (d. 42 BC), were former Pompeians whom Caesar had pardoned after the battle of Pharsalus. In the meantime he had established order, begun measures to reduce congestion in Rome and to drain large tracts of marshy land, given full voting rights to the inhabitants of his former province south of the Alps, revised the tax laws of Asia and Sicily, resettled many Romans in new homes in the Roman provinces, and reformed the calendar, which, with one minor adjustment, is the one in use today (see Appendix 1, p. 207).

In Shakespeare's play *Julius Caesar*, the best lines, and the poetry, are given to Mark Antony's defence of Caesar's actions and his denial of any exercise of 'ambition' on Caesar's part, while Brutus, the leading conspirator in his murder, is left to justify himself in prose: 'As Caesar loved me, I weep for him; as he was fortunate, I rejoice at it; as he was valiant, I honour him; but, as he was ambitious, I slew him' (III. 2). The judgement of history is that Caesar's driving ambition and energy led him to try to make too many changes too quickly, without ensuring that there were workable substitutes for the traditions he was sweeping away. Further, the senate was concerned not so much with reverting to democracy, but with preserving rule by the aristocracy, and their positions in that rule. Later in the same scene in *Julius Caesar*, Mark Antony is made to say,

> You all did see that on the Lupercal,
> I thrice presented him a kingly crown,
> Which he did thrice refuse.

(III. 2.101–3)

This is historical fact. Caesar's position was that of a king, but his refusal of the crown was for reasons of diplomacy, not modesty. In that the *imperium* that Caesar assumed gave him the position of sole ruler, he was in effect the first emperor of Rome. The word *imperium* is related to *imperator*, which came to mean 'emperor' but was originally the title bestowed on a victorious military commander by his troops. Emperors got into the habit of collecting such a salutation each time a commander won a victory in their name: hence on coins of Domitian, for example, 'IMPERATOR XIIII' indicates that he had been acclaimed as victor in war fourteen times.

The package of powers that Julius Caesar's successor assumed in 27 BC gave him the constitutional right to greater *imperium* than anyone else at the time. It is for this reason that the establishment of the rule of Rome by emperors is said to have begun then.

AUGUSTUS

Gaius (Julius Caesar) Octavi(an)us: born on 23 September 63 BC in Rome, son of Gaius Octavius (d. 59 BC) and Atia (d. 43 BC), niece of Julius Caesar, who made him his heir. Consul 43, 33, 31–23 BC. Named *princeps* ('chief' or 'first') 28 BC. Effectively became emperor in 27 BC, with extended civil powers in 23 BC. Married [1] Claudia (divorced); [2] Scribonia (divorced 39 BC), one daughter, Julia (39 BC–AD 14); [3] Livia Drusilla (58 BC–AD 29), mother of Tiberius. Died at Nola, 19 August AD 14. Deified on 17 September AD 14.

> He was of distinguished and extremely handsome appearance for the whole of his life, though for himself he did not care what he looked like. He would have several barbers working feverishly on him simultaneously, and while he was being shaved or having his hair clipped (it was all one to him) he read or even carried on with his writing . . . He had bad teeth, small and widely set apart; his hair was fair and wavy; his eyebrows met in the middle of his forehead; his ears were of average size; his nose jutted out at the top and then bent downwards.
>
> **(Suetonius, *Augustus*, LXXIX)**

The owner of this indubitably Roman nose was in Apollonia in Epirus, pursuing his military studies, when he heard of his great-uncle's murder, and that in his will Caesar had named him not only his principal heir, but also, according to several classical sources, his son by adoption. It was late April when he got back to Rome, by which time Marcus Antonius (*c.* 83–30 BC) – Mark Antony – and Marcus Aemilius Lepidus (*c.* 90–13 BC), who had been Caesar's chief assistants, had assumed control of the state, and of Caesar's personal fortune, and Brutus and the other conspirators had, at the prompting of Cicero, been granted an amnesty by the senate. A confused series of battles and comings and goings resulted in Octavian (as he is usually styled) being elected consul, at the age of 19, and forcing through a motion to the effect that he, Antony, and Lepidus should formally be recognized as the ruling triumvirate for five years in order to re-establish the constitution. Their first act was to revive the fearful Sullan policy of proscription.

> As soon as they were on their own, the three of them drew up a list of those who were to die. They proscribed, both then and later, those of whom they were suspicious because of their ability, as well as their personal enemies, trading with each other for the lives of their own relations and friends. They decreed death and confiscation of property for about 300 senators and 2,000 equestrians, among them their own brothers and uncles, as well as senior officers serving under them who had had cause to offend them or their own colleagues. As they left the conference table for Rome they decided to postpone most of the killings, but as a warning secretly to send out assassins to execute twelve, or some say seventeen, of the most important victims, including Cicero.
>
> **(Appian, *Civil Wars*, IV. 2)**

Cicero was too ill to escape his murderers, but was bundled into a litter by his slaves. He was tracked down and killed by a swordcut to the neck. His head and hands were cut off and sent to Rome, where they were nailed up in the forum on the orders of Antony, who was the stepson of Cornelius Lentulus Sura, the most senior state official executed in the wake of the Catiline conspiracy.

While the triumvirate formally remained in power beyond its statutory term, the twelve years until 31 BC were almost entirely taken up with wars between its members, and against other fellow Romans. Brutus and Cassius were defeated in two battles at Philippi in Macedonia in 42 BC, and committed suicide. Sextus Pompey (son of Pompey the 'Great' by his third wife), having obtained a large fleet and taken possession of Sicily, was finally murdered by his own troops in 35 BC. Antony's long-standing affair with Caesar's former mistress, Cleopatra, and his preference for her company and Alexandria over that of his wife (who was Octavian's sister) and Rome, culminated in Octavian's defeat of the Egyptian fleet at the battle of Actium in 31 BC.

> The queen was the first to take flight, the golden stern and purple sails of her galley disappearing into the open sea. Antony soon followed, with Octavian surging in his wake . . . Antony was the first to commit suicide, by the sword. Cleopatra threw herself at Octavian's feet, and tried her best to attract his gaze: in vain, for his self-control was impervious to her beauty. It was not her life she was after, for that had already been granted, but a portion of her kingdom. When she realized this was hopeless and that she had been earmarked to feature in Octavian's triumph in Rome, she took advantage of her guard's carelessness to get herself into the mausoleum, as the royal tomb is called. Once there, she put on the royal robes which she was accustomed to wear, and lay down in a richly perfumed coffin beside her Antony. Then she applied poisonous snakes to her veins and slipped into death as though into a sleep.
>
> **(Florus, *Abridgement*, II. 21)**

With Lepidus now edged into the background and Caesarion murdered, Octavian was in charge of the Roman world. He needed to assemble his powers into an acceptable constitutional form, avoiding any suggestion of a return to a monarchy or even to a dictatorship, which had caused so much trouble in the past. He achieved this gradually over a number of years, and in a manner which did not appear to undermine the authority of the senate, at least as a consultative body. While continuing to hold successive consulships, in 27 BC he formally resigned all the special powers he had been granted, but accepted in return for ten years the strategic provinces of Cilicia, Cyprus, Gaul, Spain, and Syria, for which troops were required, together with his confirmation as divine successor to the pharaohs in Egypt. (His own version of the process was incorporated into one of the statements engraved on bronze tablets at the entrance to the family mausoleum which he built: 'During my sixth and seventh consulates [28 and 27 BC], when I had put down the civil wars and was universally acknowledged to be in complete control, I transferred the management of affairs of state to the senate and the Roman people' (*Res Gestae Divi Augusti*, 34).) In addition, he renounced the name of Octavianus in favour of the more dignified Augustus – on his adoption, he would have become Gaius Julius Caesar Octavianus, but in the event, he never himself used the name Octavianus, preferring to be called 'Gaius Caesar, son of Caesar', or, even better, *Divi filius* (son of a god). In 23 BC, because of illness, he gave up his apparent claim to hold the office of consul for life. This was diplomatically a sound move, as it opened up to others an additional chance of honour if not much responsibility; especially as in its place he was granted for life the privileges of a tribune of the people, with powers to apply a veto at will and to take matters direct to the popular assemblies.

That particular illness proved to be only a minor set-back in a reign that lasted over forty years and gave to the western world the term 'Augustan' to denote an age

FIGURE 6 The Ara Pacis Augustae (Altar of Augustan Peace) was commissioned by the senate in 13 BC to mark Augustus' safe return from Gaul and Spain, where he had been settling provincial matters. It was dedicated on the Campus Martius in 9 BC. This section of the south frieze celebrates members of the imperial family. The central figure in the military cloak is usually taken to be Drusus, younger brother of Tiberius and stepson of Augustus, who died of a fall from his horse on military duty in Germany in 9 BC. He is facing his wife, Antonia Minor, daughter of Mark Antony and Octavia; she is holding the hand of their son Germanicus. Identification of the other figures is more problematic.

Source: VRoma: Barbara McManus: Museo dell'Ara Pacis

of glittering literary achievement. Though the boundaries of the Roman empire had not yet reached their widest extent, Augustus consolidated them by reorganizing and strengthening the army, and removing it from Italy to patrol the provinces. He remodelled the civil service and largely rebuilt parts of Rome itself, appointing 3,500 firemen under a chief fire officer to guard against conflagration.

Augustus died in the family house at Nola in Campania, at the age of 76. He was married three times, but his only child was a daughter by his second wife. He had, however, taken the precaution, after several attempts to do so had been aborted by deaths, of nominating a successor, his stepson Tiberius, to whom the previous year he had granted a form of power of attorney over affairs of state.

TIBERIUS

Tiberius Claudius Nero (Caesar Augustus): born on 16 November 42 BC, son of Tiberius Claudius Nero (d. 33 BC) and Livia Drusilla (*c.* 58 BC–AD 29), who married

Augustus in 39 BC. Consul 13, 7 BC, AD 18, 21, 31. Became emperor in AD 14. Married [1] Vipsania Agrippina (divorced 12 BC), one son, Drusus (13 BC–AD 23); [2] Julia (39 BC–AD 14), daughter of Augustus. Died at Misenum, 16 March AD 37.

> He was a large, strong man of above average height, with broad shoulders and chest, and well proportioned all the way from head to toe. He was left-handed, and his joints were so strong that he could bore through an apple with one finger, and break open a boy's or even a teenager's head with a mere rap of the knuckle. He wore his white hair long at the back, covering his neck, a family habit, apparently. He had a handsome face, which would, however, suddenly erupt into a fierce rash.
>
> **(Suetonius, *Tiberius*, LXVIII)**

Though Tiberius had been groomed by Augustus as his successor, he was actually fourth choice after Agrippa, husband of Augustus' only daughter Julia, and their sons, Gaius and Lucius, all three of whom died in the lifetime of Augustus. Thus to an already diffident nature was added a sense of inferiority. On Agrippa's death, Augustus compelled Tiberius to divorce his wife Vipsania and become Julia's third husband. Five years later, in 6 BC, in spite of his recent appointment to a five-year term as the equivalent of chief tribune of the people, a highly influential function up until then performed by Augustus himself, Tiberius asked for and was granted leave of absence, and retired to Rhodes. Of the reasons which have been suggested for this voluntary exile at such a critical point in his career, the behaviour of Julia seems not the least unlikely. Certainly, by the time he returned in AD 2, she had been banished by her father for adultery. In AD 4, Tiberius, now adopted son of Augustus, was sent to command the imperial armies, all of them based outside Italy. From then until Augustus' death, which happened while he was travelling, he hardly had occasion to visit Rome.

Tiberius was summoned back not by the senate, but by his elderly mother, Livia, widow of Augustus. The circumstances of her marriage were bizarre, whatever interpretation is put on them. It is said that Livia's first husband was forced to divorce her, and that she married Augustus when she was six months pregnant with Tiberius' younger brother, Drusus; Augustus had just divorced his own second wife, Scribonia, according to him because he was 'sick of her perpetual bitching' (Suetonius, *Augustus*, LXII), on the very day she gave birth to their only child. Livia had been 16 when Tiberius was born: now in her seventies, she was a matriarch and she wanted a share in ruling the country, too. Tiberius would have none of that, but it is reported (by Tacitus) that, in order to secure his position, he had Agrippa Postumus, the last surviving grandson of Augustus, murdered on the prison island to which he had been exiled for his antisocial behaviour. According to Suetonius, this could equally well have been done without Tiberius' knowledge on instructions left by Augustus, or on an order by Livia in Augustus' name.

There followed several years of intrigue and counter-intrigue, as candidates to succeed Tiberius (and their wives or mothers on their behalf) jockeyed for position or were jockeyed completely out of the way, as happened to Drusus, the emperor's only son. Tiberius probably had no part in any of this, but merely to sense what was going on unsettled him, and further contributed to his indecision in matters of government. Finally, in AD 26, he had had enough. Because he had probably always been happiest when away from Rome, he simply upped and departed to his holiday mansion on the isle of Capri, never to return to the city. He left administration in the hands of Lucius Aelius Sejanus (d. AD 31), praetorian prefect (commander of the imperial guard), who was, in his own mind at least, a contender for the post of emperor when it next fell vacant, and was conspiring against Tiberius while removing people in his own path. Tiberius, however, when moved to do so, could still exercise power even from a distance, and wrote a letter to the senate expressing his suspicions. Sejanus was executed, and his corpse dragged through the streets and then thrown into the Tiber. His family and many of his cronies suffered the same fate. The treatment of his children casts a chilling sidelight on the logic of the Roman penal system:

> Though the fury of the people was quietening down and many had been pacified by the earlier executions, it was then decided to attend to the two surviving children of Sejanus. They were therefore taken to jail, the boy realizing what was in store for them, the girl so innocent that she kept asking what she had done, crying that she would do nothing wrong again and that surely a gentle spanking would be enough this time. The archivists of the time record that because there was no legal precedent for the execution of a virgin, the hangman had intercourse with her beside the noose. The pair were then strangled and their bodies, young as they were, thrown on the steps by the Capitol.
>
> **(Tacitus, *Annals*, V. 9)**

Tacitus, who was born about twenty-five years after these events, was one of the Roman historians who suggested that Tiberius' retirement home was what might be termed a palace of sexual varieties, but he does add that Tiberius left for it 'with only a few companions: a former consul [and] . . . a Roman knight of the higher rank . . . the rest being intellectuals, mainly Greek, whose conversation he enjoyed' (*Annals*, IV. 58). Tiberius' last years were still fraught with morbid mistrust, reports of flagrant and not-quite-so-flagrant family adulteries, and a continual narrowing down, by natural and unnatural death, of candidates for the succession. Whether Tiberius, who was then 78, died naturally or was murdered, is uncertain, but by then the field had been reduced to two: his own grandson, Tiberius Gemellus (*c.* AD 20–37), who was, however, suspected by many, including Tiberius, to have been an outcome of his mother's affair with Sejanus; and his last surviving great-nephew, Gaius Caesar, now 24, nicknamed Caligula ('Bootsie') after the miniature army boots he used to wear as a child. With typical vacillation to the last, Tiberius named them joint heirs.

CALIGULA

Gaius Caesar (Augustus) Germanicus: born in AD 12, son of Germanicus Caesar (15 BC–AD 19), nephew of Tiberius, and Agrippina (14 BC–AD 33), granddaughter of Augustus. Became emperor in AD 37. Consul AD 39–41. Married [1] Junia Claudilla (died); [2] Livia Orestilla (divorced); [3] Lollia Paulina (divorced); [4] Milonia Caesonia, one daughter, Julia. Assassinated on 24 January AD 41.

> He was very tall, with an enormous body supported on spindly legs, a thin neck, and an extremely pallid complexion. His eyes and temples were sunken, and his forehead broad and glowering. His hair was thin and he was bald on top, though he had a hairy body. For that reason it was a crime punishable by death to look down on him from above as he passed by, or for any reason whatsoever to mention a goat in his presence. He was by nature ugly, but he made himself even more so by practising gruesome faces in a mirror.
>
> **(Suetonius, *Caligula*, 1)**

The question as to who would succeed Tiberius was resolved easily enough. Naevius Cordus Sutorius Macro (d. AD 38), a former chief of the fire service in Rome and now commander of the imperial guard in succession to Sejanus, had met Caligula in Capri, and they got on well together. When he proposed Caligula's name to the senate as emperor, there was no objection. At first, it seemed that the choice was correct, for Caligula was everything a young and charismatic ruler should be – generous to the public (and to the imperial guard), genuinely interested, though inexperienced, in matters of government, sensible, witty, and just. He recalled many political exiles and dropped the charges against them, and banished all male prostitutes. He formally adopted his cousin, Tiberius Gemellus, and appointed his uncle Claudius (his dead father's younger brother) to be, with him, *consul suffectus* in AD 37. *Suffectus* in this context means 'deputy' or 'substitute'. Julius Caesar instituted the procedure whereby an elected consul was invited or required to stand down during his term of office in favour of a suffect consul. Especially when emperors appropriated for themselves successive consulships (a policy begun by Augustus), this device was subsequently used to increase the number of men qualified for the most senior administrative or military posts in the provinces of the empire.

FIGURE 7 Caligula: a chilling study of weakness and cruelty.

Source: Ny Carlsberg Glyptotek, Copenhagen

Then Caligula fell ill. When he recovered, the citizens of Rome found they were living in a nightmare. According to Suetonius, Caligula had since childhood suffered from epilepsy, known in Roman times as the 'parliamentary disease', since it was regarded as an especially bad omen if anyone had a seizure while public business was being conducted – Caligula's very distant cousin, Julius Caesar, probably suffered from what is now recognized as late-onset epilepsy. This, or some other cause, violently affected Caligula's mental state, and he became totally irrational, with delusions not only of grandeur but also of divinity. He put Tiberius Gemellus and Macro to death without trial. To have an altar built to himself was one thing: it was quite another to propose that a statue of himself be erected in the Temple in Jerusalem, and worshipped there. His extravagance knew no bounds, and he introduced heavy taxation to help balance his personal expenditure. In such an atmosphere, executions and displays of sheer bloodlust were commonplace, and conspiracies and plots proliferated. Finally the inevitable happened: one of the plots succeeded. He was assassinated by members of his imperial guard. Caligula had been emperor for less than four years. He had four wives, three of them during his imperial reign (the last, Caesonia, and their daughter Julia were murdered at the same time as him), and he was said, according to Suetonius, to have committed incest with each of his three sisters in turn.

CLAUDIUS

Tiberius Claudius Drusus Nero (Caesar Augustus) Germanicus: born on 1 August 10 BC at Lugdunum, Gaul, son of Nero Claudius Drusus (38–9 BC), brother of Tiberius, and Antonia (36 BC–AD 37), daughter of Mark Antony. Became emperor in AD 41. Consul AD 42, 43, 47, 51. Married [1] Plautia Urgulanilla (divorced), one son, Drusus (d. *c.* AD 26), and one daughter, Claudia; [2] Aelia Paetina (divorced), one daughter, Antonia; [3] Valeria Messalina (executed AD 48), one son, Tiberius Claudius Britannicus (AD 41–55), and one daughter, Octavia (*c.* AD 40–62); [4] Agrippina (AD 15–59). Died on 12 October AD 54. Deified in AD 54.

> He was not short of either authority or dignity when he was standing up or sitting down, still less so when he reclined: he was tall but not lanky, and good-looking, with a fine crop of white hair and a well-set neck. But his knees were so weak that he staggered as he walked, and his habits were embarrassing whether he was indulging in domestic or business affairs. He had an indecent laugh, and when he was annoyed he foamed disgustingly at the mouth and his nose ran. He stammered, and his head twitched the whole time, but faster when he was actually engaged in the slightest activity. He was always ill, until he became emperor. Then

his health improved marvellously, except for attacks of stomach-ache, which he
said even made him think of suicide.

(Suetonius, *Claudius*, XXX, XXXI)

After the assassination of Caligula, members of the imperial guard who were
systematically sacking the palace came across his uncle Claudius cowering behind a
curtain. Possibly they saw him as a useful hostage in the event of retribution, for,
instead of killing him, they pushed him into a litter and carried him off to their camp.
There he was made an offer: to be the imperial guard's nominee as emperor.
Obviously feeling that to be emperor was a fate not quite as bad as immediate death,
Claudius cemented the deal by promising a special bonus in return for their support,
thus creating a precedent which future aspirants had to follow. In the absence of any
other obvious candidate, the senate confirmed the choice of the imperial guard.
Claudius was then 50. He was a scholar, being the author of historical works in both
Latin and Greek, though none has survived, and the inventor of three new letters of
the alphabet, which have come down to us in inscriptions. He had, however, no
experience of administration, let alone of government.

In history and in the accounts of ancient historians, Claudius comes across as a
positive mishmash of conflicting characteristics: absent-minded, hesitant, muddled,
determined, cruel (by proxy), intuitive, wise, and dominated by his wife and his
personal staff of freedmen. He was probably all of these. If his choice of women
was disastrous, there are countless instances of this particular failing on the part of
prominent public figures. And he may, with sound reasoning, have preferred the
advice of educated and trained executives from abroad to that of potentially suspect
aristocratic senators, even if some of those executives did use their influence to their
own financial advantage. It was a thoroughly sound if not glittering reign, which lasted
almost fourteen years.

Claudius revived the office of censor, which had fallen into disuse, and took
on the job himself, introducing into the senate as new members several chiefs from
Gaul. With the help of his personal staff, he reorganized and rationalized the financial
affairs of the state and empire, setting aside a separate fund for the emperor's private
household expenses. Almost all grain had to be imported, mainly from Africa and
Egypt. To encourage potential importers and to build up stocks against winter months
and times of famine, Claudius offered to insure them against losses on the open sea,
an unusual provision in ancient times. To make unloading easier and to relieve
congestion on the river Tiber, he carried out a scheme originally proposed by Julius
Caesar, and constructed the new port of Ostia on the coast. Unfortunately it was built
to the north of the Tiber mouth, with a channel connecting the two, which meant that
the prevailing current from the sea deposited in the harbour accumulations of silt
brought down by the river.

FIGURE 8 First-century AD head of Claudius, wearing a civic crown of oak leaves. There is a little weakness about the face, perhaps, but no doubt about the intelligence.

Source: VRoma: Barbara McManus: National Archaeological Museum, Naples

Claudius' most far-reaching initiative led to the first successful full-scale invasion of Britain, after a reconnaissance by the expedition's leader, Aulus Plautius. Rome could no longer pretend that Britain did not exist, and a potentially hostile and possibly united nation just beyond the fringe of the existing empire presented a threat which could not be ignored. Besides, Claudius, for so long the butt of his family, wanted a piece of military glory, and here was a chance to get it. The force which sailed in AD 43 was a formidable one, even by Roman standards. Whether Plautius had instructions to call on Claudius if he got into difficulties or simply to invite him over to preside at the kill is not clear. He did get into difficulties, however. The only surviving account of the campaign is by Cassius Dio, of Nicaea, governor of Africa and then Dalmatia, writing in Greek at the beginning of the third century AD:

> Shortly afterwards Togodumnus [son of the British king Cunobellinus – Cymbeline – who died between AD 40 and 43] was killed, but the Britons, so far from giving up, were all the more united now in a determination to avenge his death. Plautius, unwilling to advance any farther, consolidated the territory he had gained and sent for Claudius. His orders were to do this if he met any resistance, and extensive preparations for just such an eventuality, including the mobilization of an elephant corps, had already been made. When he received the message, Claudius handed over the administration of affairs at home and abroad, including military operations, to his consular colleague Lucius Vitellius (having fixed for both of them a further full six months in office), and then himself took the field. He went by river to Ostia, and then sailed along the coast to Massilia [Marseilles], From there, travelling overland and by river transport, he reached the sea and crossed to Britain, where he met up with his troops, who were encamped by the river Thames.
>
> Assuming command, he crossed the river, engaged the barbarians, who had rallied together at his approach, defeated them, and took Camelodunum [Colchester], Cunobellinus' capital. Then he put down many other tribes, defeating them or accepting their surrender, and was hailed *imperator* numerous times, which was against the rules, for no-one could receive this honour more than once in the same campaign. He confiscated the tribes' weapons, which he handed over to Plautius with orders to subdue the rest. He then returned to Rome, sending news of his victory ahead with his sons-in-law, Magnus and Silanus. When the senate heard about his achievement, it granted him the title of Britannicus and authorized him to celebrate a triumph.
>
> **(Roman History, LX. 21)**

Claudius was in Britain just sixteen days. Plautius followed up the advantage gained, and was from AD 44 to 47 governor of this newest province in the Roman empire. When Caratacus (brother of Togodumnus) was finally captured and brought to Rome in chains, Claudius pardoned him and his family.

Claudius was married four times; in spite of his physical disadvantages he was more successful in fathering progeny than any of his imperial predecessors, if rather less lucky in love. At his succession, he was on his third wife, his distant cousin Valeria Messalina, who three weeks later presented him with a son (afterwards known as Britannicus, the title having been conferred on him by a grateful, or perhaps astonished, senate at the same time as on his father). Eventually Messalina was discovered too many times *in flagrante delicto*, and in AD 48, at the age of about 24, she was duly disposed of by tried Roman methods. Speculation was rife as to who would be the next imperial consort. It turned out to be Agrippina, Caligula's sister and Claudius' own niece, to marry whom he had first to have a law enacted permitting such unions. By a former marriage Agrippina had a teenage son, later known as Nero. She persuaded Claudius to adopt him formally, and to give Nero his daughter Octavia in marriage. Then, according to Tacitus, she poisoned him.

NERO

Nero Claudius Caesar (Augustus) Germanicus: born Lucius Domitius Ahenobarbus on 15 December AD 37 at Antium, son of Gnaeus Domitius Ahenobarbus, consul in AD 32, and Agrippina (AD 15–59), sister of Caligula, who then married Crispus Passienus and, later, in AD 49, her uncle Claudius. Became emperor in AD 54. Consul AD 55, 57, 58, 60. Married [1] Octavia (divorced); [2] Poppaea Sabina (d. AD 65), one daughter, Claudia Augusta, who died in infancy; [3] Statilia Messallina. Committed suicide in AD 68.

> He was of average height, fair-haired, with features that were pretty rather than handsome, weak blue eyes, a fat neck, a pot belly, skinny legs, and a body which smelt and was covered with spots . . . He was so insensitive about his appearance that he used to wear his hair in rows of curls, and when he was on his Greek trip he let it grow down his back. He usually appeared in public in a dressing-gown without a belt, a scarf round his neck, and no shoes.
>
> **(Suetonius, *Nero*, LI)**

Nero was artistic, sporting, brutal, weak, sensual, erratic, extravagant, sadistic, bisexual – and latterly almost certainly deranged. He was 16 when his mother secured for him the office of emperor, by engineering his being presented to the troops as their candidate and by promising what was now the customary bonus. Shortly afterwards the only other possible contender, Claudius' son Britannicus, was removed, probably by poison. During the early years of his reign, however, Nero was kept in hand by his tutor, the distinguished philosopher and writer Lucius Annaeus Seneca, now in his early sixties, and Sextus Africanus Burrus, praetorian prefect, though exceptionally persuasive tactics had to be employed to get the emperor to withdraw, and forget, a proposal to abolish all indirect taxation. Nero's excesses of behaviour were hushed up, if not entirely restrained, and between the three of them they managed also to avert attempts by Agrippina to exert imperial influence. The turning point came largely through Nero's inherent lust and lack of self-control, for he took as his (not uncomplaisant) mistress Poppaea, wife of his partner in frequent debaucheries, Marcus Salvius Otho, five years his senior, whom in AD 58 he dispatched to be governor of Lusitania. Agrippina, presumably seeing this as an opportunity to assert herself, sided with Nero's wife, Octavia. Nero retaliated, according to Suetonius, with a grotesque and abortive series of attempts on his mother's life, including three by poison and one by engineering – the ceiling above her bed was geared to collapse while she was asleep. Finally (and here the accounts of Suetonius and Tacitus agree) he had a collapsible boat constructed, which was meant to deposit her in the Bay of Naples. It did, but she swam ashore. Nero sent a man to her house to use more conventional means. She was clubbed and stabbed to death.

That happened in AD 59. Nero celebrated by redoubling his outbreaks of excessive licentiousness and by creating two new festivals of chariot-racing, athletics, and musical contests, which gave him further opportunities to demonstrate in public his talent for singing while accompanying himself on the lyre. No-one was allowed to leave the auditorium while he was performing, for whatever reason. Suetonius writes of women giving birth during a Nero recital, and of men who pretended to die and were carried out as if to burial.

Burrus died in AD 62. Soon after that Seneca retired, whereupon Nero became totally subject to corrupt and evil advisers, indulging to the exclusion of everything else his passions for sport, music, preposterous parties, at which he and his guests publicly performed sexual acts of unimaginable ingenuity, and murder. Having divorced Octavia in AD 62 and then had her executed on a trumped-up charge of adultery, he married Poppaea, now divorced and pregnant with his child. He then killed her, too – Suetonius says he kicked her to death when she complained about his coming home late from the races. In AD 65 there was a genuine conspiracy to assassinate him; when it was discovered, there was terrible retribution in which Seneca and his nephew, the poet Lucan, died. There was never anything even resembling a trial: people whom Nero suspected or disliked or who merely aroused the jealousy of his advisers were sent a note ordering them to commit suicide. Gaius Petronius, man of letters and former 'director of imperial pleasures', died in this manner in AD 66. So did countless senators, noblemen, and generals, including in AD 67 Gnaeus Domitius Corbulo, hero of the Armenian wars and supreme commander in the Euphrates region.

In AD 64 fire had ravaged Rome for six days on end. According to Tacitus, who was about 9 years old at the time, of the fourteen districts of the city, 'four were undamaged, three were utterly destroyed, and in the other seven there remained only a few mangled and half-burnt traces of houses' (*Annals*, XV. 40). This is the famous occasion on which Nero is said to have 'fiddled while Rome burned', a phrase which in that form seems first to have emerged in the seventeenth century. Suetonius has him singing from a tower overlooking the conflagration. Cassius Dio records that he 'climbed on to the palace roof, from which there was the best overall view of the greater part of the fire and, assuming the garb of a lyre player, sang "The Capture of Troy"' (*Roman History*, LX. 18). Tacitus has a similar story: 'At the very time that Rome burned, he mounted his private stage and, reflecting present disasters in ancient calamities, sang about the destruction of Troy' (*Annals*, XV. 39), but he is careful to qualify it as *rumor*, 'an unauthenticated report'. The mere report, however, made people suspicious of the genuine relief measures which Nero immediately initiated. Nor was faith in his motives increased when he used a vast tract of ground razed by the fire between the Palatine and Esquiline hills on which to build Domus Aurea, his golden palace, a vast luxury complex (with two different kinds of running water) set in rambling pleasure gardens, specially designed for his amusements. It did not matter that he had residential areas elsewhere in the city rebuilt at his own expense to a proper grid pattern, with broad streets and open spaces. People said that they missed the cool shade of the original alleys and the towering, ramshackle tenements. Rumours of arson surfaced again, and Nero, looking around for scapegoats, found them in the members of the latest religious sect, Christianity, many of whose adherents were rounded up and torn to death by dogs or crucified as a public spectacle. The killings went on throughout the day and into the night, when more victims were burned to death to serve as street lighting, while Nero mingled with the crowds, driving his personal chariot.

Finally the tide of organized revolt gathered pace. In AD 68 one of the governors in Gaul, Gaius Julius Vindex, himself Gallic born, withdrew his oath of allegiance to the emperor and encouraged the governor of northern and eastern Spain, Galba, a hardened veteran of 71, to do the same. The revolutionary army was suppressed by legions who marched in from Germany, and Vindex committed suicide. Galba, having informed the senate that he was available, if required, to head a government, waited, and presumably sweated. The senate, obviously relieved that someone else was prepared to take personal responsibility, not only declared Nero a public enemy, but sentenced him to death by flogging. Nero thought of flight, dithered, and then killed himself with the help of his secretary.

GALBA

Servius Sulpicius Galba (Caesar Augustus): born on 24 December 3 BC near Tarracina. Governor of Hispania Tarraconensis AD 61–8. Consul AD 33, 69. Became emperor in AD 68. Married Lepida, two sons; all three died early in his career. Assassinated on 15 January AD 69.

He was of medium height, almost completely bald, blue-eyed, hook-nosed, and with feet and hands so crippled by arthritis that he could not wear shoes, or hold a book, let alone unroll it. His left side had grown outwards and hung down so far that it could only be held in with difficulty by a truss.

(Suetonius, *Galba*, XXI)

Galba, who was the direct and sole surviving descendant of an ancient patrician family, was consul in AD 33, and subsequently governed Upper Germany and Africa. He moved in high circles, and received advancement through Livia, mother of Tiberius. According to Suetonius, she left him in her will 500,000 gold pieces, which, because the sum was written in figures, Tiberius altered to 5,000 with a stroke of the pen. Galba was in his early sixties when Nero called him out of retirement to become governor in Spain. He was old and extremely distinguished, but he was also a disciplinarian whose methods owed much to cruelty, and notoriously mean. His accession was notable on two counts. It marked the end of what is known as the Julio-Claudian dynasty – he assumed the title of Caesar when Nero's death was reported to him – and it proved that it was feasible for an emperor to emerge from, and be appointed, outside Rome itself. Nero died in the summer of AD 68; it was October before Galba arrived in the city, having in the meantime organized from a distance the murder of two other regional commanders-in-chief who had been slow to get their troops to swear allegiance to him as emperor. He then committed the solecism of refusing to pay the traditional bonus which the imperial guard had been promised on his behalf.

Worse followed. On 2 January AD 69, the legions in Lower Germany proclaimed as emperor their commanding officer, Aulus Vitellius, to whom the troops in Upper Germany also promised their support. Galba tried to stem the threat of civil war by naming a young man of noble republican birth, Marcus Piso Licinianus, as joint ruler and his successor. It was a disastrous choice, as Piso had neither qualifications nor personal distinction, and the appointment offended Otho, the former husband of Nero's Poppaea, now back in Rome after his ten-year stint in Lusitania. Otho immediately turned attention on himself by the simple and, by now, time-honoured ploy of bribing the imperial guard to support his cause. On 15 January AD 69, they swore their allegiance, marched into the city, and hacked Galba and Piso to death. That act precipitated the Year of the Four Emperors.

OTHO

Marcus Salvius Otho (Caesar Augustus): born on 28 April AD 32. Governor of Lusitania AD 58–68. Married to Poppaea Sabina, future wife of Nero. Became emperor on 15 January AD 69. Committed suicide on 14 April AD 69.

> He was quite small, with bow legs, and feet that stuck out at each side. He was
> almost as fastidious as a woman. His body was plucked and because his hair was
> so thin, he wore a wig, so well-made and closely fitting that no-one suspected.
>
> **(Suetonius, *Otho*, XII)**

Otho's claims to a niche in history are few. It seems, however, that he performed
creditably as governor of the province of Lusitania, to which Nero had sent him
presumably to get him out of the way. As emperor, his most immediate task was to
overcome the threat of the other nominee, Vitellius, and this meant civil war. The
armies of Upper and Lower Germany advanced into northern Italy, each by a
different route across the Alps. Otho charged boldly out to meet them, crossed the
Po, and was outflanked. His army surrendered and he committed suicide. He had
been emperor for just three months.

VITELLIUS

Aulus Vitellius (Augustus Germanicus): born on 24 September AD 15. Consul
AD 48. Became emperor in AD 69. Married [1] Petroniana (divorced), one son,
Petronianus; [2] Galeria Fundana, one son, one daughter. Assassinated on 24
December AD 69.

> He used to have three, or four, heavy meals a day: at least a full breakfast, lunch,
> and dinner, and a convivial drinks' party, for each of which he had himself invited
> to a different house, at a cost to his host of never less than 400,000 sesterces
> a time. He was easily able to consume the lot by indulging in frequent bouts of
> self-induced vomiting . . . He was enormously tall, with a face usually purple with
> drink, a vast belly, and one thigh permanently damaged by a blow from a chariot,
> sustained while he was acting as Caligula's co-driver in a race.
>
> **(Suetonius, *Vitellius*, XIII, XVII)**

Vitellius, son of a former consul, was a man of some learning but little military skill
or experience – his appointment, by Galba, to his command in Lower Germany had
taken most people by surprise. In mid-July AD 69, he reached Rome and was officially
recognized as emperor, though he refused the title of Caesar. He immediately
celebrated with bouts of extravagant entertaining and betting on the races, and
was sufficiently out of touch with public feeling that, after assuming the office also
of *pontifex maximus*, he made a pronouncement about worship on a day which
was traditionally regarded as unlucky. Even before this, on 1 July, the forces in
the eastern Mediterranean had repudiated him and sworn their allegiance to Titus
Flavius Vespasianus, military commander in Judaea. The legions of the Danube, who

had originally supported Otho, did likewise, and, while Vespasian waited in the wings, they marched into Italy without waiting for support. They met, and defeated, the imperial army near Cremona, and then made a dash for Rome, which capitulated. Vitellius was hunted down, driven out into the streets with his hands tied behind his back, and tortured to death. The date was 24 December AD 69. Within one year three successive emperors of Rome had died violently, and now a fourth was acclaimed.

VESPASIAN

Titus Flavius (Caesar) Vespasianus (Augustus): born on 17 November AD 9 at Reate. Served in Thrace, Crete and Cyrene, Germany, Britain, and Africa. Military commander in Judaea AD 66–9. Became emperor in AD 69. Consul AD 70–2, 74–7, 79. Married Flavia Domitilla (d. *c.* AD 65), two sons, Titus and Domitian, and one daughter, Domitilla. Died at Reate on 24 June AD 79. Deified in AD 79.

> This was his usual daily routine while emperor. He rose early, even while it was still dark. Then, after reading his letters and abstracts of official reports, he let in his friends, and while they chatted to him put on his shoes himself and got dressed. When he had dealt with any business that cropped up, he would find time for a drive and then a lie down with a concubine, of whom he had several to take the place of his dead mistress, Caenis. After that he had a bath and then went through to dinner; it is said that he was at his most approachable and amenable at that time, so his household were eager to seize the opportunity of asking him something then.
>
> **(Suetonius, *Vespasian*, XXI)**

If a temporary return to a dynastic succession can be said in itself to represent a constitutional change for the better, then sanity and internal peace were for a time restored with the appointment of Vespasian. He was almost 61 when he arrived back in Rome in October AD 70, but he was still fit and active, and he had two sons, Titus (29) and Domitian (19). Titus remained in Judaea to continue the campaign against the Jews, who had precipitated the First Jewish War in AD 66 by revolting against the consistent malpractices and insensitivity of the Roman administration. This he did with undoubted, if misguided, skill and panache, taking Jerusalem in September AD 70. On Titus' return to Rome in AD 71, Vespasian formally made him his associate in government, granting him too the title of Caesar, and appointed him commander of the imperial guard, a sound move in the light of the success that body had had in altering the balance of power.

FIGURE 9 A contemporary likeness of Vespasian: even the loss of the nose cannot detract from the impression of a tough but inherently kindly man.

Source: Ny Carlsberg Glyptotek, Copenhagen

FIGURE 10 The rock-fortress of Masada, originally King Herod's mountain retreat, from the north-west, with (centre) the remains of the man-made ramp rising to a height of 140 metres. It testifies to Roman tenacity and engineering skill, and to the desperate determination of 960 men, women, and children, who in AD 73–4, three years after the fall of Jerusalem, became the final symbol of Jewish resistance. Archaeological evidence largely confirms the account of Josephus' history of the Jewish wars, written at the command of Vespasian. All materials, as well as provisions and water, had to be carried over a vast stretch of plateau. The defenders finally committed mass suicide rather than surrender. The remains of Herod's palace are at the north end of the summit. The Dead Sea is over to the left.

Source: Todd Bolen/BiblePlaces.com

Vespasian was of equestrian birth on both sides of the family. His father was a tax-collector, and his elder brother had served as *consul suffectus*. His mother's father had been a senior army officer, and one of her brothers had sat in the senate and had reached the rank of praetor. He himself was a professional soldier who as legionary commander had served with considerable distinction during the first assault by Aulus Plautius on Britain, and had been responsible for taking the Isle of Wight. This success led to Vespasian's appointment as *consul suffectus* in AD 51, and later to his appointment as governor of Africa, before being sent by Nero to Judaea. More significantly for the present predicament of Rome, he had neither the time nor the liking for the extravagant life, and he was a brilliant and tireless administrator, with a gift, so often lacking in his predecessors, of picking the right man for a job. In AD 74 he had recognized the potential of Gnaeus Julius Agricola (AD 40–93), who in AD 77 became the father-in-law of Tacitus:

> When Agricola returned from the command of his legion [in Britain], the divine Vespasian made him a member of the patrician class and appointed him governor of Aquitania, a post of great distinction from the point of view of both the status of the job and the promise it offered of a consulship, for which Vespasian had marked him out.
>
> **(Tacitus, *Agricola*, IX)**

In AD 78, after he had duly been *consul suffectus*, Agricola was appointed by Vespasian governor of Britain, a job he carried out, according to his biographer, with efficiency and not a little wisdom.

Vespasian had insight and sense in other directions, too. Though the destruction of Jerusalem and the retaliation against the Jews were carried out with unnecessary severity, and restrictions placed on certain of their practices, Jews were excused Caesar-worship. And in AD 71 he instituted the first salaried public professorship when he appointed Quintilian (*c.* AD 40–*c.* 100) to a chair of literature and rhetoric. He also exempted all doctors and teachers of grammar and rhetoric from paying taxes and from having the military billeted in their homes. Under Vespasian, too, a new class of professional civil servants was created, drawn largely from the business community.

Military considerations largely dictated his extending the empire into northern England and Wales, and, temporarily, southern Scotland, while advances were also made in Germany between the Rhine and Danube. He also extended Latin rights to all native communities in Spain, thus hastening its Romanization.

Vespasian died of natural causes, joking and with great dignity, according to Suetonius, in the family home in the Sabine mountains. On this occasion there were no doubts or worries about the succession.

TITUS

Titus Flavius Sabinus (Caesar) Vespasianus (Augustus): born on 30 December AD 40 in Rome, son of Vespasian and Flavia Domitilla. Legionary commander and then commander-in-chief in Judaea. Consul AD 70, 72, 74–7, 79, 80. Became associate emperor in AD 71, emperor in AD 79. Married [1] Arrecina Tertulla (died); [2] Marcia Furnilla (divorced), one daughter, Flavia Julia. Died on 13 September AD 81. Deified in AD 81.

FIGURE 11 The Arch of Titus, 15 metres high and 12 wide, was, according to the inscription on the opposite face, erected by the senate and Roman people (often abbreviated to SPQR) to commemorate the deified Titus. It particularly celebrates his exploits in the war against the Jews. A triumphal arch had a special significance: it reflected the triumph voted by the senate to a successful military commander. Under the empire, however, only emperors (or, with the emperor's permission, members of his family) were awarded triumphs; the actual commander received just the *triumphalia ornamenta*, the insignia of a triumph. The inscription on this face refers to the reinforcement of the structure in 1822 during the rule of Pope Pius VII.

Source: Photograph © copyright Allan T. Kohl/Art Images for College Teaching (AICT)

> As early as his boyhood it was clear that he was gifted physically and intellectually, and he became more and more so as he grew up. He was very good-looking, with an authoritative as well as a pleasing manner, and exceptionally strong, though he was short and had a small pot belly. He had an excellent memory and excelled at practically all the arts of war and peace.
>
> **(Suetonius, *Titus*, III)**

As a young man, Titus was dangerously like Nero in his charm, intellect, lavish ways, and sexual appetite and proclivities. He lived long enough, however, to demonstrate that he had, obviously thanks to the guidance of his father, some talent for government, but not long enough for any judgement to be made as to how effective a ruler he would have been. Yet, in curious ways to which nature has contributed, we have more tangible evidence from his reign of just over two years than from that of many emperors who ruled for much longer.

The massive Arch of Titus, celebrating his triumph over the Jews, still stands in Rome. So does much of the Colosseum, originally known as the Flavian Amphitheatre, begun in AD 72 in the grounds of Nero's Domus Aurea and finished in AD 80, the year before Titus' death. Oval in shape and almost 200 metres long and over 150 wide, it housed an arena roughly 75 by 50 metres and could seat some 45,000 spectators. It was the first amphitheatre to be built entirely of stone, and its three tiers of arches, each in a different architectural order, surmounted by pilasters in the Greek style and a deep cornice, provided a model for Renaissance architects. Today tourists wonder and eat pizzas where, in the time of Titus and his successors, men and wild beasts were slaughtered to please the Roman public.

In August AD 79 the volcanic Mount Vesuvius erupted. We have an eyewitness account by Pliny the Younger (*c.* AD 61–*c.* 112), writing to Tacitus:

> To us at a distance, it was not clear which mountain was belching out the cloud, but it was later discovered to be Vesuvius. In form and shape the column of smoke was like a tremendous pine tree, for at the top of its great height it branched out into several skeins. I assume that a sudden burst of wind had carried it upwards and then dropped, leaving it motionless, and that its own weight then spread it outwards. It was sometimes white, sometimes heavy and mottled, as it would be if it had lifted up amounts of earth and ashes.
>
> **(Letters, VI. 16)**

Within an hour or so Pompeii and Herculaneum, among several other towns and villages in the area, were engulfed; many of the survivors managed to escape with the help of the fleet stationed at Misenum, where Pliny was staying. The red-hot ash

FIGURE 12   The façade of the Colosseum, with its three rows of arches, each representing a different order of architecture, identified by the design of the capital at the top of each column: Doric, flat and plain (bottom row); Ionic, with spiral ornamentations (centre); Corinthian, decorated in the form of leaves (top).

Source: Photograph © copyright Allan T. Kohl/Art Images for College Teaching (AICT)

and lava destroyed, but when it cooled, it preserved, so that modern generations can see what the towns and some of the victims were like at the moment when the disaster struck. Some people suggested that it was divine retribution on Titus for his destruction of Jerusalem. Be that as it may, though he had been emperor for only a few weeks, he immediately announced a state of emergency, set up a relief fund for the homeless, to which was diverted the property of any victims who died intestate, offered practical assistance in rehousing survivors, and appointed a team of commissioners to administer the disaster area.

Titus was twice married; according to Suetonius he divorced his second wife shortly after she gave birth to his only legitimate child, a daughter. While he was in Judaea he had a passionate affair with the Jewish princess Berenice, daughter of King Herod Agrippa, and brought her back with him to Rome. She was twelve years older than Titus, had had three husbands, including her uncle Herod, king of Chalcis, and was rumoured to be having at the time an incestuous relationship with her brother, the Jewish king Agrippa II. The pressure of public opinion in Rome, not unmixed with anti-Semitism, had prevailed, and Titus was forced to send her home. She turned up again in AD 79, with her brother, who had come to demonstrate his allegiance to Rome, but Titus declined to resume the liaison with his 51-year-old former lover.

Titus was 40 when he died suddenly. Some people suspected that it was the work of his younger brother, Domitian.

DOMITIAN

Titus Flavius (Caesar) Domitianus (Augustus): born on 24 October AD 51 in Rome, younger son of Vespasian and Flavia Domitilla. Consul AD 73, 80, 82–8, 90, 92, 95. Became emperor in AD 81. Married Domitia Longina, one child, who died young. Assassinated on 18 September AD 96.

> From his boyhood he was scarcely polite, being insolent and arrogant in his conversation and behaviour. Once when his father's mistress Caenis came back from Istria and bent forward to kiss him as usual, he offered her his hand instead . . . He was tall, with a red face, an unassuming expression, and large eyes, though his sight was weak. For all that, he was good-looking, and, especially when he was young, well-proportioned all over, except for his feet; for his toes were slightly deformed. Later on he went bald and developed a paunch . . . [Towards the end] he used to say that it was a rotten life being an emperor: no-one believed in rumours of conspiracies until you were dead!
>
> **(Suetonius, *Domitian*, XII, XVIII, XXI)**

By all accounts, and by the evidence of many of his actions, Domitian was a thoroughly nasty person, but a reasonably effective ruler. First Vespasian, then Titus, kept him at a distance from playing any part in the administration, perhaps to avoid any further suggestions of nepotism, or simply because they felt he did not have the necessary qualities. The public offices which he did hold (including five brief terms as *consul suffectus*) were largely honorary, and this no doubt soured him. So when supreme power finally came his way, he accepted it as his right and positively gloried in it, especially after arrogating the office of censor, to which he had himself elected for life in AD 85. The usual methods of address were not for him: he preferred to be known as 'our master, our god' (Suetonius, *Domitian*, XIII).

Under the Flavian emperors, the economy of the empire was rationalized further, to the extent that expenditure could at last be projected. Existing dependent kingdoms became provinces of the empire. Rome itself and its aristocracy took further strides towards cosmopolitanism. Domitian's contribution was to help these processes by efficient administration, combined with a refreshing pedantry – he insisted on spectators at public games being properly dressed in togas – and a meanness which verged on the neurotic. He was particularly rigorous in exacting from the Jews the tax per head which was statutory throughout the empire, though the historian Flavius Josephus (AD 37–*c.* 100), who was himself Jewish, suggests that it was imposed by Domitian himself in return for allowing them to practise their own faith. Many Christians were tracked down and made to pay up, on the grounds that in reality they were Jews masquerading as something else. Suetonius records that as a young man he was present in court when a 90-year-old man was publicly examined to ascertain whether or not he was circumcised.

FIGURE 13 Gold *aureus* (AD 87) of Domitian, with (reverse) Minerva, goddess of crafts and industry, and also of war. The inscription, which begins under the neck and runs clockwise, reads in full: 'The emperor Caesar Domitian Augustus Germanicus, Imperator for the fourteenth time, Consul for the thirteenth time, perpetual Censor, Father of the Country'. Twice actual size.

Source: Photograph © copyright Hunterian Museum and Art Gallery, University of Glasgow

Domitian was often unsure in handling measures which required initiative. He attempted to resolve the problem of the Italian 'wine lake' by forbidding any new vines to be planted and ordering the destruction of vineyards on the other side of the Alps. Though he was popular with the army – he raised their pay, the first emperor to do so since Augustus – and he had a successful campaign in Germany in AD 83, two or three years later he allowed himself to be deceived into leading his army into battle against a combined force of German tribes who were merely creating a diversion on the Danube, and was heavily defeated. His recall of the popular Agricola from Britain, which had been 'completely conquered and [was] then immediately let go' (Tacitus, *Histories*, I. 2), neither of which statements is supported by the facts, can be justified from both a military and an economic point of view, as well as on the grounds that Agricola had served as governor for seven years (he was now 44), a long time for the holder of such a post. Tacitus was of course Agricola's son-in-law: more plausible is his suggestion that Domitian was jealous of Agricola and may have had him poisoned. In his will Agricola named the emperor joint heir with his daughter, Tacitus' wife: 'Domitian's mind was so circumscribed and corrupted by flattery, that he did not see that a good father only makes a ruler his heir if he is a bad one' (Tacitus, *Agricola*, XLIII).

Under Domitian, widespread execution returned. He used a vague charge of *maiestas* (treason) to justify all manner of persecutions and killings: 'A woman was tried and executed for undressing in front of a painting of Domitian' (Cassius Dio, *Roman History*, LXVII. 14. 2). In the wholesale slaughter in AD 95, there died Manius Acilius Glabrio, consul in AD 91 and a member of Domitian's council of state, and Flavius Clemens, consul that year with Domitian, husband of Domitian's great-niece, and father of two boys whom Domitian had adopted as his own sons. Conspiracies, real and imaginary, abounded, but Domitian's ultimate murder was not political. It was engineered by his wife, Domitia, whom he had exiled but was later reconciled with. He was stabbed by a steward, ironically while reading the report of yet another fictitious plot. It was the end of the Flavian dynasty. The senate, no doubt relieved that none of its members was openly involved, was at last in a position to make its own choice of ruler. Its members nominated a respected lawyer, Marcus Cocceius Nerva (AD 32–98), consul in AD 71 and 90, to take over the government. It was a decision of great significance. Domitian was denied a state funeral, and his name was obliterated from all public buildings.

FURTHER READING

* indicates sourcebook
Alston, R., *Aspects of Roman History, AD 14–117*, Routledge, 1998.

Barrett, A.A., *Caligula: The Corruption of Power*, Routledge, 1993.

Eck, W., *The Age of Augustus*, Blackwell, 2000.

Gelzer, M., tr. Peter Needham, *Caesar: Politician and Statesman*, Harvard University Press, new edn 2006.

Griffin, M.T., *Nero: The End of a Dynasty*, Routledge, 1987.

Kamm, A., *Julius Caesar: A Life*, Routledge, 2006.

Levick, B., *Claudius*, Routledge, reissue 1993.

Levick, B., *Tiberius the Politician*, Routledge, 1999.

Levick, B., *Vespasian*, Routledge, new edn 2005.

*Lewis, N. and Reinhold, M., *Roman Civilization: A Sourcebook*, vol. 1: *The Roman Republic and the Principate of Augustus*; vol. 2: *The Empire*, Columbia University Press, 3rd rev. edn 1990.

Morgan, G., *69 AD: The Year of Four Emperors*, Oxford University Press, 2006.

Potter, D. (ed.), *A Companion to the Roman Empire*, Blackwell, 2006.

4   RELIGIONS AND MYTHOLOGY

The Romans had a pragmatic attitude to religion, as to most things. Insofar as they had a religion of their own, any more than they could claim to have an indigenous mythology, it was not based on any central belief, but on a mixture of fragmented rituals, taboos, superstitions, and traditions which they collected over the years from a number of sources, including their own Indo-European roots. To the Romans, religious faith was effectively a contractual relationship between mankind and the forces which were believed to control people's existence and wellbeing. The result was essentially twofold: a state cult whose significant influence on political and military events outlasted the republic, and a private concern, in which the head of the family supervised the domestic rituals and prayers in the same way as the elected representatives of the people performed the public ceremonials. As circumstances and people's view of the world changed, individuals whose personal religious needs remained unsatisfied turned increasingly to the cults of the east, to Christianity, and to the tenets of the Greek philosophers.

ROMAN DIVINITIES

Many of the gods and goddesses worshipped by the Romans had their equivalents in Greek mythology. Some came by way of the Etruscans or the tribes of Latium. The Diana to whom Servius Tullius built the temple on the Aventine Hill was identified with the Greek Artemis, but some of the rites attached to her at Aricia, the centre from which he transferred her worship, went back to an even mistier past. The priest of Diana at Aricia, who was always a runaway slave, held the title of king. He took office by killing his predecessor, and held it for as long as he was able to defeat other runaway slaves in single combat. A fugitive slave could challenge him by breaking off

Gods, goddesses, and spirits

Aesculapius (Greek Asclepius)   God of healing

Annona   Mythical personification of the annual food supply

Apollo (Greek)   God of healing and prophecy

Attis (Phrygian)   Beloved of Cybele

Bacchus (Greek as Dionysus)   God of wine

Bellona   Goddess of war

Bona Dea   'Good Goddess': unnamed spirit whose rites were attended only by women

Cardea   Household goddess of door hinges

Castor & Pollux (Greek: also as Dioscuri)   Two legendary heroes

Ceres (Identified with Greek Demeter)   Goddess of agriculture

Consus   God of the granary

Cupid (Greek Eros)   God of love

Diana (Identified with Greek Artemis)   Goddess of light; also of unity of peoples

Dis (Greek as Hades and also Pluto)   God of the underworld

Faunus (Identified with Greek Pan)   God of fertility

Flora   Goddess of fertility and flowers

Forculus   Household god of doors

Fortuna (also Fors, Fors Fortuna)   Goddess of good luck

Genius   Protecting spirit

Hecate   Underworld goddess of fertility

Hercules (Greek Heracles)   God of victory and of commercial enterprises

Hermes   *See* Mercury

Isis (Egyptian)   Goddess of the earth

Janus   God of doorways

Juno (Identified with Greek Hera)   Goddess of women

Jupiter (also Jove: identified with Greek Zeus)   God of the heavens

Jutuma   Goddess of fountains

Juventas (Greek Hebe)   Goddess of youth

Lar (plural Lares)   Spirit of the household

Larvae (or Lemures)   Mischievous spirits of the dead

Liber (Greek Dionysus and also Bacchus)   God of fertility and vine-growing

Libitina   Goddess of the dead

Limentinus   Household god of the threshold

Luna   Goddess of the moon

Magna Mater (Phrygian as Cybele)   'Great Mother', goddess of nature

Manes   Spirits of the dead

Mars (Greek Ares)   God of war

Mercury (Identified with Greek Hermes)   God of merchants

Minerva (Identified with Greek Athena)   Goddess of crafts and industry

Mithras (Persian)   God of light

Neptune (Identified with Greek Poseidon)   God of the sea

Nundina   Presiding goddess at the purification and naming of children

Ops (Identified with Greek goddess Rhea)   God of the wealth of the harvest

Osiris (Egyptian)   Consort of Isis

continued

Gods, goddesses, and spirits (continued)

Pales   God/goddess of shepherds
Penates   Household spirits of the store cupboard
Picumnus & Pilumnus   Agricultural gods associated with childbirth
Pomona   Goddess of fruit
Portunus   God of harbours
Priapus   God of fertility in gardens and flocks
Proserpina (Greek Persephone)   Goddess of the underworld, wife of Dis
Quirinus   State god under whose name Romulus was worshipped
Robigus   God of mildew
Sabazius (Phrygian)   God of vegetation
Salus   Goddess of health
Sarapis (Egyptian)   God of the sky
Saturn (Identified with Greek Cronos)   God of sowing
Silvanus   God of the woods and fields
Sol   God of the sun
Tellus   Goddess of the earth
Terminus   God of property boundaries
Venus (Identified with Greek Aphrodite)   Goddess of love
Vertumnus (also Vortumnus)   God of orchards
Vesta (Identified with Greek Hestia)   Goddess of the hearth
Volturnus   God of the river Tiber
Vulcan (Greek Hephaestus)   God of fire

a branch from a particular tree in the sacred grove; so naturally the resident priest kept a close watch. Aricia is modern Ariccia, near Lake Nemi, the ancient lake into which a stream flowed from a sacred grotto beside the temple. The lake was known as 'Diana's Mirror', from the fact that at one time the reflection of the moon upon it could be seen clearly from the temple. *Nemus* means grove, and the priest of Diana had the title of *Rex Nemorensis*.

Some vestiges of earlier magic accompanied Diana to her new site in Rome.

> In the country of the Sabines there was bred on the property of a certain head of family a heifer of astonishing size and perfection of form; to which its horns testified, for they hung in the entrance court of the temple of Diana for many years. The beast was held to be the subject of an omen, as indeed it was: seers prophesied that the state whose citizens sacrificed it to Diana should be the leading power in the land. This prediction came to the notice of the priest of the temple in Rome. On the first day which seemed appropriate for the sacrifice, the Sabine brought the heifer to Rome, drove it to the temple of Diana, and stood with it before the altar. The Roman priest, much impressed by the size of the victim, which was famous, and knowing the prophecy, said to the Sabine: 'What are you

doing, stranger? Would you sacrifice to Diana in a state of uncleanliness? You must purify yourself in running water. The Tiber is at the bottom of the valley.' The Sabine, conscious of correct procedure and wanting to do everything by the book so that the prophecy might be fulfilled, immediately went down to the river. While he was away the priest sacrificed the heifer to Diana, for which the king and his subjects were exceptionally grateful.

(Livy, *History of Rome*, I. 45)

Occasionally tradition threw up a deity whose antecedents had been forgotten. Such a one was the goddess Furrina, who gave her name to the grove in which Gaius Gracchus met his death. Her festival was regularly observed on 25 July; by the middle of the first century BC, no-one could remember who she was or why she was being celebrated.

The Romans inherited their preoccupation with examining every natural phenomenon for what it might foretell from the Etruscans, who had developed the practice if not into a science, then at least into an art. The Etruscans employed three main kinds of divination, which were said to have been communicated to them by a mysterious lad called Tages, who appeared to them having literally been ploughed up from the earth while it was being tilled:

1   Divining the future from examining the entrails of victims sacrificed at the altar – the liver was of particular significance.
2   Observing and explaining the meaning of lightning and advising on how sinister predictions might be averted.
3   Interpreting any unusual phenomena and taking necessary action.

Many early societies practised animism, the belief that natural and physical objects are endowed with mystical properties. Alongside an appreciation of the divinity that resided in gods and goddesses with human attributes and human personalities, the Romans invested trees, springs, caves, lakes, animals, even household furniture with *numina* (singular *numen*), meaning the 'divine will' or 'divine powers' of a deity. Significant gods and goddesses had multiple functions; minor administrative roles were often undertaken by attendant spirits, known as *indigitamenta*, into whom the deity projected the *numen* of that particular activity. Ceres, for instance, in her capacity as goddess of the grain harvest, employed no less than twelve individual spirits, to whom reference should be made in all prayers appropriate to the occasion. These included Vervactor (first plougher of the season), Reparator (second plougher of the season), Occator (harrower), Sarritor (hoer), and Surruncinator (raker).

Boundary stones between one person's property and the next had especial significance. The word for a boundary stone was *terminus*: there was even a great

FIGURE 14 Sixth- or fifth-century BC Etruscan bronze plaque of a *haruspex* at work; his function was to examine the entrails of sacrificed animals and foretell the future from what he saw.

Source: C.M. Dixon

god Terminus, a massive piece of masonry which stood permanently in the temple of Jupiter on the Capitoline Hill, because, according to the poet Ovid (43 BC–AD 18) in his *Fasti*, a calendar of rites and traditions, it refused to budge even for Jupiter.

PRAYER AND SACRIFICE

The contractual relationship between mankind and the gods involved each party in giving, and in return receiving, services. The Romans believed that powers residing in natural and physical objects had the ability to control the processes of nature, and that man could influence these processes by symbolic action. The first is a primitive form of religious creed; the second is a type of magic.

The 'services' by which Romans hoped to influence the forces that guided their lives were firmly established in ritual – the ritual of prayer and the ritual of offering. In either case, the exact performance of the rite was essential. One slip, and you had to go back to the beginning and start again. The very multiplicity of deities caused problems. 'Whether you be god or goddess' is a common formula in Roman prayers, introduced to offset a lack of knowledge of a particular deity of a location or situation, or to avoid giving offence to a deity of foreign origin. The poet Horace (65–8 BC) dedicated to Augustus an ode calling for divine assistance to restore the fortunes of Rome, but is clearly in doubt as to whom his appeal should be addressed: 'Upon which of the gods should the people call to revive the failing empire?' (*Odes*, I. 2). He plays safe by starting at the top of the hierarchy: 'To whom will Jupiter assign the task of receiving atonement for our crimes?' He then cites four candidates in turn: Apollo, Venus, Mars, Mercury.

Many Roman deities went by a variety of names, and might not respond if wrongly addressed. So Catullus (*c*. 84–54 BC), in a hymn to Diana (Poem XXXIV), is careful also to invoke her as 'Latona's daughter, splendid child of Jove . . . called Juno Lucina by those in childbirth's pangs, and also queenly Trivia, and Luna, she who shines with borrowed light'. The poem ends on a note of respectful exasperation, and with a ritual escape clause: 'Accept our prayer under any name by which it pleases you to be addressed.' These lines throw up another identity problem in that Juno Lucina (Lucina here means 'bringing into the light') is not Diana, but Juno, consort of Jupiter, appearing here in her guise as goddess of childbirth. Juno had at least ten other names or surnames for use on special days or in particular circumstances, including Juno Moneta (Juno the 'Mint'), because her temple on the Capitoline Hill housed the state mint where money was coined and stored.

There were few occasions on which a prayer was inappropriate. There was a prayer for the return of stolen property and another for the diversion of some

FIGURE 15 Silver statuette of the god Mercury (*c.* AD 150–220), twice actual size. Mercury, god of merchants and business transactions, is identified with the Greek god Hermes, herald and messenger of the gods and guide of travellers. He is thus often represented as wearing a *petasus*, the wide-brimmed hat worn by travellers to protect them from the rain and sun.

Source: British Museum

unspecified piece of ill-fortune to someone else. Some prayers were realistic and modest, for example Horace's 'Poet's Prayer', which ends: 'I pray, Apollo, let me be content with what I have, enjoy good health and clarity of mind, and in a dignified old age retain the power of verse' (*Odes*, I. 31). This is, however, about the nearest any Roman usually got to praying for anything but material blessings.

Prayer was almost invariably accompanied by some form of offering, or sacrifice. This did not necessarily involve the ritual slaughter of an animal, as long as the offering represented life in some form: it could be millet, cakes made from ears of corn which had been picked a month earlier, fruit, cheese, bowls of wine, or pails of milk. Each deity, however, had his or her own preference of sacrificial animal – a ram for Janus, a steer for Jupiter. For Mars it was usually a combination of ox, pig, and sheep, but on 15 October it had to be a race-horse. In fact it had to be the winner: the near-side horse of the winning pair in the chariot race that day was immediately taken to the altar and slaughtered. Then its tail was cut off and the blood that dripped from it preserved as a charm. The sex of a chosen animal was also significant: male for gods, female for goddesses. So was its colour. White beasts were offered to deities of the upper world, black to those of the underworld, but a red dog was sacrificed to Robigus, symbolizing the destruction of red mildew.

The sacrificial routine was elaborate and messy. The head of the victim was sprinkled with wine and bits of sacred cake made from flour and salt. The *victimarius* then stunned the animal with an axe or mallet before cutting its throat and disembowelling it to ensure there was nothing untoward about its entrails. If there was, it was not only a bad omen, but the whole process had to be repeated with a fresh animal until it came out right. The vital organs were burnt upon the altar and the carcase cut into pieces and eaten on the spot, or else laid aside. Then the priest (or presiding sacrifant), with his toga drawn up over his head, would say prayers, speaking under his breath, while a flute was played, possibly to drown any ill-omened noise. Any unintentional deviation from the prescribed ritual meant not only a new sacrifice, but an additional one in expiation of the error. The victim in this case was usually a pig. On high occasions, on which a replay of the entire ceremony might be an embarrassment, an expiatory sacrifice was performed as a matter of course on the previous day, in the hope of atoning for any sin of omission or error on the day itself.

Multiple sacrifices were commonplace: the word hecatomb, which derives from the Greek, means the sacrifice of a hundred head of oxen. Human sacrifice was not a usual Roman practice, but was not entirely unknown. In the terrible days which followed the defeat by Hannibal at Cannae in 216 BC, two vestal virgins were convicted of having sexual relations. One was walled up alive, the traditional punishment for this offence; the other committed suicide. Whereupon the *pontifex maximus* got hold of one of the men in the case and personally clubbed him to death.

FIGURE 16   First-century AD altar relief from the Sanctuary of the Genius of Augustus in the forum at Pompeii. It depicts a bull led to a tripod altar in front of a temple hung with bunting. The *victimarius* holds an axe with which to stun the victim before its throat is cut, while the presiding officer, his head veiled, holds out a *patera*, the dish used for offerings.

Source: VRoma: Barbara McManus

The original acts of sacrilege were regarded as symptoms of impending doom, and recourse was had to the Sibylline Books, the national storehouse of prophetic utterances, for remedies against further disasters: 'Among other sacrifices, a Gaulish couple and a Greek couple were walled up alive in the cattle-market, in an underground tomb which had once before [in 228 BC] been stained with human victims, an un-Roman practice' (Livy, *History of Rome*, XXII. 57).

The act of self-sacrifice known as *devotio* is also recorded by Livy. During the Latin war of 340 BC, an engagement was fought near Mount Vesuvius, in the course of which the Romans found themselves sorely beset. One of the consuls, Decius Mus, called out to his consular colleague that a sacrifice was called for to redress the situation. Instructed by an attendant priest, he went through the ritual of dedicating himself and the enemy to the gods of the underworld. Then, wearing his toga in the manner which left both arms free, he leaped on his horse and rode full-tilt deep into the enemy lines, causing much consternation, until he was buried beneath a hail of missiles. The Roman formations rallied, and won the day.

OMENS

A sibyl was a Greek prophetess. The story goes that one of her kind offered to Tarquinius Superbus at a high price a collection of prophecies and warnings in the form of nine books. When he refused, she threw three of them into the fire and offered him the remaining six at the original price of the nine. He refused again; she burned three more and offered him the surviving three, still at the same price. This time he bought them, for what he could have paid for all nine. The Sibylline Books were consulted on the orders of the senate at times of crisis and calamity, in order to learn how the wrath of the gods could be allayed. They were accidentally burned in 83 BC, and envoys were sent all round the known world to collect a set of similar utterances. Augustus had the new collection put in the temple of Apollo on the Palatine Hill, where it remained until it was finally destroyed in the fifth century AD.

Disasters were seen by the Romans as manifestations of divine disapproval, and unusual phenomena as portents of catastrophe. In the winter of 218/217 BC, just before the battle of Trasimene, but with Hannibal already ensconced in Italy, the following portents were said to have been observed:

> In Rome a 6-month-old freeborn infant shouted 'Victory' in the vegetable market; in the cattle market an ox climbed up three flights of stairs on its own and then jumped out of a window in fright when the inhabitants screamed; phantom ships glowed in the sky; the temple of Hope, in the vegetable market, was struck by lightning. In Lanuvium a sacrificial corpse moved and a crow flew down into the temple of Juno and alighted on her sacred couch. In the district of Amiternum, ghostly men in shining garb materialized in many places but did not approach anyone. In Picenum it rained stones. At Caere oracular tablets shrank. In Gaul a wolf stole a sentry's sword from its sheath and ran off with it.
>
> **(Livy, *History of Rome*, XXI. 62)**

Reports of phenomena such as these could cause panic among a people for whom superstition was a way of life, especially at times of national uncertainty. The Sibylline Books were duly consulted, except apparently about the case of the raining stones, which it was felt could be dealt with by an official period of nine days' prayer. Various methods of appeasement emerged for the rest, including the ceremonial purging of the entire city of Rome, sacrifices, gifts to temples of Juno of gold ingots (each weighing 40 lb) and bronze statues, and a series of symbolic feasts at which statues of the gods were laid in reclining positions on couches round a banqueting table. At the end of it all, Livy reports, the Roman people felt considerably relieved.

The awe in which the Sibylline Books were held and the reverence with which their revelations were treated illustrate their significance in the Romans' relationship with their gods. The taking of auspices – the literal meaning of which is 'signs from birds' – was a standard procedure before any state activity, as is illustrated by the story of the legendary founding of Rome itself (see page 2). An official augur, who was present on such occasions merely as a consultant, marked out and prepared the statutory square measure of ground and then handed over to the state official who was to perform the ritual. He took up his position and observed the flights of any birds he could see, their kind, height, position, speed, direction of flight. If there was any doubt about the interpretation of what the official saw, the augur was called upon to advise. Later, armies took with them a portable auspice-kit, consisting of a cage of sacred chickens, in front of whom bits of cake were placed to see what would happen. It was a bad sign if they refused to eat: good if they ate the cake and let bits of grain fall from their beaks. The consul Claudius Pulcher, newly arrived in Sicily from Rome to take up his command in 249 BC, 'began a sea-battle though the sacred chickens had refused to eat when he took the auspices. In contempt of religious practice, he threw the chickens into the sea, remarking that if they would not eat they could drink' (Suetonius, *Tiberius*, II). He was very lucky to escape from the ensuing debacle, during which ninety-three Roman ships and their crews were captured by the Carthaginians.

Public business was frequently interrupted so that the omens (Latin *omina*, singular *omen*) could be consulted. A law passed by an assembly or an election could be declared invalid if the correct procedure had not been carried out. There was no need in political assemblies to resort to the tactic of filibustering to obstruct proceedings: religious grounds could suffice. In 59 BC Julius Caesar's consular colleague, Marcus Calpurnius Bibulus, announced that he proposed to offer religious justification for the assemblies to reject Caesar's legislation. Fearful, in the prevailing unrest, of venturing out of his house, he sent messages that he was watching the sky for omens. As bad omens had to be announced in person before the start of business to be valid, this raised an awkward precedent. Caesar overruled Bibulus' tactics, but for some time these particular laws were regarded with suspicion.

There was a distinction between signs that were solicited and those which appeared without invitation. The more startling or unexpected the sign, for instance a sudden flash of lightning or an epileptic fit on the part of a member of an assembly, the more seriously it was taken. It was not unknown for an interested party to throw a feigned fit in order to obstruct proceedings. Lightning which appeared while auspices were being taken was good news: not so when it came unbidden. In 114 BC the unthinkable happened and a vestal virgin was struck by lightning. A special commission was set up which by dubious means procured the conviction of several other vestals for sexual offences. Hysteria was still not abated, and the senate called for a reading from the Sibylline Books. The same answer was returned as just over a century before, and a Greek and a Gallic couple were buried alive.

WORSHIP IN THE HOME

Two national deities had their place in private worship too: Vesta, goddess of the fire and the hearth, and Janus, god of doorways. Janus, who gave his name to the month of January, is often depicted as having two faces, one looking in each direction. For this there are several interpretations: that it represents opening and closing a door, going in and coming out, or viewing (and thus guarding) both the inside and outside of a house. The door itself was so highly regarded that it required the attention of three more deities: Cardea, goddess of hinges, Limentinus, god of the threshold, and Forculus, who presided over the individual leaf or leaves. To trip as one went through a door was regarded as a thoroughly bad omen, so it was customary for brides to be carried over the threshold. Vesta was particularly important to the women of the household, for the open hearth was where the food was prepared and cooked, and beside it the meal was eaten. Prayers were said to Vesta every day, and during a meal a portion of food might be thrown into the fire as an offering, and also to seek omens from the way in which it burned.

The particular gods of the household were its *lares* and *penates*. The *lares* (one of them was designated *lar familiaris* or 'family spirit' and was special to that household) were supposed to be the spirits of dead ancestors, and had a shrine of their own which they inhabited in the form of tiny statuettes. Daily prayers and offerings were made to them, with more elaborate ones on the sacred days of each month – the calends, ides, and nones (see Appendix 1, p. 207) – and on notable occasions such as a birth, wedding, birthday, a departure or return, or the first word spoken by a son of the house. The *penates* looked after the larder, its contents and their replenishment, and also had their own cupboard. The statuettes of the *penates* used to be taken out and put on the table at mealtimes, and were sometimes given the names of particular state gods. When the family moved, its *lares* and *penates* went, too.

Each household had in addition its *genius*, whose image was a house-snake. *Genius* might be described as a 'spirit of manhood', since it was supposed to give a man the power of generation, and its particular sphere of influence was the marriage-bed. The household *genius* was especially honoured on the birthday of the head of the family.

FIGURE 17 Wall painting in the *lararium* (shrine of the *lares*) of the House of the Vettii, Pompeii. The *genius* of the household is flanked by two *lares*.

Source: Photograph © copyright Allan T. Kohl/Art Images for College Teaching (AICT)

Births and deaths had their special rituals. Juno Lucina was, as we have seen (p. 79), the main deity of childbirth, but there were other spirits who watched over the embryo child and its mother from the moment of conception to the birth itself. Immediately after the birth, a sacred meal was offered to Picumnus and Pilumnus, two jolly rustic deities, for whom a made-up bed was kept in some conjugal bedrooms. A positive string of child-development deities watched over the baby's breastfeeding, bones, posture, drinking, eating, and talking, even its accent. Levana helped it get up from the ground; Statanus taught it to stand; Abeona supported its first steps.

On the ninth day after the birth of a boy, the eighth in the case of a girl, the ceremony of purification and naming was enacted, presided over by the goddess Nundina. Free-born children received an amulet – gold for a child of the rich, bronze or merely leather for poorer families – which a girl would wear until her marriage, and a boy until he exchanged his *toga praetexta*, the robe of a child which was also worn by girls, for the *toga virilis*, the garb of a man, at the age of between 14 and 17.

While a spirit of some kind watched over a person at most times and on most occasions from conception to death, at the actual moment of death there was none.

The religious element in the funeral rites was directed towards a symbolic purification of the survivors. After the burial or cremation, a sow was sacrificed to Ceres to cleanse the house, and any refuse in it was solemnly swept out, while the family was sprinkled with water, and then invited to step over a ceremonial fire. After that, everyone sat down to a feast. Once the corpse was buried – and even in the case of cremation one bone was preserved and put in the ground – its own spirit joined all those other spirits of the dead, which were known collectively as *manes* and required regular worship and appeasement. There were also mischievous spirits of the dead, known as *larvae* or *lemures*, which could, however, be exorcized by the master of the house performing an elaborate ritual, involving the spitting out of black beans and the clanking of brass pots.

WORSHIP IN THE FIELDS

To the countryman, the natural world teemed with religious significance. The fields, orchards, vineyards, springs, and woods all had their attendant deities or spirits – every oak tree, for instance, was sacred to Jupiter. Silvanus, god of the woods and fields, guarded the boundary between farmland and forest, and the estate had regularly to be protected from natural and supernatural hazards by lustration, the ritual of purification involving sacrifice and a solemn procession round its perimeter. The country year was crowded with festivals of appeasement, prayer, and rejoicing.

The farmer's annual round began in the spring, which the original Roman calendar reflected by the year beginning on 15 March. The establishment of what is now New Year's Day in Christian countries at 1 January was for sheer administrative convenience. In 153 BC, in order to enable the arrival in Spain of the incoming consul to coincide with the start of the campaign season, the beginning of his term of office, and thus of the year, was advanced to 1 January, and there it remained. The first celebration of the country year was the Liberalia on 17 March, in honour of Liber, god of fertility in the fields and vineyards. It was also the traditional date on which a teenage boy abandoned his *toga praetexta* for the *toga virilis*.

The latter part of April was a riot of festivals, each with its special significance. At the Fordicia on 15 April, pregnant cows were sacrificed to the earth-goddess Tellus, and in Rome itself foetuses were burned and the ashes kept for use at the festival of the Parilia the following week, at which the sheep were purified by being driven through bales of blazing straw. Ceres, goddess of agriculture and especially of corn, had her festival on 19 April, as Virgil records in his verse handbook on farming, the *Georgics*:

> First thing of all is to revere the gods, especially Ceres: to her greatness dedicate the yearly rites. Perform them on the grass which burgeons at the very end of winter, in the bright days of spring. The lambs are fat, the wine is at its softest, sleep is sweet, and all the shadows thicken on the hills. This is the time when all your country folk should worship Ceres. Mix the mellow wine with milk and honey, lead the sacrifice three times the circle of your new-grown crops, while all your fellow workers follow on behind, chanting and calling Ceres to their homes. Let no-one put his sickle to the corn without a wreath of oak-leaves on his head, or giving Ceres an impromptu dance, and singing verses to her bounteousness.
>
> **(*Georgics*, I. 338–50)**

Here again we have the lustration ritual as an act of purification and bringing of luck. According to Livy, writing of the Macedonian army in 182 BC, there were other ways of achieving the same end:

> A dog is cut in two and the front half placed on the right-hand side of the road, and its rear part, with the entrails, on the left. The army then parades between the two parts in full battle order. At the head of the column are carried the arms and banners of all the kings of Macedonia from its beginnings. Then comes the present king with his children, followed by the royal cohort and the king's personal bodyguard, and after them by the troops themselves.
>
> **(*History of Rome*, XL. 6)**

In Rome itself, there was a macabre finale to the festival of Ceres. Flaming torches were attached to the tails of foxes, which were let loose in the space below the Capitoline Hill that later became the Circus Maximus. After the Vinalia Rustica, probably a drunken revel to celebrate the end of winter, and the sacrifice of the red dog to Robigus, god of mildew, the month closed with the Floralia, a festival ostensibly to petition for the healthy blossoming of the season's flowers. It lasted from 28 April to 3 May, and appears to have been celebrated with the greatest licence.

As the crops ripened, there were several rites of a more serious nature, including the movable feast of the Ambarvalia, during which the ritual lustration was renewed and the farmer sacrificed a pig, a sheep, and an ox, together with items from the previous harvest and the first fruits of the new. When the corn was cut in August, there were celebrations to Consus, god of the granary, and Ops, god of harvest wealth, and a further Vinalia Rustica; the real festival of thanksgiving for the wine crop, the Meditrinalia, was observed on 11 October. Sowing took place in December, during which there were repeats of the festivals of Consus and Ops. The Saturnalia was on 17 December. This festival was observed in the country as a genuine celebration of seed-time: in towns it was a longer celebration which embodied some of the secular traditions later associated with Christmas, including holidays from school, candles, exchanges of gifts, the mingling of household staff with the family, and the wearing of party hats.

THE RELIGION OF THE STATE

The religion of the Roman state reflected the ways of private worship, while retaining traditions from the period of the kings. Under the nominal direction of the *pontifex maximus*, administrative and ritualistic matters were the responsibility of four colleges, whose members, with one or two exceptions, were appointed or elected from the ranks of politicians and held office for life.

The members of the Pontifical College, the senior body, were the *rex sacrorum*, *pontifices*, *flamines*, and the vestal virgins. *Rex sacrorum* (king of religious rites) was an office created under the early republic to maintain the tradition of royal authority over religious matters. Though in later times he still took precedence at religious ceremonies over all other dignitaries including the *pontifex maximus*, it had by then become largely an honorary position.

The sixteen *pontifices* (priests) were the chief administrators and organizers of the religious affairs of the state, and authorities on procedure and matters of the calendar and festivals, and on the designation of particular days on which certain public business could not be conducted.

The *flamines* were priests of particular gods: three for the major gods, Jupiter, Mars, and Quirinus, and twelve for the lesser ones. These specialists had the technical knowledge of the worship of the particular deity to whom, and to whose temple, they were attached, and performed the daily sacrifice to that deity. The *flamen dialis* (priest of Jupiter) was the most important of them, and on certain occasions he ranked alongside the *pontifex maximus* and *rex sacrorum*. His life was hedged around with taboos and hazards. Aulus Gellius recorded, in the second century AD, 'those I can remember':

> He may not ride a horse . . . If a person is brought into the house of the *flamen dialis* in fetters, he must be untied and the bonds pulled up through the open skylight onto the roof and then let down into the street . . . Only a free man may cut his hair. It is the custom that the *flamen dialis* may not touch or even mention a nanny-goat, uncooked meat, ivy, or beans . . . He may not go out without his cap of office; it has only recently been decided by the priests that he can take it off indoors . . . If he loses his wife, he must resign his office. His marriage cannot be ended except by death.
>
> **(Attic Nights, X. 15)**

The six vestal virgins were chosen from ancient patrician families at an early age to serve at the temple of Vesta. By tradition, they normally served ten years as novices, the next ten performing the duties, and a further ten teaching the novices, though staying on seems to have been an option. They had their own convent near the forum, and their duties included guarding the sacred fire in the temple, performing the rituals of worship, and baking the salt cake which was used at various festivals throughout the year. Punishment for any lapse in ritual or conduct was rigorous: whipping for letting the sacred fire go out; whipping and being walled up underground, with a few provisions, for a breach of the vow of chastity. The last-known case of this ultimate punishment occurred during the rule of the emperor Domitian (AD 81–96). There is a contemporary record in the letters of Pliny the Younger, who also suggests that severities of this kind were based on Domitian's misplaced belief that they conferred distinction on his rule (see also p. 72).

> [Cornelia, the chief vestal,] continued to protest right up to the place of punishment; whether she was guilty or innocent, I don't know, but she certainly had the demeanour of innocence. And here's another thing! As she was being conducted into the underground vault, her gown caught on something. She turned to pull it free. When the executioner offered to give her a hand, she recoiled in horror from his touch, an unspeakable violation of her purity and chastity.
>
> **(Letters, IV. 11)**

The prestige of being a vestal virgin, however, was considerable. She was preceded in the street by a lictor, and any criminal condemned to death who happened to see her passing was automatically reprieved. The disappointment of not being selected appears to have been profound, at least to the girl's parents:

> The emperor [Tiberius in AD 19] then brought up the question of a replacement for Occia, who had for fifty-seven years presided over the rite of Vesta with supreme sanctity. He proposed a vote of thanks to Fonteius Agrippa and Domitius Pollio for the public-spirited way in which they had offered their daughters for selection. Pollio's child had been chosen, for no other reason than that her mother was still living with her husband; Agrippa had divided his household by his divorce. The emperor, however, gave the rejected candidate a surety of a dowry of a million sesterces as a consolation prize.
>
> **(Tacitus, Annals, II. 86)**

The fifteen members of the College of Augurs exercised great learning, and presumably also diplomacy, in the interpretation of omens in public and private life, and acted as consultants in cases of doubt. Each carried a crooked staff, without any knot in it, with which he marked out the square space of ground from which official auspices were observed.

The members of the College of 'Quindecimviri Sacris Faciundis' (Fifteen for Special Religious Duties) were the keepers of the Sibylline Books, which they consulted and interpreted when requested to do so, and ensured that any actions prescribed were properly carried out. Their functions were originally performed by two officials, then ten, and in the time of Sulla by fifteen; Julius Caesar added another *quindecimvir* to the board, but the name stayed. The college also had responsibility for supervising the worship of any foreign deity which was introduced into the religion of the state from time to time, usually on the recommendation of the Sibylline Books. Such a one was Cybele, the Phrygian goddess of nature, whose presence in Rome in the form of a sacred slab of black meteoric rock was recommended in 204 BC after, as Livy records, it had rained stones more often than usual. The cult itself, symbolized by noisy processions of attendant eunuch priests and flagellants, was exotic and extreme, in direct contrast to the stately, methodical practices of state religion; Roman citizens were discouraged from participating in its rites until the time of Claudius. The annual public games, however, in honour of Cybele, the 'Great Mother', were held in considerable style from 4 to 10 April, and were preceded by a ceremonial washing and polishing of her stone by members of the college.

The three, later seven, office-holders of the College of 'Epulones' (Banqueting Managers), belonged to the smallest and most junior of the four colleges. It was founded in 196 BC, presumably as a result of the amount of organization required to put on the official feasts which had become integral parts of the major festivals and games. A day each, for instance, was allocated to the public banquets in honour of Jupiter which took place during the Great Roman Games in September and the People's Games in November.

The earliest state religious festivals were celebrated with games, such as the very first one recorded at Rome, the festival to Consus at which the Sabine women were kidnapped (see p. 3). The Consualia, traditionally celebrated in Rome on 21 August, was also the local Derby Day, the main event of the chariot-racing calendar. Whether it was a case of cause or effect, the underground granary, which housed the sacred shrine of Consus where the opening sacrifice was conducted, was conveniently situated in the middle of the Circus Maximus, where the racing took place. Another of the original racing-festivals was the Equirria to Mars on 15 October, this time on the Campus Martius, with its grisly climax that has already been described (p. 81).

Religious festivals could be grave as well as joyful. February saw both kinds. During the nine days of the Parentalia, during which the family dead were worshipped, state officials did no business, temples were closed, and marriages forbidden.

In complete contrast were the ancient rites of the Lupercalia, at which the deity honoured was probably Faunus, god of fertility, but the proceedings reflected the origins of Rome itself. They started in the cave where Romulus and Remus were supposed to have been suckled by the wolf. Several goats and a dog were sacrificed, and the blood smeared over two youths of noble family. The pair then ran a prescribed cross-country course, wearing goatskins and carrying strips of hide, with which they whipped people as they passed. The blows were supposed to promote fertility, and women wanting to become pregnant would place themselves at strategic points on the course to receive their stripes. The discovery, near the remains of the palace of Augustus, of a ritual cave purporting to be that in which the ceremony opened, was reported in 2007.

The marathon festivities for Mars from 1 to 19 March were even more exhausting for the participants. Two teams each of twelve celebrants known as *salii* (jumpers) put on the helmets, uniform, and armour of Bronze Age warriors and leapt through the streets, chanting and beating their shields. Each night they rested, and feasted, at a prearranged hostelry or private house. Once a member of the *salii*, always a member! It was a rule of the order that if you were out of Rome while the celebrations were taking place, you had to stay where you were for the duration of them. In 190 BC, this held up a military campaign, when a Roman army waited at the Hellespont while its commander was immobilized by the festival on his way to join his troops.

The festival of Vesta in June was a more sedate and dignified affair. For a week, the storehouse of treasures in the temple was open to the public (but to married women only), who came barefoot with offerings of food. On 15 June the vestal virgins swept the place out, and public business, which had been suspended during the festival, was resumed. As an extra touch, on 9 June mill-donkeys were hung with garlands of violets, decorated with loaves of bread, and given the day off. There was not a month in the Roman calendar which did not have its religious festivals. August, the sixth month of the old calendar, hosted, in addition to the Consualia, festivals to Portunus (god of harbours), Vulcan (god of fire), Volturnus (god of the river Tiber), and Hercules, god not just of victory but also of enterprise in business. In the course of his life on earth, Hercules pulled off some celebrated, but decidedly shady, commercial deals. He was thus popular with the business community, who were in the habit of offering him a proportion of their profits as a thank you for services and a security for further assistance. On one occasion Crassus (see pp. 37–39) pledged one-tenth of his whole resources, though this was taken as a demonstration to the public of how rich he was. August was the month, too, in which the ancient festival of Diana was remembered on the Aventine.

That January should find itself the first month in the revised calendar was entirely appropriate. Janus, who gave his name to it, was a god unique to the Romans and has no equivalent in any other mythology. He was the god of beginnings as well as of the door, which you meet when you first enter a house. He not only began the year, and received the first state sacrifice of the year at the Agonia on 9 January, but the first hour of the day was sacred to him, and his name took precedence over all others in prayers. His bearded, double-headed image appeared on the first round bronze coin of the republic, the basic *as*, in about 300 BC, and also on the earliest silver coins, minted in Capua. The gates of his temple in the north-east corner of the forum were, it is said on the orders of Numa, kept wide open in times of war. According to Livy, this meant that they were closed only twice in the succeeding seven centuries.

Augustus, as a part of his national morale-boosting campaign, reaffirmed the traditional forms of worship. He restored eighty-two temples in and around Rome, it is claimed all in the space of one year. In 12 BC, after the death of Lepidus (see p. 47), who had held the post since 44 BC in succession to Caesar, he had himself appointed *pontifex maximus*, an office which thereafter was restricted to emperors. Thus the head of state was once again the head also of religious affairs. He especially promoted the god Apollo, with whom his own family was said to have special affinities, to the status of a major deity, and dedicated a magnificent new temple to him on a site on the Palatine Hill which was his personal property. He did not take the connection between religion and rule so far as to allow himself officially to be regarded as a god in his own lifetime, but he prepared the way to being deified after his death by confirming the divinity of Julius Caesar and dedicating a temple to him.

Augustus, however, was happy to accept the worship of non-Romans, provided that his name was coupled with that of Rome (or Roma, the goddess who personified Rome). His deification enabled the proliferation throughout the empire of Rome's most potent export: the imperial cult, or emperor worship. In this way, the loyalty of inhabitants of the provinces of Rome could be focused on an individual rather than on a concept of government. Even one of the most pragmatic of Augustus' successors, Vespasian, dedicated a new temple to the divine Claudius; he also encouraged the establishment of emperor worship in the provinces of Baetica (south-east Spain), Gallia Narbonensis, and Africa, to strengthen ties between their inhabitants and his family.

Emperor worship bound together the largely Hellenized eastern empire and the predominantly Celtic and Germanic provinces of the west. In the west, however, traditional Roman deities infiltrated local religions, which were often reinterpreted along Roman lines. Roman interference, however, only occurred in cases of obnoxious practices, such as human sacrifice, or for political reasons. Except in army camps and Roman colonies, the Roman religion and attendant culture had little impact on the Hellenized east, where the responsibility for temples and their priesthoods was largely left to the local authorities.

FIGURE 18 Maison Carrée, Nîmes, probably finished in 16 BC, is the most complete surviving temple of the Augustan era. Dedicated to Gaius and Lucius, sons of Agrippa and Augustus' daughter Julia, it reflects the loyalty of the local provincial community to the imperial family. The slender columns, each just over 9 metres high, are surmounted with capitals in the Corinthian style.

Source: Photograph © copyright Allan T. Kohl/Art Images for College Teaching (AICT)

CULTS OF THE EAST

The survival of a religious faith depends on a continual renewal and affirmation of its beliefs, and sometimes on adapting its ritual to changes in social conditions and attitudes: expansion is possible only through active and organized proselytizing, and by the relevance of its teachings to those to whose attention it is brought. To the Romans, the observance of religious rites on occasions of state was a public duty. Their beliefs were founded on ancient rituals and on a variety of mythological traditions, many of them derived from Greek rather than Italian models. Without any basic creed to counter, foreign religions made inroads into a society whose class-structure was being blurred and whose constitution was being changed by the increased presence of freed slaves and of incomers from abroad. The brilliance of some of the major foreign cults had considerable attraction for those brought up on homespun deities of the hearth and fields. The first of these to reach Rome was that of Cybele, according to Livy in 204 BC. The worship of Mithras, the emissary of light who symbolized the fight to disseminate life-giving forces in the face of the powers of darkness and disorder, was practised from the first century AD and had a particular appeal to the army. Tacitus dramatically illustrates the preliminaries to the second battle of Cremona during the civil war in AD 69. After Antonius Primus, leader of Vespasian's faction, had harangued his troops, 'There was a shout from the whole army, and the men of the Third Legion turned to the east and saluted the rising sun, in accordance with the custom in Syria' (*Histories*, III. 24).

The worship of the Egyptian goddess Isis came to Rome in the early years of the first century BC. Its significance is powerfully reflected in the fictional prose narrative *Metamorphoses* (also known as *The Golden Ass*) by Lucius Apuleius (*fl. c.* AD 160), who became a priest of Isis and her consort Osiris. The protagonist, also called Lucius, is accidentally turned into an ass while experimenting with an ointment supplied by the maid of the house. After several adventures and misadventures he appeals for help to Isis, having realized the omnipotence of the 'supreme goddess'. She duly appears to him:

> I come in answer to your prayers, Lucius: I, mother nature, ruler of all the elements, original child of time, most powerful of divine spirits, queen of the dead, supreme in the heavens, the single face of all gods and goddesses. With a nod I arrange the glowing arch of the sky, the healthy sea breezes, the bitter silence of the underworld. I am one god, worshipped throughout the world in many forms, with different rites, and under a variety of names . . . The Egyptians, who are skilled in ancient lore, celebrate my being with forms of worship which are unique to me and address me by my real name, Queen Isis.
>
> **(Metamorphoses, XI. 5)**

This is not just a description of a powerful deity, or even of a chief divine: it is an expression of monotheism.

The worship of Isis in the Roman empire was just one of the cults known as 'mysteries', which were of Greek origin. The mysteries based on those practised at Eleusis, to whose ancient annual festival initiates flocked from the Greek-speaking world, and those of Cybele and Bacchus, were also significant. They all have in common a ceremony of purification of the initiate, a sense of personal relationship with the deity, and an understanding of a life beyond death. Of the ultimate rite of initiation into the mysteries of Isis, Lucius of the *Metamorphoses* of Apuleius protests:

> Perhaps, interested reader, you want to know what was said and done. I would tell you if it was permitted to do so: you would learn if you were permitted to listen . . . But since you have, for all I know, a religious justification for your curiosity, I will not keep you in an agony of suspense. Listen, now, but believe: this is all

true. I travelled to the verge of death, I trod on Proserpina's threshold, I was borne through all the elements, and returned. In the middle of the night I gazed on the sun, dazzlingly clear; I approached the gods of the underworld and the gods of the heavens above, and I worshipped them from so near that I could have touched them.

There now: I have told you what you are forbidden to know, though you have heard it.

(Metamorphoses, XI. 23)

The rituals of the mysteries were supposed to be known only to initiates. What do remain, however, apart from literary allusions, are fascinating glimpses, preserved by nature in the lava from the eruption of Vesuvius in AD 79, of the cults of Isis and Bacchus, in the form of wall paintings uncovered at and near Pompeii.

RELIGIOUS PHILOSOPHIES: STOICS AND EPICUREANS

Philosophy, in the same way as religion, is concerned with the nature and conduct of life. The state religion of the Romans, however, put the observance of ritual above individual beliefs. Those who wished to explore the meaning and purpose of existence largely did so through the teachings of philosophers. The term Stoicism comes from the Greek *stoa*, referring to the colonnaded portico in Athens in which the philosopher Zeno (335–236 BC) held discussions with his disciples. Its teachings were brought to Rome in 156/5 BC by his successor, Diogenes of Babylon. They reflected some of the traditional characteristics which Romans aimed to emulate, and which were to be enshrined in Virgil's *Aeneid* (see p. 159) and endorsed by Cicero (see pp. 37 and 170) in his philosophical work, *Tusculanae Disputationes* (Discussions at Tusculum). Seneca (see pp. 58, 115, 122, and 169) and Marcus Aurelius (AD 121–80), the 'philosopher emperor' (see p. 188), were devotees.

To be stoical means in English to carry on regardless, in a state of impassiveness or resignation to fate, as does Virgil's hero, Aeneas. This is a simplification of a basic Stoic credo, that a single divine will (or God) controls everything in the universe. All activity is incorporated in the *logos* (Greek), the 'rational order' or 'meaning' of the universe. Everything is part of a wider 'reason' or good, a concept which Christianity was to accept. The Romans valued *virtus*, which comes from the word *vir* (man), and means something akin to manliness or mental as well as physical strength. With the help of *virtus*, one can more readily accept the circumstances of life and one's station in it. At the same time, and in their own times, Stoics declared that there was no difference between people of one station and another: whether male, female, Greek, barbarian, enslaved, or free.

FIGURE 19 The 'Villa of the Mysteries' at Pompeii was built in the middle of the second century BC and remodelled and redecorated in about 60 BC. One hall carries round its walls a continuous series of paintings in bright tones. These have been taken to symbolize the preparations of a bride for marriage, while reflecting elements which have been associated with the mysteries of Dionysus (Bacchus). In this section, which goes round a corner, a kneeling woman (left) begins to uncover an object which has been guessed to be an enormous phallus. Next, a winged female figure raises a whip to strike a half-naked girl whose back is being bared by the woman in whose lap she buries her face. On the right a clothed woman holds the *thyrsus*, the wand carried by Bacchus and his adherents, while a naked companion, clashing cymbals above her head, dances in ecstasy.

Source: C.M. Dixon

By tradition, the spirits of Roman dead lived on in the form of *manes*. When Julius Caesar, as the elected *pontifex maximus* the head of the religion of the state, stood up in the senate during the debate on the fates of the colleagues of Catiline (see p. 38) and argued, 'Death is not a torment but a relief from suffering; it is the end of all human misfortunes, beyond which there is no place for grief, or joy' (Sallust, *Conspiracy of Catiline*, 51), he was denying a fundamental religious belief. To the Romans, however, impiousness was not so much disrespect to the gods, but to the rituals of their worship. Whatever personal religious doubts Caesar, and other intellectuals, may have had, this particular one was shared by followers of the Epicurean school of philosophy. Epicurus (341–270 BC) was born in Samos and in about 306 BC bought a house in Athens with a garden, where his disciples met. Epicureans believed in a primitive atomic theory of the universe, that there was nothing to fear in God or from the supernatural, that pleasure was the ultimate good, that death was the end of all things, and that competition, deep emotional involvements, and conflict were to be avoided.

Whether Caesar subscribed fully to Epicureanism is not known, but in addition to his attitude to death, he demonstrated an Epicurean scepticism of the supernatural: on one memorable occasion, when informed that the sacrificial beast had no heart, he observed, 'The omens will be more favourable when I wish them to be' (Suetonius, *Julius Caesar*, 77). There is some evidence, however, that his third wife Calpurnia, whom he married in 59 BC shortly after his daughter Julia's marriage to Pompey, shared an interest in Epicureanism with her father, Lucius Calpurnius Piso (consul 58 BC). Piso was patron of the Epicurean philosopher Philodemus (*c.* 110–*c.* 40 BC), who gave seminars at the splendid villa at Herculaneum which is believed to have been owned by Piso. Known as the 'Villa of the Papryi', its archaeological secrets are still being uncovered.

JEWS AND CHRISTIANS

Traditional beliefs were also affected by the Jewish diaspora. By the time of Augustus' death in AD 14, there were considerable areas of Jewish settlement throughout the eastern empire, in the provinces of Africa and Mauretania, in southern Spain and Gaul, and in Italy, Corsica, Sicily, and Sardinia, with major communities in Rome, Alexandria, Ephesus, Antioch, and Damascus. A Jewish force enabled Julius Caesar to extricate himself from an embarrassing military situation in Egypt in 47 BC, and he in return granted Jews in communities outside Judaea privileges which included freedom of worship, the ability to remit contributions to the Temple in Jerusalem, answering to their own laws, and exemption from conscription into military service. A significant part of the Jewish community in Rome was founded by the prisoners brought back by Pompey from Jerusalem in 63 BC as spoils of war taken in the course of sorting out Roman problems in the east (see p. 39). Freed by their owners, they, and their descendants, were allowed by Augustus to observe their traditions and worship while still holding Roman citizenship. If the handout of the monthly grain ration fell on the Jewish Sabbath, his agents had his instructions to hold back the supplies due to the Jewish population until the following day.

Roman policy was that other cultures within the empire should be allowed to maintain their own traditions while being helped to become Romanized, provided that there were no breaches of the peace. Opposition to Jews occurred mainly in Hellenized cities, though conflicts of culture emerged once the Romans began worshipping their emperors. The most significant charge that could be brought against the Jews in Roman times was that they were *different*. To them, religion had such a bearing on daily life that it was impossible to eat with their fellow citizens or join them at festivals. Though they were at times exempted from emperor worship as long as they offered sacrifices and prayers for his health and wellbeing, this could still be interpreted as disloyalty to the state. Slaves in Roman households worked all day, every day, including festivals. Servants in Jewish households did not work on the Sabbath. The injunction that agricultural land should lie fallow every seventh year gave Jews an undeserved reputation for idleness.

Many Romans, however, responded to a creed much of whose tradition was based on written law and sound medical practice. A form of semi-Judaism became fashionable, especially among women: one did not have to be a full convert to attend services in synagogues. These followers were known as 'god-fearers'; among them, according to Josephus, the Jewish historian who accompanied Titus back to Rome after the fall of Jerusalem in AD 70, was Nero's empress Poppaea Sabina.

During the rule of Tiberius, a devout young Jewish thinker and teacher, son of a carpenter in Nazareth, had been executed in Jerusalem under Roman law. His name was Jesus, and he was held to be the Messiah. His death was hardly noticed by Roman historians, but if he had not died, he might have been completely forgotten, for it is central to the Christian faith that he came back to life.

His original adherents were the Jewish Christians. That this sect of Judaism became a separate and vibrant movement was due to another Jew, Saul, from Tarsus. His name in Greek was Paul, and the Roman citizenship acquired by his father extended also to him. Though he was in Jerusalem towards the end of Jesus' life, they never met, but Paul was violently opposed to the Jewish Christians, and supported the death by stoning in AD 36 of the deacon Stephen, accused of preaching 'against the Temple and the Law'. Sent by the Temple authorities to assist in rounding up Jewish Christians in Damascus, he had a searing vision on the road and experienced the voice of Jesus; he was subsequently baptized in Damascus by Ananias, a member of the local Jewish-Christian community.

Paul's mission became to establish across the Roman empire a faith based on the life, death, resurrection, and divinity of Jesus, instead of on Jewish law. Pagans were allowed to be Christians without first becoming Jews. Christianity appealed especially to the lower orders, to whom this new and personalized religion seemed to offer a bond of unity with one another, and a means of worshipping a single spiritual god by giving honour to a being with whom they could identify. In the course of his lengthy, tireless, and often dangerous missionary travels, described in the Acts of the Apostles, Paul was (as is recounted in chapter 22) arrested by the Roman authorities in Jerusalem for being the cause of a riot against himself. The commander of the guard ordered him to be interrogated under flogging. As he was being tied up, Paul demanded to know whether it was legal to flog a Roman citizen who had not been found guilty. This was reported to the commander, who asked him, 'Are you a Roman citizen?' Paul said that he was. The commander observed, 'It cost me a large sum to become a Roman citizen.' To which Paul replied, 'I am a citizen by birth.' The charges were hastily dropped.

In AD 61, Paul arrived in Rome, which he now used as a base for his mission. He was arrested, and probably executed, in about 67, during one of Nero's anti-Christian periods. There were now more Christians in the known world than there were Jews. The story of both religions under Roman rule is picked up in chapter 9 (pp. 183, 185, 198, and 201).

FURTHER READING

* indicates sourcebook

Adkins, R. and Adkins, L., *Dictionary of Roman Religion*, Oxford University Press, 2001.

Beard, M., North, J. and Price, S., *Religions of Rome*, vol. 1: *A History*, *vol. 2: *A Sourcebook*, Cambridge University Press, 1998.

Clark, G., *Christianity and Roman Society*, Cambridge University Press, 2004.

Clauss, M., tr. R. Gordon, *The Roman Cult of Mithras: The God and his Mysteries*, Routledge, 2001.

Ferguson, J., *The Religions of the Roman Empire*, Thames and Hudson, new edn 1985; Cornell University Press, new edn 1993.

Grant, M. and Hazel, J., *Who's Who in Classical Mythology*, Routledge, reissue 2001.

Lane Fox, R., *Pagans and Christians: In the Mediterranean World from the Second Century AD to the Conversion of Constantine*, Penguin, new edn 2006.

North, J., *Roman Religion*, Oxford University Press, 2000.

Price, S. and Kearns, E., *The Oxford Dictionary of Classical Myth and Religion*, Oxford University Press, 2004.

Rüpke, J. (ed.), *A Companion to Roman Religion*, Blackwell, 2007.

Scheid, J., *An Introduction to Roman Religion*, Edinburgh University Press, 2003.

Turcan, R., *The Gods of Ancient Rome*, Routledge, 2001.

5 SOCIETY AND DAILY LIFE

Roman society under both the republic and the empire was rigidly and recognizably structured, while inherent social and economic factors ensured that inequality was maintained. The top ranks in society had the wealth and status to control and exploit property, and to manipulate the legal system. The lower ranks depended for their position on how far they were able to influence the means of production. Land meant wealth, and remained in the family as long as there were natural or adopted heirs. When a family ceased to exist, it was often favoured freedmen or even slaves who reaped the benefit.

The old patrician aristocracy died out when republicanism took hold, to be replaced by the nobility, comprising the families of patricians and wealthy plebeians who had successfully stood for office and then entered the senate. Through their strings of hereditary hangers-on, their clients (*cliens*, plural *clientes*, means listener, and thus 'follower'), the nobility became the ruling class. With senators barred from participating in state contracts and restricted in trading overseas, a new equestrian class emerged, to whom Gaius Gracchus (see chapter 2, p. 30) effectively granted the status of an order of society by giving non-senators who possessed 400,000 sesterces (the same qualification as senators) the right to bid for tax collection in the provinces, and to have control over the jury-courts.

Augustus created a senatorial order, membership of which was at his discretion. Senators, and their sons, were entitled to wear a toga with a broad stripe (*latus clavus*) of purple (more accurately, a reddish pink). To promote the dynastic principle, senatorial status was also conferred on senators' wives, and three generations of his descendants. To maintain an aristocratic strain, senators were now barred from marrying freedwomen. To avoid bad publicity, senators and their families (and also equestrians) were forbidden to participate in public spectacles.

Augustus also raised the qualification portal for senators from 400,000 sesterces (the same as for equestrians) to 1 million sesterces. A decree in the time of Tiberius stipulated that a prospective equestrian and his two previous generations must be free born. Otherwise, it is not generally known whether membership was automatic or conferred by the emperor. Certainly the equestrian ranks provided the state with a host of army officers and provincial officials (including provincial governors), and latterly palace dignitaries.

As the rich grew richer and the poor poorer, the *plebs urbana* (city plebs), originally composed mainly of artisans and shopkeepers, became less of a respectable class of society and more of an uncontrolled and uncontrollable rabble, comprising also ruined peasants from the country vainly seeking work and those attracted by the grain dole. They had voting power, for they were always on the spot to exercise it. In AD 14, responsibility for the election of state officials was transferred to the senate. A new division of society emerged in Rome: plebs who were professional people (teachers, architects, physicians, tradesmen) and *plebs quae frumentum accipiebat* (plebs who received the grain dole). Especially because the latter could still cause trouble on the streets, Augustus had also interested himself in the supply of housing and water, had provided them with public games, and had distributed cash benefits.

There was a distinction between society in the capital and society in the towns (*municipia*) of Italy. Each despised the other. When, in the time of Augustus, the powers of the city officials diminished, and the towns themselves received attention from the centre of government, politically minded local citizens began to look for recognition in their own town, rather than in Rome, laying a basis for local government which has been one of Rome's most significant legacies.

As the status of non-citizens in the provinces became of more concern, a new division of society emerged which did not discriminate between citizens and non-citizens when it came to the administration of the law. From the early second

---

FIGURE 20 (opposite) Model of imperial Rome in the Museo della Civilta Romana: a view from the south. The river Tiber is on the left, and beyond it (centre, far left) the temple of Jupiter stands on the Capitoline Hill. The Circus Maximus is in the foreground; behind it, on the Palatine Hill, is the imperial palace complex, from which the Claudian aqueduct snakes out. The larger columned building to the north of the palace is the temple of Venus and Roma, to the west of which are the Basilica of Constantine, the temple of Peace, and the Basilica Aemilia, which fronts on to the east end of the forum. To the north-east of the palace is the Colosseum, behind which are the baths of Trajan. The large building to the south-east of the Colosseum is the temple of Claudius.

Source: C.M. Dixon

century AD, citizens and non-citizens alike were either *honestiores* (men of privilege) or *humiliores* (men of humble rank), with separate punishments for the same crime. Whereas *humiliores* could be sentenced to hard labour in the mines, *honestiores* were merely banished for a short term. The most common form of punishment for a minor offence was flogging, from which *honestiores* were immune.

TRADITIONAL VALUES AND CUSTOMS

The Romans were sticklers for tradition as well as for order – Julius Caesar stressed in public that he was, through his mother, descended from the fourth historical king of Rome and through his father from the goddess Venus, and it was not unknown, under the empire, for successful entrants to the new nobility to invent for themselves fictional genealogies. To support an obsession with the passing of laws, in which everyone was able to participate, and the creation, in the form of the Twelve Tables in 451/450 BC (see chapter 2, p. 17), of a digest of current legal practice, the Romans claimed a system of *mos maiorum*, the 'way (or "custom") of our ancestors'. The application of tradition and precedent often had more potency than the law itself, and in addition methods of resolving legal situations covered all aspects of public and daily life, including the conduct of the family and the inviolability of the home. It was not so much the law that the brothers Gracchus breached in their pursuit of common justice, as the *mos maiorum*, and this presaged the downfall of the republic (see chapter 2, pp. 28–31).

The Latin term *familia* is usually translated as 'family' or 'household', while *domus* stands for 'house' or 'home'. In Roman times, however, each had a variety of connotations, depending on the circumstances. Thus, *familia*, according to the legal writer Ulpian (d. AD 223), could refer to all those subject to the father's authority (*patria potestas*), including his wife (if married under rites which gave him this authority, known as *manus*), children, adopted children, and sons' children; all those related through the male line (*agnates*) to the household, such as brothers and their children, unmarried sisters, but not the sisters' children; all those related through the male line to a common ancestor (also known as *gens*); or all the slaves belonging to a house or farm.

In practice, *domus* also came to be used to refer to relatives outside the particular household, but often including those descended through the female line.

We have already met the term *virtus* (chapter 4, p. 96), describing a male quality of steadfastness. Women, as well as men, were expected to possess to a considerable degree that essentially Roman quality of *pietas*, which is untranslatable except as a combination of duty, devotion, and loyalty, especially to the gods, but also to one's country, parents, and other relatives. The Romans also prized *gravitas*, which, too, implies a sense of duty, but in the context of dignified reserve and integrity. Its opposite, *levitas*, frequently had the meaning of inconstancy.

ECONOMY AND MONEY

Most of the hard and menial work was done by slaves. Leisure hours for citizens of Rome were comparatively long and leisure pursuits were subsidized. Public holidays were plentiful and public entertainment was free. In the times of Julius Caesar and Augustus, 150,000 of the inhabitants of Rome received free grain. Nero was in the habit of handing out gifts of astonishing value and variety during the games which he inaugurated:

> Every day all manner of free gifts were thrown to the people: on a single day 1,000 birds of different kinds, a variety of food parcels, and tokens for corn, clothing, gold, silver, jewellery, pearls, paintings, slaves, farm beasts, even wild animals, as well as ships, tenement blocks, and agricultural land.
>
> **(Suetonius, *Nero*, XI)**

The economy of ancient Rome was an issue of the greatest complexity, and Roman numerals were not in any case designed for easy computation. Imports into Italy, especially of grain, olive oil, and wine, were astronomical, as were those of luxury goods from other parts of the Roman world. Consumer spending was restricted in that so many of the population were slaves, and others, especially in Rome itself, were on the bread line; while the army, whose presence anywhere had the effect of boosting the local economy, was spread around the provinces. The provinces themselves were meant to be self-supporting and to provide the fiscal treasury with taxes, as well as to supply Rome with staple goods. Some of them were more successful at this than others. There was mass production of pottery, especially the distinctive and often decorated red-coated bowls, plates, serving dishes, cups, and lamps that have been found even on sites of dwellings of the rural poor. Archaeological evidence has further revealed that branches of Italian potteries began to operate in Germany and Gaul, which then became major manufacturing countries in their own right, exporting their wares to other provinces, and even back to Italy.

Vast sums were expended on public works and entertainments, and on the armed forces. At the end of the day, the emperor was usually blamed for shortages, shortfalls, and anything else to do with the economy.

> [In AD 32] the exorbitant price of corn almost led to rioting; as it was, there were frantic demands made in the theatre for several days, even more outspoken

FIGURE 21 The basic coinage instituted by Augustus comprised the copper *quadrans*, brass *semis*, copper *as*, brass *dupondius* and *sestertius*, silver *denarius*, and gold *aureus*. Other coins were introduced from time to time to meet inflation. Caracalla introduced the *antoninianus*, a silver coin worth two *denarii*, which gradually became debased. Constantine replaced the *aureus* with the gold *solidus*. a) *quadrans* of Nero (reverse), with laurel branch; the smallest coin, it is frequently mentioned as the entrance fee to the public baths. b) *semis* of Domitian (= 2 *quadrantes*). c) *as* of Vespasian (= 2 *semisses*). d) *dupondius* of Marcus Aurelius (= 2 *asses*). e) *sestertius* of Hadrian (= 2 *dupondii*). f) *denarius* of Julius Caesar, the first living person to be depicted on a Roman coin (= 4 *sestertii*). g) *aureus* of Augustus (= 25 *denarii*). h) *solidus* of Zeno, emperor in the east at the time of the end of the western empire. Portraits on coins of the later empire reflect eastern influence and have less personality than those of earlier times. All actual size.

Source: Photographs © copyright Hunterian Museum and Art Gallery, University of Glasgow

against the emperor [Tiberius] than was customary. Stung by these, he repri-
manded the state officials and the senate for failing to use their authority
to control the people, listing the provinces from which he had obtained corn and
emphasizing that he had imported greater quantities than Augustus. In response
the senate drafted a statement censuring the people in old-fashioned terms of
severity, and the consuls issued one which was equally tough. Tiberius' public
silence on the matter was not, as he thought, regarded as a constitutionally tactful
move, but as arrogance.

(Tacitus, *Annals*, VI. 13)

The emperor always had, however, considerable resources of his own on
which to draw, particularly from estates which were bequeathed to him or acquired
by other means – according to Pliny the Elder, Nero confiscated the entire properties
of six men who between them owned almost all the grain land in north Africa, and
these were still being cultivated as imperial possessions under the rule of Hadrian,
sixty years later. The whole of Egypt, too, had from the time of Augustus constituted
an imperial perquisite, in that he had (in his estimation) acquired it by right, and he
passed on to his successors the tradition that the ruler owned the land and those who
worked it were his tenants. Nerva and his immediate successors, Trajan, Hadrian,
Antoninus, and Marcus Aurelius, inherited from Domitian and his father the habit of
moderation in personal expenditure. During their rule, however, there was considerable improvement in the provision of roads and harbours, central government
money was granted for new buildings in the provinces, and new public assistance
programmes were introduced, particularly for the children of poor families in the
municipalities, and increased allowances of wine and olive oil, as well as of grain,
made to the public in Rome. The successful conclusion of Trajan's invasion of Dacia,
begun in AD 101, and especially the output of the Dacian gold and silver mines,
boosted the imperial exchequer, but it needed a period of comparative peace, and
the careful and dedicated attention of Antoninus and Marcus Aurelius to the levying
and collecting of taxes, before comparative liquidity was finally, but only temporarily,
achieved.

WORK

Romans rose early and usually worked a six-hour day. The woman's place was firmly
in the home: even queuing for the little wooden token entitling a family to the monthly
grain dole appears to have been a male prerogative. Free men and freedmen who
had work were out and about on their business for the whole morning, contributing
to the noise and bustle of urban activity, of which the poet Martial (*c.* AD 40–*c.* 104)

wrote: 'There's no place in Rome for a poor man to think or rest. Schoolmasters disturb life in the morning, bakers at night, while the coppersmiths hammer all day long' (*Epigrams*, XII. 57). The import business was centred on Ostia, where goods from overseas were unloaded, checked, and stored in warehouses before being transferred to barges for the journey upstream. The building industry accounted for a continual supply of skilled labour in the form of architects, surveyors, supervisors, foremen, sculptors, stonemasons, carpenters, and brickworks' managers. In the cities and towns, wholesale and retail markets operated, craftsmen plied their trades, and the little shops, taverns, and inns did their business. They in their turn were supplied with raw materials and foodstuffs by the agricultural estates. In accordance with the *mos maiorum*, sons tended to follow the trades of their fathers. Apart from the army, the only respectable occupations for the upper classes were the law and politics, since so many professional posts in such fields as architecture, medicine, surgery, dentistry, teaching, and agricultural management were held by freedmen. This left a sizeable group of educated, if not always aristocratic, unemployed, many of whom pursued the calling of client. Queues of them formed at dawn at the houses of the rich, waiting patiently in their best clothes for some pathetic gift of money or food, which the patron solemnly dispensed to each in order of social seniority.

> Now the toga-clad mob compete for the little baskets of hand-outs on the doorstep. Your patron, however, first looks you in the face, anxious to avoid the fraudsters who give false names; if he recognizes you, you'll get your dole. Then he tells his crier to call the noble-blooded sons of Troy, for they, too, block the doorway, just like us. 'The praetor first, and after him the tribune.' But a freedman is at the head of the queue. 'I was here first,' he complains to deaf ears. 'Why should I be frightened off or be denied my place?'
>
> **(Juvenal, *Satires*, I. 95–102)**

The more humble or poorer clients would do the rounds of patrons to collect as many donations as possible. That done, the client returned to his writing, if he was a poet like Martial, or mingled with the crowds in the forum or market, which were as much meeting places as centres of public or private business, read the daily newspaper which was posted up in various public spots, or took an early bath. For after work, for women as well as men, a visit to the public baths was usually the order of the day (see also chapter 6, p. 142). For the better-off poet, or one such as Horace who boasted a generous patron, the day was less active:

> I lie in until 8 o'clock, then take a walk or, after reading or writing something which will satisfy me during times of contemplation, rub myself down with oil . . . But

FIGURE 22 Mosaic from Ostia, the port of Rome, showing an amphora of wine being loaded on board. Roman merchant ships had a single mast amidships supporting a regular sail, and were steered by an oar at the stern. If it had no other cargo, a ship might carry in layers 6,000 amphorae, each weighing 50 kilos.

Source: Richard Stoneman

> when the noonday sun tells my exhausted frame that it is time for the baths, I avoid
> the Campus and the game of ball. After a light lunch, enough to prevent my having
> to last out the day on an empty stomach, I loaf around at home.
>
> **(*Satires*, I. 6, 122–8)**

THE ROLE OF WOMEN

'Our ancestors, in their wisdom, considered that all women, because of their innate weakness, should be under the control of guardians' (Cicero, *Pro Murena*, XII). The guardian might be the father, husband, or a male relative, or someone appointed by the will of the father or husband, or by an official of the state. The only exceptions up to the time of Augustus were the six vestal virgins; after Augustus the rule was relaxed in cases of free-born women who had had three children and freed-women who had had four, provided that there was no father or husband to exercise control.

It was customary for marriages to be arranged. Pliny the Younger wrote to a friend about one which, sadly, had to be cancelled.

> She was only 13, but she had the wisdom of an older woman and a matronly dignity, combined with the sweet nature of a girl and the innocence of a maiden . . . She was engaged to an excellent young man; the wedding day was fixed and we had all been invited . . . I cannot express in words my heartfelt despair when I heard her father (grief finding ever more ways of increasing sorrow) laying out on incense, perfumes, and spices for her funeral what he had budgeted for gowns, pearls, and jewellery for her wedding.
>
> **(Letters, V. 16)**

Nothing, it seems, was a woman's own.

> Your maidenhead is not entirely yours: a third belongs to your father, and a third to your mother. You own the rest. Don't resist your parents: they have handed over their rights of guardianship to their son-in-law, together with your dowry.
>
> **(Catullus, Poem LXII. 63–6)**

The size of the dowry was expected to match the social standing of the prospective bridegroom.

> *To Quintilian*
> Though you yourself have few needs and have brought up your daughter as befits a child of yours and a grandchild of Tutilius, she is, however, to be married to a man of great distinction, Nonius Geler, whose status in the community demands a certain ostentation by way of gowns and attendants (not that these enhance a bride's value, only show it off to its best advantage). Now I know that you are not blessed with as much wealth as you are with intellect. So I am taking upon myself part of your responsibility and, in the capacity of an additional father, propose to settle on our girl fifty thousand sesterces. It would be more, but I reckon only an insignificant sum could prevail over your modesty and, that being so, you will not refuse it. Yours.
>
> **(Pliny the Younger, Letters, VI. 32)**

In the history of letter writing, there can be few to match this one for tact as well as generosity.

There were several ways of celebrating a marriage, of which the simplest involved the consent of both parties, without rites or ceremony. There were three others, each giving the husband legal power over his wife (*manus*):

1   By cohabiting for a year without the woman being absent for more than a total of three nights (*usus*).

2   By a symbolic form of purchase, in the presence of a holder of a pair of scales and five witnesses (*coemptio*).

3   By full ritual (*confarreatio*), in the presence of the *pontifex maximus*. This was obligatory for patrician families, and comprised a form of religious service with prayer, a bloodless sacrifice, the offering and eating of sacred bread, and the taking of auspices. The bride and bridegroom sat on two chairs bound together and covered with lambskin.

After the second century AD a different kind of ritual emerged, which began with a formal betrothal, at which the prospective bride slipped a gold ring onto the finger now known as the 'wedding finger' in the presence of the guests. For the marriage ceremony itself she wore a veil of flaming orange-red, surmounted by a simple wreath of blossom. There was animal sacrifice and the inevitable examination of the entrails for happy omens, after which the couple exchanged vows and the wedding guests shouted their congratulations.

Women in Roman times, though discriminated against, and subjected to abuse by such poets as Horace and Juvenal (*c*. AD 55–*c*. 140), were still capable of standing up for themselves when aroused. One of the most contentious pieces of Roman legislation was the Oppian Law, brought in after the defeat by Hannibal at Cannae in 216 BC with the object of reducing spending on luxury goods. Livy picks up the story when describing events of the year 195 BC.

> In between concerns of great wars either just finished or about to begin, there occurred an incident which is brief enough to record but which, because of the intensity it generated, blew up into a major confrontation. The tribunes of the people Marcus Fundanius and Lucius Valerius proposed to the [tribal] assembly the repealing of the Oppian Law, sponsored during the consulship of Quintus Fabius and Tiberius Sempronius by the tribune Gaius Oppius at the height of the Punic War, whereby no woman could possess more than half an ounce of gold, or wear a dress dyed in a variety of colours, or ride in a horse-drawn carriage in a city or town or within a mile of it except on holy days. The tribunes Marcus and Publius Junius Brutus were for keeping the law and announced they would veto its repeal. Many representatives of the nobility rose to speak for the ayes or the noes. The Capitol was packed with voters in favour or against. Neither modesty nor the persuasion or authority of their husbands could keep the women indoors. They blocked all the streets and entrances to the forum, vociferously arguing that at a time of prosperity, when men's personal fortunes were increasing

daily, women too should be restored to their former splendours. The press of women increased day by day, as they came in from the towns and outlying districts. They even grew so bold as to waylay and interrogate the consuls, praetors, and other officials.

(History of Rome, XXXIV. 1)

There was a prolonged and impassioned debate, during which Cato the Elder, needless to say, spoke against the motion.

The next day an even greater crowd of women poured out of their houses into the streets, and mass-picketed all the entrances to the homes of the two Brutuses, who had announced that they were vetoing their colleagues' proposal. Nor would they let up until the tribunes agreed to withdraw the veto. There was now no doubt that all the tribes would vote for the motion: the law was duly rescinded, twenty years after it had first been passed.

(History of Rome, XXXIV. 8)

FIGURE 23 A family (father, mother, baby) rides in the countryside in a horse-drawn carriage. From a sarcophagus in the National Museums, Rome.

Source: John Pittaway

In such a restricted environment it is not surprising that there seems to have been a comparatively small number of women in professional jobs. There are, however, records of a few female doctors, clerks, and secretaries; also hairdressers, for whom training was obligatory, teachers, and the occasional fishmonger, vegetable seller, dressmaker, and wool or silk merchant. There were certainly female gladiators: Martial makes a point of mentioning them in his book celebrating the shows put on by Titus in AD 80 in the recently completed Colosseum:

> You demand more, Caesar, than to be served under unconquerable arms by warlike Mars: Venus herself is also at your command.
>
> Noble tradition tells how Hercules slew the lion in the wastes of the Nemean valley. Let the ancient tale be reduced to silence: after your shows, Caesar, we can say that we have seen such deeds performed by a woman's hand.
>
> **(Spectacles, VII, VIII)**

It would seem, from a relief now in the British Museum, that when women fought each other in the arena, they did not wear helmets.

There were also prostitutes, who were required to register with the aedile. A law of Augustus declared adultery by women a public offence. A subsequent court ruling forbade men to have sex with an unmarried or widowed woman of the upper class, and banned upper-class women from having any sexual relationship outside marriage. This led some women of the upper classes to register as prostitutes, though this barred them from receiving legacies. In AD 19, under Tiberius, the senate eliminated this loophole by making daughters, granddaughters, and wives of senators or equestrians ineligible to register as prostitutes. Caligula was the first to tax prostitutes, probably on a monthly basis, the levy being the sum they normally charged for a single sexual encounter.

Another side to the legislation against adultery by women is reflected in the story of Lucretia (see chapter 1, p. 9), as told by Livy. She is technically, and under laws passed in Livy's lifetime legally, guilty, and feels she must pay the penalty. Her nobility and constancy in legend are matched historically by Cornelia, mother of the brothers Gracchus (see chapter 2, pp. 28–31). With her husband, Tiberius Sempronius Gracchus, censor, twice consul, and twice awarded a triumph for his victories, she had twelve children, only three of whom lived to adulthood. He died in 154 BC. Though she was still nubile, to judge from the fact that she had a proposal of marriage from King Ptolemy VIII, she preferred to remain a widow and dedicate herself to the upbringing and education of her children. That both her surviving sons were inspired by civic, rather than mere political, duty to bring about changes in the system, suggests some maternal influence. Whether she actively motivated them, or tried to control their excesses of enthusiasm for their causes, is a subject of debate. Certainly,

FIGURE 24 Erotic floor mosaic (sometimes captioned: prostitute with client) of the second half of the fourth century AD in a bedroom of Villa del Casale, Piazza Armerina, Sicily.

Source: Photograph © copyright Allan T. Kohl/Art Images for College Teaching (AICT)

according to Plutarch, she prevailed upon Gaius to withdraw a law aimed at banning from public office anyone who had once been voted from office by the people, as had the tribune who tried to get his elder brother's land bill referred to the senate.

After the death of her son Tiberius, she retired to a villa near Misenum, where she was brought news twelve years later that Gaius too had been killed supporting his beliefs. It was said that she bore their loss with the greatest nobility of spirit, and for the rest of her life devoted herself to literary and other cultural pursuits, and to entertaining learned men, particularly Greeks, who flocked to see her. Only a single whiff of scandal was ever attached to her name, that she was implicated in the death of her daughter's husband, Cornelius Scipio Aemilianus Africanus, conqueror of Carthage, who had nullified the operations of the Gracchi's agrarian commission by initiating a senatorial decree passing its powers to the consuls. After her death, the citizens of Rome erected a bronze statue of her, with the inscription, 'Cornelia, mother of the Gracchi'.

Women were expected to possess to a considerable degree that essentially Roman quality of *pietas*, particularly to one's husband. The most patient wife, in this respect, seems to have been Octavia (*c.* 70–11 BC), sister of Octavian. She had only recently been married to Gaius Claudius Marcellus when, in 54 BC, Caesar's daughter Julia, wife of Pompey, died. Caesar now made a bizarre proposition. He would divorce his wife Calpurnia, and marry Pompey's daughter Pompeia, who was married to Sulla's son: Pompey, now a widower, would marry Octavia. Pompey declined all offers, and Octavia remained married to Marcellus, with whom she had a son and two daughters. When Marcellus died in 40 BC, she was immediately married off to Mark Antony, as his third wife, to cement the agreement between him and Octavian to divide responsibility for the empire. That same year, Antony and Cleopatra's twins were born.

Antony and Octavia's daughter Antonia (grandmother of Nero) was born in 39 BC. Octavia spent the winter of that year and the following year in Athens with her husband, after which, pregnant with their second child, she was sent back to Italy, while Antony dallied with Cleopatra in Antioch. In 35 BC, she went on behalf of Octavian to Athens with troops, money, and supplies for Antony, who accepted them but sent Octavia home without even bothering to see her. With Octavian and Antony now at loggerheads in the senate, Octavian begged her to leave her husband. Octavia refused. Her reward was to be divorced by Antony in 32 BC, while her brother now went to war against her ex-husband and his mistress. After the death of the lovers, Octavia brought up her three children with Marcellus and her two daughters with Antony, together with Antony's three children with Cleopatra and his surviving children with his previous wife.

None, however, displayed the quality of *pietas* more sublimely than Pompeia Paulina, young wife of the aged Seneca, when Nero's men came to order him to commit suicide while he was at dinner with her and two friends. After asking for, and being refused, the tablets comprising his will, he commended himself to his friends, made a few guarded comments about Nero's habitual cruelty, and embraced his wife.

> He asked her, entreated her, to temper her grief, and not to allow it to be a permanent burden; rather to take genuine consolation for the loss of her husband in the contemplation of his virtuous life. Paulina assured him that she had every intention of dying with him, and demanded a share of the fatal knife. Seneca, by no means averse to her having her moment of glory, and at the same time moved by an affection which would not allow him to risk exposing to possible outrage someone he loved so deeply, said: 'I offered you the comfort of life: you have chosen the dignity of death. I shall not deny you the chance to show such an example. May the steadfastness of such a brave ending bring honour to us both,

but the greater fame be accorded to your death.' Then they sliced open the veins in their arms with a single stroke of the knife.

(Tacitus, *Annals*, XV. 63)

That, however, was by no means the end of the story. Because of Seneca's age and the spareness of his frame (the result of 'frugal living'), his blood was so sluggish that he had to cut open the veins in his legs, too. After persuading Paulina, streaming with her own blood, to retire into another room, he dictated a long statement to his secretaries, and then ordered his doctor to administer poison to him. When this did not do the trick, he had himself lifted into a hot bath and was asphyxiated by the steam.

Meanwhile Nero, hearing what had happened and being unwilling to be held responsible for the death also of Paulina, gave orders that she should be revived. While soldiers stood over them, her staff bandaged her arms and staunched the bleeding. She lived a few years longer, 'faithful to her husband's memory to a most praiseworthy degree, the pallor of her face and body testifying to the extent to which her soul had been destroyed' (Tacitus, *Annals*, XV. 64).

Certainly some women were able to attain a degree of education and to absorb and reflect the culture of the times. Some even had some fun, as well as influence: notably Sempronia, whom Catiline earmarked as a potential recruit to his revolutionary cause in 63 BC.

> She used to behave with the outrageous audacity of a man. Yet this woman was of an excellent family, and was blessed with beauty, and then with a husband and children. She had studied Greek and Latin literature; she sang to her own accompaniment on the lyre; she danced more gracefully than a respectable woman needs to do, and had many other superfluous gifts. But there was nothing she respected less than decorum or modesty. It was not easy to decide whether she was more spendthrift with her money or her reputation. She was so oversexed that she made passes at men more often than they did at her. She often broke promises, reneged on debts, and was an accessory to murder; she would get herself into deep trouble because of both her luxurious living and her lack of cash. Yet she was a woman of ability: she wrote poetry; she was witty; her conversation could be modest, sympathetic, or provocative. She was, in fact, an exceedingly amusing and charming person.

(Sallust, *The Conspiracy of Catiline*, XXVI)

Sempronia was the mother of Decimus Junius Brutus (d. 43 BC), Caesar's naval commander during his Gallic wars and subsequently one of the leading conspirators in his assassination. Sallust (86–35 BC) was an aspiring politician at the time of the

Catiline affair. He retired from public life in about 44 BC after doubts were cast about his activities as governor of the province of Africa Nova. *The Conspiracy of Catiline* (published *c.* 41 BC) is one of two historical monographs which he then wrote. The character he draws of Sempronia reflects his general theme of decline and his policy of emphasizing Catiline's guilt by blackening his associates. At the same time, though there was not necessarily any connection between intellectual accomplishments and sexual freedom, some Roman matrons did behave with abandon, some did get into debt, and prominent people who knew her would still be alive when Sallust's account appeared.

We are on shakier ground when trying to make an assessment of the characters of two undoubtedly talented and politically aware imperial consorts, Livia (58 BC–AD 29), wife of Augustus and mother of Tiberius (see also chapter 3, pp. 50–51), and Agrippina the Younger (AD 15–59), wife of Claudius and mother of Nero (see also chapter 3, pp. 58–59) – and Tacitus implies that both poisoned their husbands. Whether or not suggestions of strings of other murders and, in the case of Agrippina, of lovers too, including her brother and her own son, are justified, both women undoubtedly manipulated the system to ensure that their sons by an earlier marriage became emperor, and both sons grew actively to demonstrate distaste for their mothers.

Livia had a distinguished aristocratic pedigree, besides having been married to Tiberius Claudius Nero (d. 32 BC), who had, however, had a chequered political career. One of Caesar's right-hand men, he had advocated that the dictator's assassins should be rewarded. He then supported Mark Antony's brother against Octavian, then with his wife and baby son joined Sextus Pompey in Sicily, and then switched his allegiance to Mark Antony in Greece. He and his family were allowed to return to Rome under the terms of the treaty of Misenum (39 BC) between Octavian, Antony, and Sextus Pompey. Soon afterwards, 19-year-old Livia, six months pregnant, was forced to divorce, or be divorced by, her husband, in order to marry Octavian, who had conveniently divorced his own wife. After they had faced down the public out-cry at the circumstances of their marriage, the union, during which she received unprecedented honours, lasted for 53 years.

Though they had no children (a premature baby died), she was in other respects a traditional and successful Roman upper-class wife who even spun and wove material for her husband's clothes. And as a traditional Roman wife, she organized the household. She also organized much else besides: she received imperial clients and provincial embassies, commissioned public buildings and dedicated them in her name, established charities, presided at banquets, and is said to have interceded on behalf of a man accused of plotting against Augustus. As a Roman wife should, she helped her husband with his correspondence, and altogether eased his imperial burden, while undoubtedly increasing her own influence. This unprecedented crossing of the boundary between private and public spheres made ancient historians such as Tacitus and Cassius Dio uneasy, and may be the reason for their hostility. But there had never been a Roman empress before, and someone had to lay down some ground rules.

Livia filled the position very well indeed, as is suggested by Augustus' public recognition of her role. Statues were erected to her. She sat with the vestal virgins at public shows, she had the right to manage her own affairs, and she was even granted the same tribunician privileges as her husband. In his will, Augustus formally adopted her into his line, with the name Julia Augusta – subsequent empresses came to adopt the title of Augusta for themselves. Livia's prestige was such that she was awarded the services of a lictor to walk before her, but there is some confusion as to whether he ever materialized. When she died, the senate voted a triumphal arch in her memory – her son Tiberius accepted it on her behalf, agreed to meet the cost, and then forgot about it. She was finally deified in AD 42, at the instigation of her grandson Claudius.

Claudius may have had Livia's role in public affairs in mind when he decided to marry his 34-year-old niece Agrippina – he was then 59. As with Livia, much of what we know about her comes from historians to whom the notion of a woman wielding political clout was anathema. The eldest daughter of Claudius' brother Germanicus and Vipsania Agrippina, granddaughter of Augustus, she was, however, no stranger to public controversy. With her two sisters, she was, during the rule of Caligula, officially cited in prayers, but in AD 39 she was implicated in a plot to assassinate Caligula in Germany, and banished. She was recalled to marry Claudius, and by intrigue certainly, and organizing ability probably, established herself, and her son by her first marriage, in virtually unassailable positions.

She was granted the title of Augusta, which even Livia had not received until after her death. Her portrait, and details of her honours, appeared on the reverse of coins of Claudius, an unprecedented privilege for a ruler's wife during her lifetime. She rode in a ceremonial carriage such as was usually reserved for priests and holy statues, and extended her geographical influence by founding a settlement for army veterans at her birthplace in Germany. She had Seneca recalled from Corsica, to which Claudius had banished him for alleged adultery with her sister, and ensured that her own nominee, Burrus, became sole commander of the imperial guard: she had jobs for them both, as her son's tutors. She also persuaded Claudius to betroth his own daughter Octavia to him. Octavia had been betrothed before, to Lucius Junius Silanus, a young man of impeccable aristocratic lineage and ability, whom Agrippina had neatly put out of the reckoning by having him accused of incest with his sister. Silanus committed suicide on the day she married Claudius.

The following year, AD 50, her son was formally adopted by Claudius and took the name Nero. Being three years older than Claudius' son Britannicus, he took

FIGURE 25 Gold *aureus* issued in AD 54, the first year of Nero's reign, showing the new emperor and his mother face to face. The inscription is hers: his is relegated to the reverse. The design was changed the following year. Both figures now faced in the same direction, with Nero partially obscuring Agrippina. Twice actual size.

Source: Photograph © copyright Hunterian Museum and Art Gallery, University of Glasgow

precedence over his stepbrother, now his brother by adoption. If Agrippina was responsible for Claudius' death in AD 54, then it may have been because her husband's unpredictable nature made her position precarious, and because she wanted to exercise full control while Nero was still too young to do so himself.

Not only was she now the widow of a god, but in the east she was herself hailed as divine. Even in Italy, she made her position clear. Gold and silver coins of AD 54 carry portraits of her and Nero facing each other, but it is her inscription that surrounds them: 'Agrippina Augusta, wife of the divine Claudius, mother of Nero Caesar'. Nero's inscription is relegated to the reverse of the coin. She was, in effect, regent for her teenage son, but he was influenced still by Burrus and Seneca. When matters began to unwind for Agrippina, the situation was reversed. Both heads still appear on the coin's obverse, but facing in the same direction, with Nero slightly obscuring his mother: the inscriptions have also changed places. Several factors, or a combination of them, have been suggested for Nero deciding, or being persuaded, to get rid of her. Nero revelled in the power that his new position gave him, and it may be that his tutors realized that the activities of Agrippina were bad for the state. Agrippina wished to be seen to be in control. In the time of Claudius, she had been used to attending meetings with foreign diplomats, but sat apart from the emperor. Now, on one occasion, it was clear as she entered the hall that she intended to sit beside Nero on the platform. Seneca managed, by quick thinking, to circumvent a major lapse in protocol, by whispering to Nero to rise and go to meet her.

Agrippina interfered, too, in the emperor's emotional entanglements. Nero was also psychotic about his personal safety, and it is more than likely that fear motivated him to take the actions he did. So, after several botched attempts, the murder was contrived of a woman with a most remarkable curriculum vitae: to successive Roman emperors she was respectively great-granddaughter, granddaughter (by adoption), sister, wife (also niece), and mother.

SLAVES AND SLAVERY

In using slave labour, the Romans were perpetuating an institution which had existed in Egypt since at least 2600 BC, and had been carried on under the empires of China, India, and Babylon, and by the Greeks. Nor does it seem that the treatment of the slaves who worked the vast farmlands of Italy was very much harsher than or different from that meted out to African slaves on the American and West Indian plantations in the eighteenth century, or that the majority of household slaves were worse off than many domestic staff in Europe at an even later date. The Romans, however, especially after the gradual decline of peasant farming in Italy from about 200 BC, based much of the social and economic fabric of their empire on slavery. When attitudes changed, fuelled partly by Christianity, which was not so much anti-slavery as pro-benevolence, and the supply of slaves from abroad dwindled, that part of the fabric began to disintegrate. Under the empire, emancipated slaves were joining the free-born poor in the struggle for existence.

One of the functions of official provincial tax-collectors, especially in Asia Minor, was to kidnap potential slaves and ship them to the specialist slave-markets, one of the biggest of which, at Delos, could process 10,000 men, women, and children in a day. Acquisition of slaves by conquest was a standard practice. Julius Caesar records laconically of one of his campaigns of aggression: 'The next day the gates were broken down, there being no-one to defend them, and the troops marched in. Caesar sold off the whole town lock, stock, and barrel. The dealers gave him a receipt for 53,000 head of people' (*Gallic War*, II. 33). This was not excessive by the standards of the time, especially as the warriors inside had broken their word. He was, however, more uncompromising on another occasion:

> Caesar, aware that his compassion was widely recognized, was not at all concerned that harsher treatment of the inhabitants of the town might be regarded as innate brutality, but at the same time he could not see any satisfactory outcome of his plans if more of the population in other parts of the country took the same action. He therefore decided to make an example of them to deter the rest. He spared the lives of those who had taken up arms against him, but cut off their hands, a punishment intended clearly to demonstrate the evil of their ways.

> **(Gallic War, VIII. 44)**

Until the empire, marriage between slaves was not recognized, and their children automatically assumed the status of slave. A slave could keep what he could save towards buying his freedom, but if he ran away and was caught, the punishment was branding or death. There was hardly any aspect of daily life, or of work or the leisure industry, in which slaves were not involved, and their treatment, which was entirely the responsibility of their owner, varied according to their skills and the labour which was required of them. They were trained to fight each other, and wild animals, to the death in the arenas of the empire; it was from a training establishment for gladiators that Spartacus the Thracian led out a band of slaves and in 73 BC began his two-year campaign of revolt. During the later republic, gangs of slaves worked in fetters on the agricultural estates and were chained up in semi-underground barracks at night. Others did not suffer so much. Great numbers of herdsmen were required, and in 8 BC Gaius Caecilius Isodorus, himself a former slave, left a staff of 4,116, most of whom would have been employed in this capacity. Cato the Elder, who acquired young slaves as an investment and sold them at a profit after training, laid down that a staff of twelve (a manager, his wife, and eleven hands) was the right number to work a farm of 150 acres devoted to olive-growing and sheep. There is little doubt that Roman technology could have devised many labour-saving devices, particularly for use on the farm, were it not that an abundance of slave labour was an economic fact of life.

Slaves worked in the mines, and also in the potteries. They constituted the state's labour force for building and maintaining public works, and in other government services such as the mint and the grain supply; they were also its 'white-collar' workers, who kept the machinery of bureaucracy and administration working. They served as clerks and accountants in private businesses, and as secretaries, teachers, librarians, doctors, scribes, artists, and entertainers. And they were the private staff of villas, town houses, and palaces. Household slaves had perquisites – even in the house of the bombastic and vulgar freedman Trimalchio, portrayed in Gaius Petronius' novel, *Satyricon*, they got what was left over from the dinner-party. Some, however, suffered unusually severe hazards:

> Vedius Pollio, Roman knight and a friend of the divine Augustus, practised his barbarity with the assistance of moray eels, into whose tanks he threw condemned slaves: not that wild animals would not do, but because with no other creature could he watch a man being torn to pieces utterly and instantaneously.
>
> **(Pliny the Elder, *Natural History*, IX. 39)**

The poet Martial, by his own account, laid into his cook if a meal was not up to scratch:

> You think me barbaric, Rusticus, and too fond of my food, because I beat my cook when my dinner is below standard. If that seems to you a trivial reason for the lash, what other excuse is there to flog a cook?
>
> **(*Epigrams*, VIII. 23)**

Was it ambivalence that inspired another poem? 'You say your hare is not cooked and call for the whip. You'd rather cut up your cook, Rufus, than your hare?' (*Epigrams*, III. 94).

Pliny the Younger used to invite the better-educated members of his staff to join him after dinner for conversation, and remarked of his villa at Laurentum that most of the rooms in the wing which housed his slaves were also perfectly suitable for putting up guests (see also chapter 6, p. 139). This kind of sentiment is echoed by Seneca, expressing one of the principles of Stoicism (see chapter 4, p. 96):

> Remember that he whom you call your slave came into life by the same route as you, basks in the same sky, and breathes, lives, and dies in the same way as you do. You can observe the free man in him just as he can see the slave in you. In the proscriptions of Marius many high-born men, on the military ladder to a seat in the senate, were reduced by fate to being shepherds or janitors. You look down at your peril on someone in whose place you could come to be even while you look down on him. I don't want to get too involved in the broader issues of the treatment of slaves, to whom in general we are extremely arrogant, cruel, and abusive. This, however, is the sum of my advice: treat your inferiors as you would want to be treated by your masters.
>
> **(Epistles, XLVII)**

A contrary view is illustrated by an incident shortly before Seneca's enforced death and during the lifetime of Tacitus, who describes it:

> [In AD 61] the city prefect, Pedanius Secundus, was killed by one of his own slaves; the murderer had either been refused his freedom after the price had been agreed, or had fallen in love with a youth and could not bear to have his master as a rival. Whatever the reason, when the time came to take out to execution all the slaves of the household, as was the time-honoured tradition, there was almost a revolution as the people, bent on sparing innocent lives, got together and besieged the senate. In the senate-house itself there were those who protested that the punishment was unfair, though the majority saw no reason why the law should not be observed.
>
> **(Annals, XIV. 42)**

Among the latter was the jurist Gaius Cassius, who made an impassioned speech upholding the status quo.

> While no-one dared speak openly against Cassius, his words were greeted by a confusion of voices expressing pity at the number of victims involved [said to be

400], their ages, sex, and the fact that most of them were indubitably innocent of any crime. In spite of that, the pro-hanging lobby prevailed. The decision could not be put into effect as an enormous crowd gathered, armed with stones and flaming missiles. Nero issued an edict reprimanding the public, and gave orders that the entire route along which the condemned slaves were being led to execution should be lined with soldiers. Cingonius Varro had proposed additionally that the freedmen who had been in the house at the time should be deported. This was vetoed by the emperor on the grounds that an ancient custom, which had withstood pleas of mercy, should not be stretched to incorporate the exercise of unreasonable cruelty.

(Annals, XIV. 45)

A slave could purchase his freedom or achieve it by a process of manumission which was at the discretion of the owner, but which became such a popular practice at the beginning of the empire that Augustus introduced laws restricting it. A freedman had full rights of citizenship except that of holding public office. Some freedmen became even richer than the masters they had once served. Others, at the same time, influenced affairs of state, as did Claudius' personal advisers. Only in about AD 100, did equestrians replace freedmen as senior civil servants.

EDUCATION

At the beginning of the republic, education was a case of *mos maiorum*, being left entirely to the parents, and consisting of a mixture of martial and practical arts. Boys were expected to emulate their fathers, and girls their mothers. From about 250 BC, largely as a result of the influx of educated Greek slaves, tutors were employed in richer homes or were set up as teachers of informal schools. Towards the end of the republic, a two-tier educational system evolved, leading to higher education in oratory and philosophy. At about the age of 7, children of the privileged classes were sent to a primary school (often presided over by a single teacher), where from dawn to the middle of the afternoon, with a break for lunch at home, they learned reading, writing, and arithmetic. Girls as well as boys could benefit from this basic schooling, which seems often to have been in premises designed as shops, with an open front on the street. Pupils sat on wooden benches and wrote out their exercises on tablets which they rested on their knees.

Formal education ceased for girls at the age of 12, but boys who showed academic promise were sent on, if their parents could afford the fees, to 'grammar' school, where they stayed until they assumed the *toga virilis*, pursuing a curriculum which emphasized Greek as well as Latin literature. Much has been made, from allusions in literature and from an often reproduced fresco uncovered at Herculaneum, of the brutality of schoolmasters. There seems, however, to be no evidence that corporal punishment in Roman times was any more frequent or severe than it was in many schools in Britain in the twentieth century. And though Horace writes of remembering verses 'dictated to me as a boy by flogger Orbilius' (*Epistles*, II. 1, 70–1), Suetonius describes a man who was less of a disciplinarian:

> Marcus Verrius Flaccus, a freedman, was renowned for his teaching methods. He stimulated his pupils' efforts by competition: setting those at the same level of attainment a subject on which to write and offering a prize for the best essay. This would be a book of antiquarian interest for its beauty or rarity. As a result of his success he was chosen by Augustus to teach his grandsons, and moved into the palace with his whole school on the understanding that he would not take on any more pupils.
>
> **(On Teachers, XVII)**

According to Suetonius in the same book, rhetoric was 'in the early days' taught in schools. By the time of Quintilian towards the end of the first century AD, it had become accepted that rhetoric should be taught in special schools at a higher level, though a pupil might be expected to have had an introduction to the subject before embarking on higher education.

Rhetoric as a subject as well as an art originated in Sicily in the fifth century BC, and was developed in Athens and in Asia Minor, before becoming an accepted study in Rome. There were basically three branches of oratory: the display of one's art, often in the form of a panegyric or invective (the latter had its counterpart in the medieval Scottish flyting); the persuasion of an audience to a point of view; and the defence or prosecution of a defendant in a court of law. Each of these involved five separate skills: selection of content, arrangement, language, memory, delivery.

While the schools taught traditional religious observances and supplemented the training children received at home in conduct and morality, older boys, as they grew up, were exposed to the influence of the various branches of Greek philosophy, in which the upper classes at least came to find a more acceptable guide to life than in the religion of the state. Leading citizens employed resident philosophers. When Cicero was about 18, he attended lectures in Rome given by Phaedrus the Epicurean; shortly afterwards he listened to Philo of Larissa, head of the Academic school of philosophy, to whose doctrines he remained generally faithful for the rest of his life. When he was 18, Horace studied philosophy in Athens, where in addition to the Academics and the Epicureans he would have come under the influence of the Stoics and the Peripatetics (see also chapter 4, pp. 96–98).

DRESS

The Romans applied their ingenuity and use of basic materials and principles not only to solving complicated architectural and engineering problems, but also to their clothes. These had to be simple. Only wool and, to a lesser extent, linen were available, and because needles were of bronze or bone, and thread only of the coarsest quality, stitching or sewing was neither elegant nor particularly effective. Buttons and buttonholes were therefore rarities, and clothes were fastened or held together mainly by enormous safety-pins, belts, knots, or not at all.

To say that the Romans slept in their underwear is not to suggest, as would be true of many later civilizations, that they did not wash, for bathing was a feature of daily life. It was simply that the time for taking one's bath was in the afternoon. A woman might have a brassiere in the form of a band, the purpose of which was to keep the breasts up rather than in. Otherwise, both men and women wore a loin-cloth knotted round the waist, with a belted tunic or shift with short or long sleeves. The male tunic reached to the knees, but women and girls wore one that was longer, sometimes down to the ground. In winter you might wear two tunics, one on top of the other; those particularly susceptible to cold, such as was Augustus, might wear as many as four. For the poorer classes, slaves, and small children, that was the limit of their attire, though Pliny the Elder used to allow his shorthand writer to wear gloves in cold weather so that nothing would reduce the effectiveness with which his thoughts were recorded.

The outer garment, the classic toga for men and the *palla* for women, was the standard, and statutory, formal dress for a Roman citizen. It was simply a vast blanket of undyed light wool, draped round and over the body, leaving one arm free, and probably held together only by its own weight and its folds, or by faith alone. The *palla* was rectangular in shape. Archaeologists and scholars have concluded, from practical experiments, that the toga was in the form of a segment of a circle, along the straight edge of which ran the purple stripe of the *toga praetexta* (worn by children and certain officials, and latterly by men of senatorial rank), and that it was about 5 metres long and 2 metres wide at its deepest point. Putting it on, getting the folds to fall correctly, and keeping it adjusted while performing daily tasks, appear to have been almost as much of a problem to the Romans as they have proved to modern scholars, for Suetonius mentions it as a mark of admiration that Vespasian could chat to callers while he was getting dressed. Those who were standing for public office were in the habit of whitening their toga with chalk, and were thus known as *candidati* (clothed in glittering white). For dinner-parties, at which the toga could have been an intolerable burden, it was often replaced by the synthesis, a kind of dressing-gown. Martial is particularly biting about a rich acquaintance who changed his synthesis eleven times during a meal.

FIGURE 26   Man in a *toga*.

FIGURE 27   Woman in a *palla*.

Cloaks were worn out of doors in bad weather. There was little difference between the footwear of men and women; both usually wore sandals tied round the ankle with thongs, and on more formal occasions the *calceus*, a soft leather shoe.

For men, shaving was the rule between about 100 BC and AD 100, performed with iron razors by a slave or at one of the innumerable barber's shops which were a feature of urban life. Women wore their hair up in a variety of styles varying between the simple, often with a knot or lock at the back falling to the nape, and the intricately curled and over-ornate.

FOOD AND DRINK

The ordinary Roman was not a great eater of meat; the word *frumentum* (grain) also means military food supplies or rations. The army diet, which was carefully super-vised, was a balanced one of grain (which the soldiers themselves ground and made into porridge, bread, or biscuits), some meat (usually bacon), fish, poultry, cheese, vegetables, fruit, salt, olive oil, and raw wine. When there was a delay in getting the grain ration through and meat had to be substituted, the soldiers groused. Officers fared rather better, even in what has been traditionally regarded as the most uncom-fortable posting of all, northern Britain. Entries in documents (in the form of thin wooden tablets) relating to the accounts of the commanding officer's household in about AD 100, found since the 1970s at the fort of Vindolanda on Hadrian's Wall, record fresh produce in the form of pork crackling, pork cutlets, pig's trotters, piglet, ham, chicken, venison, anchovies (or other small fish), oysters, eggs, radishes, apples, lentils, beans, pork fat, lard, and butter.

At home, porridge and bread were the staple food of most Romans, many of whom in the city had to rely on the grain dole for their needs.

> Now that state officials are elected by the senate and the people have no votes to sell, they have lost interest. Those who once had a say in the election to power of everyone from consul to legionary commander have taken back seats, claiming as their rights just bread and circuses [i.e. free tokens for grain and free tickets for the games].
>
> **(Juvenal, *Satires*, X. 77–81)**

In well-to-do homes the regimen was different. *Jentaculum* (breakfast), for those who wanted it, might be bread dipped in wine, or with cheese, dried fruits, or honey. The equivalent of lunch was *prandium*, again a light meal, often consisting of left-overs from the previous day. The main meal of the day, *cena*, was eaten in the middle of the afternoon, after work and the bath, and could, and often did, go on for hours.

FIGURE 28   A family meal: the man reclines while the woman sits.

Source: John Pittaway

Dinner-parties were elaborate, and could be dignified or disgusting affairs, depending on the discrimination of the host and his choice of guests. Cicero wrote to his friend Atticus that when Julius Caesar stopped overnight at his country villa at Pozzuoli (Puteoli) in 45 BC with his retinue (who had to be entertained in three dining-rooms), Caesar 'had a bath at about one . . . oiled his body, and came into dinner. He took an emetic, and so was able to eat and drink to excess, with obvious enjoyment' (*To Atticus*, XIII. 52). Dinner guests reclined on their left elbow at an angle of about 45 degrees to the table, on couches set against three sides of it, and ate with their fingers.

The meal consisted of three parts, within each of which there could be any number of courses served individually or together. *Hors d'œuvre* might be eggs presented in a variety of ways, salads, cooked vegetables, shellfish, snails, and, occasionally, roasted and stuffed dormice. The main courses illustrate the varieties of meat, game, fish, and fowl that were available, or which were pressed into service in the form of more impressive-sounding dishes: not just beef, lamb, pork, venison, hare, bream, hake, mackerel, mullet, oysters, sole, chicken, duck, goose, and partridge, but also veal, sucking-pig, boar, wild goat, kid, porpoise, crane, flamingo, ostrich, thrush, and turtle-dove. From the only surviving Roman cookery book, we know how all these were sometimes cooked. It is attributed to a noted gourmet of the time of Tiberius called Apicius, who, it is said, having spent nine-tenths of his considerable fortune on good living, which still left him with 10 million sesterces, killed himself. The book is a later compilation, and many of the recipes have been made to work under modern conditions. They reveal that the ambitious host was usually more concerned with exotic ingredients than with exotic tastes – peacock, for instance, features, but only as rissoles. Most main dishes were served in sauce, the basic ingre-

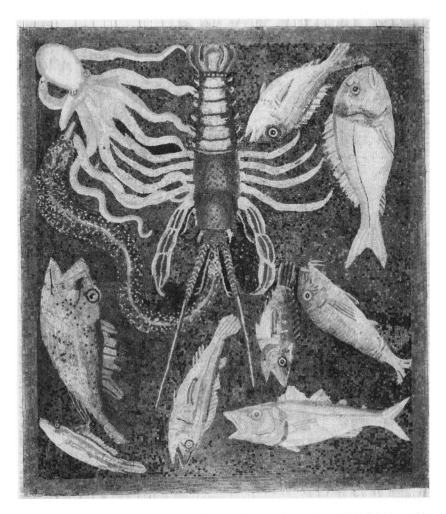

FIGURE 29 A panel from a mosaic floor (*c.* AD 100) depicting edible fish from the Mediterranean: (clockwise from top left) octopus, spiny lobster, dentex, gilt-headed bream, red mullet, comber (*serranus*), common bass (bottom right), green wrasse, rainbow wrasse, scorpion fish, moray eel.

Source: British Museum

dient of which was a factory-made fish stock called *liquamen* or *garum*, concocted from the entrails of mackerel. The meal would finish with dessert: fruit, cakes, and puddings.

Juvenal provides a hypothetical guest with a simpler country meal: home-grown asparagus and farm eggs as starters; chicken and milk-fed kid for the main course;

local pears, oranges, grapes, and apples to finish with. Martial offers his guests in the country, at a dinner-party for seven:

> Mallow leaves (good for the digestion) . . . lettuce, chopped leeks, mint (for burping), rocket leaves . . . mackerel garnished with rue and sliced egg, and a sow's udder marinated in tuna-fish brine . . . that's the *hors d'œuvre*. For the main course, all served together, tender cuts of lamb, with beans and spring greens, and a chicken and a ham left over from three previous dinners. When you are full, fresh fruit and vintage wine from Nomentum with no dregs.
>
> **(*Epigrams*, X. 48, 7–19)**

Wine was the national, and natural, drink, usually diluted with water: beer was for Britons and Gauls. Wine was also mixed with honey to make *mulsum*, a cooling aperitif which accompanied the first course at dinner. This was usually made from must, the first treading of the grapes, but Pliny the Elder recommended that dry white wine should be used instead. For those modern readers inclined to try, two tablespoonfuls of honey to a bottle of wine have been suggested. The best wine-producing region in Italy was around the border between Latium and Campania, from which came the excellent Caecuban, Setian, Falernian, and Massic vintages.

HOLIDAYS AND THE GAMES

Not only was the official Roman working day a short one by modern standards, but there were comparatively few working days in the year, except for slaves, who in any case were not allowed to attend public entertainments as spectators. In the reign of Claudius, 159 days in the year were designated public holidays, on 93 of which shows were offered at public expense: in the middle of the fifth century AD, there were 200 holidays a year, on 175 of which public games were held. Originally these games had religious significance, but under the republic more and more secular games were introduced into the calendar ostensibly to celebrate notable events, some of which lasted as long as a fortnight. There were two kinds of games: *ludi scaenici*, or theatrical events, and *ludi circenses*. That the *ludi scaenici* suffered overwhelming competition from the other forms of spectacle is attested to by the much smaller numbers that the stage theatres seated (see chapter 6, p. 143), by the fewer days allocated to them, and by the evidence of the playwright Terence (*c.* 185–159 BC). A revival of his comedy *The Mother-in-Law* was staged as a part of the funeral games in 160 BC for Lucius Aemilius Paullus, who had been twice consul, and censor, while mixing cultural sensitivity with brutality beyond the cause of duty. All was going well during the first act, Terence says in a prologue to a further performance that year, when someone

FIGURE 30 In republican times, after about 175 BC, it was usual for each of the three men appointed respectively to cast the state's bronze, silver, and gold coins to put their name on the reverse (a practice which survives, for instance, on British and US bank notes). This particular design on a silver *denarius* of 113/112 BC is a token of the promise of the moneyer (T. Didius) to mount a public gladiatorial games if he is elected curule aedile. Twice actual size.

Source: Photograph © copyright Hunterian Museum and Art Gallery, University of Glasgow

announced that the gladiatorial show was about to begin. The audience did not so much melt away as surge out.

Ludi circenses took place in the custom-built circuses, or race-tracks, and amphitheatres. In these days of live, and televised, sporting mass-entertainments – motor-racing, horse-racing, physical team sports such as soccer and rugby football, games under American and Australian rules, and even cricket played between teams wearing coloured track suits – it should not be difficult to appreciate the Romans' passion for chariot-racing. One can understand, too, their devotion to the particular team they supported, and its colours of white, green, red, or blue, though not necessarily condone the violence that often ensued between gangs of rival supporters. The public adulated the most successful drivers, and there was heavy on-course and off-course betting. The drivers were slaves, but they were also professional sportsmen, who could earn vast sums from winning. The chariots themselves were deliberately constructed to be as light as possible, and were drawn by two, four, or even more horses; the higher the number, the greater was the skill required of the driver, and the more sensational were the crashes and pile-ups. A race was usually seven laps of the track – a total of about 4,000 metres in the Circus Maximus in Rome – with a hair-raising 180 degrees turn at each end of the *spina*, the narrow wall that divided the arena. Though the start was staggered, there were no lanes and apparently no rules, yet during the first and second centuries AD several star charioteers notched up over 1,000 wins each, and there are records of individual horses being in a winning team several hundred times. Gaius Appuleius Diodes, who died at the age of 42, having driven four-horse chariots for twenty-four years, had 1,462 wins in 4,257 starts, and was placed 1,437 times. In the reign of Augustus there might be ten or twelve races in a day: during and after the time of Caligula, twenty-four a day was commonplace.

It was the *ludi circenses* of the amphitheatres, however, which have given the Romans the bad press that their thirst for blood-letting has earned them, though there is evidence that the Etruscans attached religious significance to the gladiatorial combat. The single rule of such bouts was that similarly armed contestants or teams of contestants did not normally fight each other. The most usual contest was between a moderately protected and helmeted swordsman and a *retiarius*, armed only with a net and a trident, or between teams of these. It was each man for himself, and any who appeared less than enthusiastic were prodded into activity with red-hot irons, while other attendants stood by to drag off the corpses. It was sometimes left to the crowd to signify whether a wounded and downed gladiator should be finished off by his opponent. They did so by waving their handkerchiefs for a release, or giving the 'thumbs down' signal for death. Gladiators were slaves, or condemned criminals, or prisoners of war, all of whom were regarded as expendable. So were wild animals, which were rounded up in their natural habitats and transported in their thousands to be hunted down and slaughtered in the confines of the arenas of the Roman empire, as a morning's overture to the gladiatorial contests in the afternoon. To celebrate the opening of the Colosseum in AD 80, 5,000 wild beasts and 4,000 tame animals were killed in one day. For variety, animals would be goaded to fight each other. Elephants versus bulls was a feature of a games in 79 BC. Nero introduced a novel turn, the marine contest: 'Fights between wild animals of the forests are less interesting, now that we have seen seals against bears' (Calpurnius, *Eclogues*, VII. 64–5). Alternatively, or as an additional attraction, the animals tore apart contingents of condemned and unarmed criminals.

The third and most spectacular form of combat, which involved flooding the arena or transferring the show to a suitable stretch of water, was the *naumachia*, or sea-fight. The idea seems to have originated with Julius Caesar, an impresario of great ingenuity and ambition, who had an artificial lake dug, on which he pitted against each other two fleets of 10,000 oarsmen, with 1,000 soldiers dressed up to represent men of Tyre and Egypt. Particularly popular in later years was a reconstruction of the battle of Salamis in 480 BC, which was replayed several times during the first century AD. The biggest *naumachia* ever was staged by Claudius in AD 52.

> The tunnel dug through the mountain between the Fucine lake and the river Liris had now been completed. [Brick-lined, and 5,600 metres long, it had taken 30,000 workmen eleven years to construct.] In order that as many people as possible might admire the impressiveness of the achievement, a naval battle was arranged on the lake itself . . . Claudius put 9,000 armed combatants into two fleets of ships with both three and four banks of oars. He positioned rafts round the edge of the lake to block off any escape routes, leaving enough space in the middle for the display of the power of the oarsmen, the skill of the coxes, the speed of the ships, and all the other arts of such a contest. Platoons and companies of the praetorian cohorts were stationed on the rafts, protected by ramparts, from behind which they fired catapults and missile-throwers. Covered ships manned by marines

occupied the rest of the lake . . . The battle, though contested by criminals, was fought as bravely and spiritedly as if the combatants were men of free will, and after considerable bloodshed they were excused death.

(Tacitus, *Annals*, XII. 56)

Hazards were not always confined to the arena itself. When the Circus Maximus was still used for gladiatorial contests, Pompey put up iron barriers to protect the audience during a fight between twenty crazed elephants and bands of armed hunters. The barriers buckled and some of them broke. And in AD 27, a jerry-built amphitheatre at Fidenae collapsed, throwing 50,000 spectators (according to Tacitus, 20,000 according to Suetonius) to the ground and burying them in debris. A redeeming feature of the disaster was the way in which emergency services were provided by the rich, who drafted in medical supplies and doctors from their own households. The response of the government was to issue guidelines for such entertainments: 'No-one with a capital of less than 400,000 sesterces may present a gladiatorial show, and an amphitheatre may only be built on solid ground' (Tacitus, *Annals*, IV. 63).

FURTHER READING

* indicates sourcebook

Adkins, L. and Adkins, R.A., *Handbook to Life in Ancient Rome*, Oxford University Press, new edn 1998.

Barrow, R., *Greek and Roman Education*, Bristol Classical Press, 1998.

Bauman, R.A., *Women and Politics in Ancient Rome*, Routledge, 1994.

Bradley, K., *Discovering the Roman Family: Studies in Roman Social History*, Oxford University Press, 1991.

Bradley, K., *Slavery and Society at Rome*, Cambridge University Press, 1994.

*Cooley, A.E. and Cooley, M.G.L., *Pompeii: A Sourcebook*, Routledge, 2004.

Crook, J.A., *Law and Life of Rome*, Thames and Hudson, new edn 1984; Cornell University Press, 1984.

Croom, A.T., *Roman Clothing and Fashion*, Tempus, 2002.

Dalby, A., *Food in the Ancient World from A to Z*, Routledge, 2003.

Fantham, E. et al., *Women in the Classical World*, Oxford University Press, 1994.

*Futrell, A., *The Roman Games: Historical Sources in Translation*, Blackwell, 2006.

Gardner, J., *Women in Roman Law and Society*, Routledge, new edn 1987.

*Gardner, J. and Wiedemann, T., *The Roman Household: A Sourcebook*, Routledge, 1991.

Habinek, T., *Ancient Rhetoric and Oratory*, Blackwell, 2004.

Kleiner, D.E.E. and Matheson, S.B. (eds), *I Claudia II: Women in Roman Art and Society*, Yale University Art Gallery, 2000.

*Lefkowitz, M.R. and Fant, M.B., *Women's Life in Greece and Rome: A Sourcebook in Translation*, Duckworth, 3rd rev. edn 2005; Johns Hopkins University Press, 2005.

*Lomas, K., *Roman Italy, 338 BC–AD 200: A Sourcebook*, Routledge, 1996.

Robinson, O.F., *Ancient Rome: City Planning and Administration*, Routledge, 1992.

*Shelton, J.-A., *As the Romans Did: A Sourcebook in Roman Social History*, Oxford University Press, 2nd edn 1997.

Stambaugh, J.E., *The Ancient Roman City*, Johns Hopkins University Press, 1988.

Treggiari, S., *Roman Social History*, Routledge, 2002.

Wiedemann, T., *Emperors and Gladiators*, Routledge, 1995.

*Wiedemann, T., *Greek and Roman Slavery: A Sourcebook*, Routledge, 1980.

6 ART, ARCHITECTURE, AND BUILDING

The overriding impression the material arts of Rome offer is of opulence, solid permanence, and the application of practical skills which were largely inherited but which were adapted to the economic and expansionist tendencies that resulted in the growth of the empire. Roman sculpture, learned from the Greeks and Etruscans, reached a peak in the first and second centuries AD which has hardly been matched since. The development of the arch, the vault, and the dome, and the use of concrete, gave distinction, serviceability, and grandeur to Roman domestic and public architecture and civil engineering. These physical expressions of Roman culture were in turn exported throughout the empire.

SCULPTURE

Two influences in particular drove the Romans fully to explore and develop the art of sculpture: the worship and reverence of images, not only of gods and goddesses, but also of dead ancestors; and the recording of ritualistic and triumphant events in bas-relief on pillars, arches, and tombs. Whereas the faces of Greek portrait sculptures tend to display neither expression nor emotion, those carved particularly in the time of the Flavian emperors and after have character and animation, often down to the glint of an eye, a technique achieved by using a drill to indicate the ring of the iris and the reflection of light on the pupil. Reality before flattery was demonstrably the rule rather than the exception. No less effective are some of the portraits on coins of the later republic and early empire.

The sculptural skills acquired during the later republic were breathtakingly employed to embellish the north and south friezes of the great marble edifice which is the Ara Pacis Augustae (see Figure 6, page 49). The life-size figures of Augustus and his extended family, officers of state, senators, and priests, some with their wives and children, are caught in a moment of pause as they progress towards the entrance. The children display childish traits while adults chatter decorously to each other.

Typical among outstanding historical reliefs are those on the column of the emperor Trajan, erected during his lifetime in AD 113 in the forum which bears his name, to celebrate his conquest, and acquisition for the empire, of Dacia, which equates to present-day Romania. The style of this monument has been imitated several times since: most immediately in the column of Marcus Aurelius, begun in AD 180 and completed in AD 192, recording his victories against the German tribes along the Danube, with emphasis on the agony and suffering of the enemy, and most recently by Napoleon in the Place Vendôme in Paris to celebrate his defeats of the Russians and Austrians. Trajan's column is 30 metres high, with a staircase inside lit by forty-three slit windows. A spiral band about 1 metre deep and 200 metres long winds twenty-three times round the shaft from bottom to top, carrying 155 continuous scenes. Though there is not a great deal of attention given to perspective, the effect is of activity and action in which more than 2,500 different human figures have been counted (see Figure 40, page 174).

The story of Trajan's campaign is built up stage by stage, from the commissioning of the army, its march and crossing of the Danube by a bridge specially built for the purpose, through preparations for the fighting, siege, and battle, to the grim aftermath of the torture of Roman prisoners of war and the suicide of the Dacian chief. Trajan himself appears frequently, at the head of his troops, addressing them before battle, briefing his officers, conducting the ritual sacrifice. The bridge over the fast-moving river took a year to construct, and its architect, Apollodorus of Damascus, also designed Trajan's column; it is not only a monument to the artistic skill of the men who decorated it, but the fullest pictorial source we have of the conduct, uniforms, and arms of the imperial army.

PAINTING AND MOSAIC

During the republic there was a vogue for collecting and exhibiting narrative paintings of battles and mythological scenes, mainly by artists from the Hellenistic world. Pliny the Elder is the source of information for some of these. An imaginative war artist depicted in 201 BC the victories of Cornelius Scipio Africanus over Hannibal in Africa. Lucius Hostilius Mancinus, who claimed, as naval commander in the Third Punic War, to have been the first to break into Carthage, displayed paintings of his exploits in the forum. Hostilius accompanied the exhibition with a personal commentary, a stunt which, again according to Pliny, gained him a consulship at the next election, for 145 BC. Julius Caesar dedicated the temple of Venus Genetrix in Rome to Venus, his divine ancestor. He decorated the interior with two mythological paintings by

Timomachus of Byzantium (for which he paid two million sesterces), and, according to Appian, with a statue of his current mistress, Cleopatra.

In imperial times, as far as we know, paintings ceased to be portable and were used almost exclusively to cover walls of rooms in houses. These frescoes, of which many are splendidly preserved at Herculaneum and Pompeii, are brightly coloured, and most frequently depict scenes from Greek mythology. Landscapes were employed to give the impression of picture windows – Nero's Domus Aurea even has some enclosed in window frames also painted onto the wall – while the effect of a garden was often extended and enhanced by landscape frescoes along its boundary walls. We have still-life paintings, too, of dead game birds, fish, and vegetables, which may be intended to represent the kinds of gifts which guests would take away from a party.

The art of mosaic seems to have originated in Babylon; it was widely practised in Egypt under the Ptolemies in the third century BC. Because a mosaic is comparatively indestructible and the medium spread throughout the Roman empire to its very outposts, it has come to represent Roman pictorial art to many who have never seen the sculptures and paintings which Italy has to show, and which are not viewed to their best advantage in museum surroundings.

Mosaics were of three kinds. *Opus sectile* consists of small pieces of different-coloured marble cut into various shapes and fitted together in a geometrical pattern. In *opus tessellatum*, the dice are square and all of the same size. In *opus vermiculatum*, the dice are of varied shape and size, sometimes of minute proportions, and are often set in wavy lines (*vermiculatus* means 'resembling the tracks of worms'). Sometimes more complicated works were made in a studio, and transferred to the site and embedded in concrete, either as wall decorations or pavements. These might be scenes from legend or daily life, or even portraits. A fourth mosaic style, *opus incertum*, was much employed during the second century BC to decorate the walls of concrete buildings: it consisted of pieces of rubble fitted together to make rough patterns.

GEM ENGRAVING

Romans were great accumulators of wealth rather than collectors of art, but some of their acquisitions were put to good and artistic use. It was said that Pompey started the craze by his capture of the gem collection of Mithridates, which he put on public display in the temple of Jupiter on the Capitoline Hill. Carved signet rings were widely employed to authenticate legal documents, and the wearing of a ring to denote office or status was an old custom. In the later empire, free-born men wore gold rings, freedmen silver, and slaves iron. Though the Egyptians and the Greeks had used the art of gem engraving, it was brought to a high pitch in Roman times to produce the most delicate portraits. These were cut either in intaglio, by incising the surface of the stone; or cameo, where the figure is made to stand out by carving away the background, a method which can be doubly effective if the stone has layers of different colours, as has onyx or sardonyx.

DOMESTIC ARCHITECTURE

The early Roman town house was little more than a single room known as the *atrium*. The roof sloped inwards and downwards to a rectangular opening, beneath which was a basin, *impluvium*, set into the floor to catch the rainwater. As time went on, small extra rooms were built inside the *atrium* against its walls, or separated off by partitions. In about the second century BC, the Greek influence began to be felt. The *atrium* with its *impluvium* and the little rooms remained, but now opened into a larger extension, the *peristylum*, a garden court (sometimes with a fountain in the middle) surrounded by a colonnaded passage off which were further rooms. Between the *atrium* and the *peristylum*, and opening into both, was the *tablinum*, which had various uses: dining-room, especially in summer when it would be the coolest place in the house, reception room, or office for the head of the household.

The main doors into the house from the outside were usually set back from the street and approached through the *vestibulum*. Such a house would be unlikely to consist of more than one storey, though upstairs dining-rooms are sometimes referred

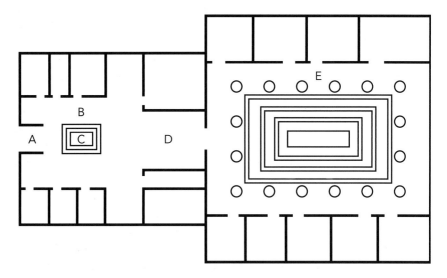

FIGURE 31   Plan of a Roman house.
A *vestibulum*; B *atrium*; C *impluvium*; D *tablinum*; E *peristylum*

to by writers of the times. Apartments above shops, however, reached by an outside staircase, were a feature of small towns. Urban congestion was a problem in Rome from early times. It has been estimated from statistics compiled at the time that in the second century AD there were 1,782 houses in the city, providing accommodation for 50,000 people, many of whom would have been household slaves. The other 1.5 million lived, as the majority do in Rome today, in tenement blocks, six or even seven storeys high. Augustus limited their height to 20 metres: Trajan lowered this to 18. Many of them were cheaply built on unsound foundations. Collapsed blocks were commonplace, rent irregularities were rife, and sanitation was superficial. Comparatively well-to-do flat dwellers lived on the ground floor and had access to a public sewer. Even in the purpose-built new-town apartment blocks in Ostia, it would appear that upstairs private latrines were not connected to any public sewer. Upper-floor tenants in Rome had to make their own arrangements, though there were public lavatories for those who could afford them. The rest had recourse to chamber-pots, the contents of which they emptied into a well at the foot of the stairs, or threw out of the window into the street below, a practice still prevailing in eighteenth-century Edinburgh, which had a similar population problem.

For the rich, there were two kinds of villa, or country house. The *villa rustica* was a glorified farmhouse which contained living-quarters for the owner of the estate when he happened to be in residence. The *villa urbana* was where you luxuriated or retreated for a holiday from the bustle of Rome, or stopped off for a night on a journey, or from which one commuted to the city. Cicero, who was by no means one of the richest men of his time, owned seven houses in the country, each of which he used from time to time. Pliny the Younger, who was very rich, had at least four, including one in Etruria where he spent the summer, and an especially opulent one on the seashore at Laurentum, where he lived in the winter, but which was near enough to Rome, with a good road between, for him to be able to ride home after a full day's business in the city.

In the villa, the principal parts of the town house were usually reversed, the entrance opening into the *peristylum*, behind which was the *atrium*. Plans of houses that have been excavated can tell us about the shape, size, and probable use to which the various rooms were put. In a letter to his friend Gallus, Pliny describes in detail what many of the rooms in his winter villa looked like, and for what they were used. Apart from the usual features, it had two towers, with bedrooms commanding magnificent views, a series of sitting-rooms, several studies (one of which had built-in bookcases and got the sun all day through a bay window), a centrally heated bedroom, an outdoor gymnasium for the staff, a tennis-court, and a swimming-pool. Some if not all of the windows were glazed. The only drawback, according to Pliny, was that there was no running water, but he adds that there were three public baths in the nearby village if for any reason it was inconvenient to heat up the water at

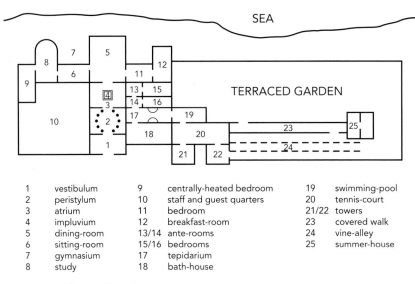

FIGURE 32 Pliny's villa at Laurentum.

1	vestibulum	9	centrally-heated bedroom	19	swimming-pool
2	peristylum	10	staff and guest quarters	20	tennis-court
3	atrium	11	bedroom	21/22	towers
4	impluvium	12	breakfast-room	23	covered walk
5	dining-room	13/14	ante-rooms	24	vine-alley
6	sitting-room	15/16	bedrooms	25	summer-house
7	gymnasium	17	tepidarium		
8	study	18	bath-house		

home. Central heating was invented by Sergius Oresta in about 100 BC, and was achieved by circulating hot air from a furnace through cavities under the floor and inside the walls. Not unnaturally, it is a particular feature of villas found in Britain.

THE ARCHITECTURE OF PUBLIC BUILDINGS

The Romans did not invent the arch, but their development of it enabled them fully to exploit their penchant for massive constructions and for resolving improbable situations by vast expense of labour. From the Greeks they took the three orders of architecture, Doric, Ionic, and Corinthian, based on different forms of column and the capital which surmounted it, and added to them a hybrid of their own, known as Composite. It was, however, a mark of eccentric extravagance to decorate the façades of public buildings, especially theatres and amphitheatres, with rows of columns in tiers, and to use a different order for each. That they could indulge their architectural ambitions was due also to the indubitably Roman invention of concrete. Its basis was pozzolana, a chocolate-coloured volcanic earth originally found near the Greek settlement of Puteoli, which when mixed with lime formed a powerful, waterproof cement. It was then discovered that vast quantities of pozzolana could be quarried around Rome. It was used to make mortar and also, when mixed with lime and strengthening materials such as chips of rock and broken brick, concrete. Judicious use of bricks and concrete together enabled massive, permanent structures to be built.

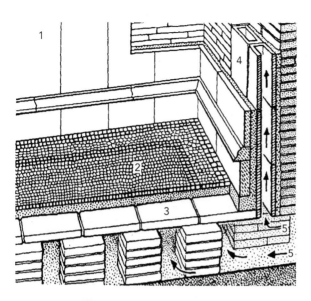

FIGURE 33
Hypocaust or central heating system.
1 Marble wall facings
2 Mosaic floor on cement
3 Bricks on brick piers
4 Wall flues
5 Hot air from furnaces

Source: Richard Leacroft

FIGURE 34 Public latrines, such as this one in Ostia, also served a social function: 'Vacerra haunts the public loos, where he sits all day – not shitting, just cadging a meal' (Martial, *Epigrams*, XI. 77). The practice extended to private houses: the villa at Settefinestre, near Cosa, built in 75 BC, sports a communal lavatory seating twenty people at a time.

Source: C.M. Dixon

Their command of materials and techniques enabled the Romans to construct circular temples, perhaps consciously imitating the round huts of the original Italians, as in the quaint, shallow-roofed temple, now the Church of Santa Maria del Sol, only 8 metres in diameter and surrounded by twenty columns, which was built in the first century BC. The most spectacular example is the Pantheon, crowned by a hemispherical dome, 43.28 metres in diameter, which if completed would exactly touch the ground. The only light falls through a circular hole, 8 metres wide, in the top of the dome. The original building was erected by Marcus Agrippa, son-in-law of Augustus and intended as his successor, in 27 BC. It was dedicated in particular to the most significant deities of the emperor's family, Mars and Venus, in the ears of a statue of whom hung earrings made from Cleopatra's pearls. The present building was constructed between AD 120 and 124 in the reign of the emperor Hadrian.

The remains of Roman buildings are a guide to the enormous areas which some of them covered. The Basilica Julia in the forum of Rome, a colonnaded hall designed primarily as a court of law, measured 100 by 36 metres. The main block of the baths of Caracalla, just outside the Appian gate to the south-east of the city, which could accommodate 1,600 bathers at a time, was 216 by 112 metres. Reconstructions of ancient Rome in model form (see Fig. 20, page 102) suggest the haphazard siting and comparative size of public buildings, and of the triumphal arches, columns, and statues crammed into this extraordinary urban complex. Neither remains nor reconstructions, however, can reliably reflect the sheer height of so many of them or the inspiration which governed their design. Roman architects were less concerned with external appearances than with the creation of interior space. This can still be experienced in the Pantheon and in the Church of Santa Maria degli Angeli in Rome, converted by Michelangelo in 1563 from just one hall of the baths of Diocletian, which was completed in about AD 305 and was capable of accommodating twice the number of customers as the baths of Caracalla. The dome, where it was employed, enhanced the impression of vastness. From constructing it on a circular base, the architects progressed to domed buildings on a polygonal plan. And in their construction of public baths as luxury-cum-cultural leisure and sports centres, the Romans combined their passion for opulence with their flair for hydraulics. The essential rooms, separate for men and women, were the centrally heated *tepidarium*, where bathers were encouraged to sweat after removing their clothes; the *caldarium*, where they bathed in tubs of hot water; and the *frigidarium*, where they took a cold plunge. The water was heated by furnaces and circulated by means of cisterns and pipes.

For their theatres, the Romans followed the Greek plan of tiers of seats in a semicircle facing the stage, but whereas the Greeks tended to take advantage of natural slopes on which to erect the seats, Roman theatres were usually built on level ground. Some of the smaller ones were covered, thus also improving the acoustics and making them particularly suitable for musical performances. The first stone

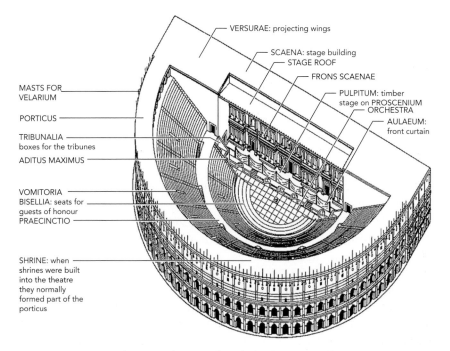

VERSURAE: projecting wings

SCAENA: stage building
STAGE ROOF

FRONS SCAENAE

MASTS FOR VELARIUM

PULPITUM: timber
stage on PROSCENIUM
ORCHESTRA

PORTICUS

AULAEUM:
front curtain

TRIBUNALIA
boxes for the tribunes

ADITUS MAXIMUS

VOMITORIA
BISELLIA: seats for
guests of honour
PRAECINCTIO

SHRINE: when
shrines were built
into the theatre
they normally
formed part of the
porticus

FIGURE 35 A typical Roman theatre. The whole theatre could be covered by the *velarium*, a great canvas roof hung on masts to protect the audience from the sun. The audience entered and left the auditorium through openings known as *vomitoria*, according to where their seats were.

Source: Richard Leacroft

theatre in Rome was opened in 55 BC, and by 13 BC there were two more. The smallest of these could seat 7,500 and the largest 14,000, compared with the 3,000 capacity of the present Scala in Milan, the 2,200 of the Royal Opera House in London, and the 3,800 of the Metropolitan Opera House in New York. These figures are minute, however, beside the Colosseum (capacity 45,000) and the 635-metre-long Circus Maximus, where 265,000 spectators at a time watched the chariot races. Present-day comparisons might be the Rose Bowl Stadium, California (92,542), Melbourne Cricket Ground, Australia (100,000), and the Millennium Stadium, Cardiff (permanent seating 74,500).

The Romans took their architectural techniques with them, wherever they settled. When they left Britain in about AD 400, it was to the marauding and looting of waves of Saxons and Danes. Even these, however, and further centuries of violent unrest, have not entirely obliterated the skeletons of an amphitheatre in Chester, a public baths in Bath, and a theatre, capable of seating 6,000, in St Albans; while traces of a huge basilica, 150 metres long, have been discovered under offices in the city of London, and ruins nearby of a second-century AD temple of Mithras. Even more solid evidence of the Romanization of their extensive empire stands in parts of north Africa and the Near East, and in what was the province of Gaul. Julius Caesar made Lutetia Parisiorum (Lutetia, tribal capital of the Parisii) a centre of provincial administration, and Paris has revealed Roman origins for some of its streets, traces of a forum, and remains of three public baths and an amphitheatre. Trier, on the Moselle, became even more significant during Roman times than Paris, and contains substantial portions of public buildings and a completely restored audience-hall. The biggest cluster of remains outside Italy is in Provence, where Arles, Nîmes, and Orange can between them boast two amphitheatres, two theatres, a temple, and a triumphal arch (see Fig. 18, page 94).

The extension and retention of an empire required the construction of town walls to discourage attackers, and in the case of Hadrian's Wall in Britain to be the empire's northernmost frontier. Roads and bridges were needed for speedy communications and the deployment of troops, and aqueducts to supply populations adequately with water. Towns on exposed ground could comparatively quickly be turned into fortresses by the raising of walls consisting of a base of large stone blocks, then a deep course of rubble faced with concrete, topped off with alternate layers of stone and tiles. More permanent defences called for an elaborate standard procedure which involved digging ditches 30 Roman feet deep and 100 feet wide – a Roman foot was 29.59 centimetres. The earth that had been excavated was built up into a mound behind the ditch and supported on either side by a retaining wall of standard-sized blocks of tufa rock: the end result was about 15 metres deep and 15 metres high. Hadrian's Wall was built between AD 122 and 127 on the orders of the emperor Hadrian, and supervised by his friend and governor of Britain, Aulus Platorius Nepos. Its purpose was to facilitate the control of the border and to keep in their native northern parts the tribes who had been defeated by Agricola at Mons Graupius, near Aberdeen, in AD 84, but who had subsequently been allowed to regroup unmolested.

The empire was kept together by a network of roads, branching out from all the main towns and joining up with the quickest and safest sea routes. The building and upkeep of roads were the responsibility of the state, and military roads in the provinces were constructed by the army, with some additional forced labour from the local people. According to an 'itinerary' compiled in the reign of Antoninus (AD 138–61), the extent of metalled or paved roads in Italy was approximately 22,400 km; in Gaul 14,000 km; in Spain 11,200 km; in Britain (parts of which were still unknown) 4,500 km; in Africa 14,000 km; in Asia 15,200 km. All were provided with milestones – there were 5 Roman feet to a *passus* (pace) and 1,000 paces to a Roman mile (*mille passus* or *mille passuum*), which was thus 1.48 km. In AD 68, a special messenger reached Clunia, in northern Spain, from Rome (2,000 km) in 6½ days;

the following year another messenger travelled from Mainz via Rheims to Rome (2,100 km) in 9 days.

A solitary triumphal arch can hardly give aesthetic satisfaction unless its proportions are in tune with its surroundings, and it is unlikely that the ancient designers of these extraordinary structures thought much about that aspect. Thus to succeeding generations the true triumphal arches of Rome are those which support the bridges which have survived, all the more impressive in that it was not always possible to employ the ingenious course of diverting the river temporarily while the bridge was being built. Early bridges were made of wood, as in later times were military bridges, which could then be destroyed to prevent them being used by the enemy. When Augustus had the roads of Italy renovated, he also built new bridges, of which the ornate, low, five-arched one at Ariminum (Rimini) is still in use. So, in very much its original form, is the much longer and earlier Milvian Bridge in Rome, constructed in 109 BC of unmortared blocks of tufa and limestone. At Alcantara in Spain, six arches of unmortared granite blocks, the two centre ones 55 metres above the water, carry the road across the river Tagus. The bridge was built in about AD 106, and an inscription in a temple nearby reads: 'The celebrated Lacer built this bridge with supreme skill to endure through the ages to eternity.' He did and it still does.

The arch enables wide spaces to be crossed by the use of the minimum of materials, thus relieving weight which would otherwise put an intolerable burden on the structure. To the countryman, the most astonishing manifestation of the civilization of Rome must have been the rows of arches, sometimes three tiers of them, which marched across the plains, bringing fresh water from the mountain springs and lakes in a covered channel gently down in an imperceptible gradient into the intricate mechanism which piped it through the towns. The Romans knew all about the rule of dynamics that water always rises to the level of its source. They did use underground pipes, and where necessary tunnelled through hills which could not easily be skirted, but building materials and labour were cheap and readily available, whereas large-bore pipes were expensive and less reliable.

The most notable survivor of these monster creations is the Pont du Gard, where it crosses the river near Nîmes. The most famous in ancient times was the Claudian aqueduct, begun by Caligula and finished by Claudius, which had a channel 70 km long and which started its final overhead descent to Rome 12 km out. This was just one of a total of eleven similar structures which brought water to the city. The municipal water board which maintained the system consisted of 460 slaves whom Claudius had taken onto his personal staff, with a special commissioner, a freedman, in charge. In AD 97 Nerva appointed as inspector of aqueducts Sextus Julius Frontinus (c. AD 40–103), a former governor of Britain. In his exhaustive report on the system, Frontinus estimated that over 1,000 million litres of water a day came into Rome through the eight aqueducts which were then operational.

FURTHER READING

* indicates sourcebook

Adam, J-P., *Roman Building: Materials and Techniques*, Routledge, 1999.

Barton, I. (ed.), *Roman Domestic Buildings*, Exeter University Press, 1996.

Barton, I. (ed.), *Roman Public Buildings*, Exeter University Press, 1995.

Beard, M. and Henderson, J., *Classical Art: From Greece to Rome*, Oxford University Press, 2001.

D'Ambra, E., *Roman Art*, Cambridge University Press, 1998.

Dunbabin, K., *Mosaics of the Greek and Roman World*, Cambridge University Press, new edn 2001.

Elsner, J., *Imperial Rome and Christian Triumph*, Oxford University Press, 1998.

*Humphrey, J.W., Oleson J.P., and Sherwood, A.N. (eds), *Greek and Roman Technology: A Sourcebook: Annotated Translations of Greek and Latin Texts and Documents*, Routledge, 1997.

Kleiner, D.E.E., *Roman Sculpture*, Yale University Press, new edn 1994.

Ling, R., *Ancient Mosaics*, Princeton University Press, 1998.

Ling, R., *Roman Painting*, Cambridge University Press, 1991.

Ramage, N.H. and Ramage, A., *Roman Art: Romulus to Constantine*, Prentice Hall, new edn 2004.

Sear, F., *Roman Architecture*, Routledge, 1998.

Stewart, P., *Roman Art*, Oxford University Press, 2004.

Ward-Perkins, J.B., *Roman Imperial Architecture*, Yale University Press (Pelican History of Art), new edn 1992.

Wilson Jones, M., *Principles of Roman Architecture*, Yale University Press, new edn 2003.

FIGURE 36 (previous page)   The Pont du Gard, 16 miles west of Avignon, carried water along a channel on top of three tiers of enormous arches towering 50 metres above the river.

Source: Photograph © copyright Allan T. Kohl/Art Images for College Teaching (AICT)

7 LATIN LITERATURE

Wandering immigrants to the Italian peninsula brought with them their own dialects of ancient speech. Three of these, Umbrian, Oscan, and Latin, emerged as contenders for the ultimate language of the region. Latin, which was spoken from about 800 BC in the comparatively small area of Latium, became enriched by features of local Sabine and Etruscan speech, and much more significantly by Greek. Legend has it that Greek settlers came to Italy shortly after the Trojan War, which took place in about 1220 BC. Certainly, there was a Greek trading post in the Bay of Naples by 775 BC. The fifty years or so following the traditional date for the founding of Rome of 753 BC coincide with the composition of the Greek epic poems, the *Odyssey* and *Iliad*, and the establishment and circulation throughout the Greek world of the Greek alphabet.

The domination of one dialect over another is usually due to external rather than linguistic features – the south-eastern dialect of English became the standard form because London, where it was spoken, was the centre of government, and where the English printing industry emerged. In the case of Latin, Roman military expansion caused it to become the common language of the Italian peninsula, the western Mediterranean, and the Balkans, and the second language, if not the first, wherever else Rome's conquests lay.

From the Latin alphabet is derived the English alphabet, and to all intents and purposes they are the same. Since no-one knows exactly how Latin was pronounced – there are several 'standard' pronunciations taught – anyone without any knowledge of Latin who reads it aloud cannot go very far wrong. This is important, because whereas the flowering of English literature, for instance, occurred after the introduction of printing, much of Latin literature was expressly written to be read or spoken aloud.

Not that the Romans were without books. The Latin word *liber*, originally the inner part of the bark of a tree which even more ancient Italians had used as a writing surface, meant to the Romans anything that was written. The equivalent of our 'book' was *volumen* (volume), meaning 'roll'. This literally was a roll of papyrus up to 10 metres long and 30 centimetres deep, with a rod fixed at each end, on which the work was written in columns about 10 centimetres wide. To read a book, rolling up the used portion with the left hand while unrolling the rest with the right, required both dexterity and strength, though reading desks were supplied in libraries. The word 'library' also comes from *liber*. Julius Caesar had the idea of opening a public library, but the project lapsed on his death; the credit for founding the first one in Rome goes to Asinius Pollio (76 BC–AD 4). Publishers employed teams of educated slaves to do the copying, and booksellers advertised and sold the results. Importunate acquaintances were an occupational hazard for authors, in precisely the same way as they can be today.

> Whenever we meet, Lupercus, you immediately say, 'May I send my boy to pick up a copy of your new book? I'll give it back as soon as I've read it.' Lupercus, don't bother the boy: it's a long way to my district, and I live up three flights of stairs, long ones, too. You'll find what you want much nearer. I guess you're often in the Argus shopping precinct. Opposite the forum of Caesar there's a bookshop whose front is covered with advertisements: you can see at a glance which poets are available. Ask for Atrectus – he's the owner – and he'll get down for you from the first or second shelf a Martial, smoothed with pumice-stone and bound in purple, for 5 *denarii*. 'You're not worth that,' I hear you say? You're a sensible chap, Lupercus!
>
> **(Martial, *Epigrams*, I. 117)**

The most striking feature of Latin is its use of inflections, that is changes in the form of a word to indicate, for example, gender, number, case, person, degree, voice, mood, or tense. The order of words in a sentence was flexible and could be varied for the sake of emphasis, different minutiae of meaning, or simply rhythm. Alliteration was widely used in both verse and prose, but rhyme only rarely, and then usually internally in prose. Poetry was written in prescribed metre patterns, made up of short and long syllables, arranged in 'feet', as in Shakespeare's line:

⌣ 1̲ ⌣ 2̲ 3̲ ⌣ 4̲ ⌣ 5̲
Uneas|y lies|the head|that wears|a crown

This is the classic iambic pentameter of five feet, each comprising one short and one long syllable, which is the basis of all the verse in Shakespeare's plays.

The equivalent line in Latin poetry is the dactylic hexameter (borrowed from Greek) of six feet, each of one long and two short syllables, or of two long syllables, with a break in the middle of the third foot called a *caesura*.

$$1 \;\smallsmile\smallsmile \quad 2\;\smallsmile\smallsmile \quad 3\;\smallsmile\smallsmile \quad 4\;\smallsmile\smallsmile \quad 5 \quad 6\;\smallsmile$$
$$- \; - \mid - \; - \mid - \; \| - \mid - \; - \mid - \; \smallsmile\smallsmile \mid - \; -$$

Which we can apply to the first line of Virgil's *Aeneid*:

$$- \;\; \smile 1 \;\smile\; - \; 2 \;\smile \;\; \smile \; - \; 3 \; - \quad - \; 4 \; - \; - 5 \;\smile \;\; \smile \;\; - \underline{6}$$

Arma vi | rumque ca | no, || Tro | iae qui | primus ab | oris

(I sing of arms and the man, who first from Trojan shores . . .) Note that in Latin, when the letter 'i' comes before a vowel in the same syllable, as in 'Troiae', it has the effect of the English 'y', as in 'you'. In modern English it is represented by, and sounded as, the letter 'j', as in 'junior' (Latin *iunior*) and 'Julius' (Latin *Iulius*).

In English prosody iambic pentameters rhyming in pairs are known as heroic couplets, a form perfected by John Dryden (1631–1700) and Alexander Pope (1688–1744). The equivalent in Latin is the graceful elegiac couplet: a dactylic hexameter followed by a pentameter, a line of five feet made up of two parts, each of two and a half feet.

$$- \;\; \smallsmile\smallsmile \quad - \;\smile\;\smile \quad - \quad \smile\;\smile \quad - \; - \quad - \smallsmile\;\smile \; - \; -$$

Cynthia | prima su | is || mise | rum me | cepit o | cellis

$$- \; - \quad - \; - \quad - \quad \smile\;\smile \; - \smile\;\smile \; - \smile\;\smile$$

Contac | tum nul | lis || ante cu | pidini | bus

(Propertius, *Elegies*, I. 1, 1–2)

(Cynthia's dear eyes were the first to ensnare my luckless self, never till then aroused by love's desires.)

Another Greek metre, the hendecasyllable, widely used, especially by Catullus and Martial, comprises eleven syllables:

$$- \; - \; - \quad \smallsmile\smallsmile \quad - \smile \quad - \quad \smile \; - \; \smile$$

Vivamus mea Lesbia atque amemus

(Catullus, *Poems*, V. 1)

(Come, Lesbia, let us live and love . . .) Note that where a word which ends in a vowel precedes one which begins with a vowel, the former vowel is 'elided' or suppressed.

A translation can never totally recapture all aspects of the original, but it can reflect its spirit: the meaning, flavour, and often the flow as well. Translation is a craft of the creative imagination. Just as a translation should be into the first language of the translator, so the translator needs to be a skilled exponent in that language of the medium into which the original is being translated, whether it is prose or verse. The flexibility as well as the precision of Latin were well suited to the verse forms which Roman poets employed, as Alfred Lord Tennyson (1809–92) acknowledged in the case of Virgil, whom he addresses by the Italian epithet of the place of his birth:

> I salute thee, Mantovano,
> I that loved thee since my day began,
> Wielder of the stateliest measure
> Ever moulded by the lips of man.
> **(To Virgil, 37–40)**

Because of the essential differences between the two languages and between the ways in which metrical weight and stress-accent are disposed, the stateliness of Virgil's lines cannot be reflected in English by the use of hexameters. English verse has been written in hexameters, notably by Arthur Hugh Clough (1819–61), but here the effect is not at all heroic, but intentionally mock-heroic:

> It was the afternoon; and the sports were now at the ending.
> Long had the stone been put, tree cast, and thrown the hammer;
> Up the perpendicular hill, Sir Hector so called it,
> Eight stout gillies had run, with speed and agility wondrous;
> Run too the course on the level had been; the leaping was over.
> **(The Bothie of Tober-na-Vuolich, I. 1–5)**

There have been numerous prose translations of Virgil, and many also in verse, of which Dryden's, though by no means the most accurate, gets nearest to the stateliness and possibly to the spirit, too.

> Arms, and the man I sing, who, forc'd by fate,
> And haughty Juno's unrelenting hate,
> Expell'd and exil'd, left the Trojan shore.
> Long labours, both by sea and land, he bore,
> And in the doubtful war, before he won
> The Latian realm, and built the destin'd town;
> His banish'd gods restor'd to rites divine,
> And settled sure succession in his line,

> From whence the race of Alban fathers come,
> And the long glories of majestic Rome.
>
> **(*Aeneid*, I. 1–7, tr. John Dryden)**

Not that the hexameter form was rigid in its application. Virgil used it also for his pastoral and didactic poems, the *Eclogues* and *Georgics*, and Juvenal for his *Satires*, brimming with cameos of city life and of contemporary mores. So Dryden, in his translations of Juvenal, represented the linguistic and narrative spirit of the original again in the medium of which he was a master, the heroic couplet: as in the reflections on the hazards of living in Rome and the tribulations of those who face the nightly fear of fire.

> Codrus had but one bed, so short to boot,
> That his short wife's short legs hung dangling out;
> His cupboard's head six earthen pitchers grac'd,
> Beneath 'em was his trusty tankard plac'd;
> And, to support this noble plate, there lay
> A bending Chiron cast from honest clay;
> His few Greek books a rotten chest contain'd,
> Whose covers much of mouldiness complain'd:
> Where mice and rats devour'd poetic bread,
> And with heroic verse luxuriously were fed.
> 'Tis true, poor Codrus nothing had to boast,
> And yet poor Codrus all that nothing lost;
> Begg'd naked thro' the streets of wealthy Rome;
> And found not one to feed, or take him home.
>
> **(*Satire* III. 203–11, tr. John Dryden)**

ENNIUS

Quintus Ennius (239–169 BC) is regarded as the father of Latin poetry. He has been referred to as the 'Chaucer of Roman literature', which is misleading in that Chaucer's birthplace was London and early on he had access to the royal court, whereas Ennius was born of Greek parentage in Rudiae in Calabria, the 'heel' of Italy. As well as Greek, however, he spoke Latin and the local Oscan dialect. As a subject of Rome, he served in Sardinia in the Second Punic War. He was still there, presumably as a member of a garrison, in 204 BC, for there he met Cato, then praetor, who took him back to Rome. Ennius lived frugally, writing and earning a living by teaching the sons of the nobility, with whom he was on good terms. He was granted Roman citizenship in 184 BC.

Ennius wrote over twenty stage tragedies, mainly on Greek themes, as well as some comedies and occasional verses. His main work, on which he was engaged for the last twenty years of his life, was a massive verse history of Rome up to his own day (omitting the First Punic War), in eighteen books. For this, he abandoned the rough and barely perceptible rhythms of earlier Latin poets for the musical measures of the hexameter, which he forged into the epic medium later used by Virgil. We have only fragments of Ennius' work totalling some 600 lines, which may not be his best, but he was often quoted by later writers.

COMEDY: PLAUTUS AND TERENCE

The first comic dramas that the Romans saw were based on the Greek 'new comedies' of the kind staged in Athens from about 400 to 200 BC. Their hallmarks included stratagems and counter-stratagems, stock characters (young lovers, scheming slave, family hanger-on), and standard situations (obstacles to young love, mistaken identities, revelations of true identity), with some musical accompaniment.

FIGURE 37   The principal writer of the Greek 'new comedy' was Menander (342–c. 292 BC), whose situation comedies influenced Plautus and Terence. This second-century or early first-century BC mosaic from Pompeii illustrates a scene from Menander's *Ladies at Lunch*, of which only a few lines survive.

Source: C.M. Dixon

Titus Maccus Plautus (254–184 BC) was not the first of these Roman dramatists, but twenty-one plays attributed to him by Terentius Varro have survived. This in itself is a measure of popularity, were it not also that in spite of being based on earlier Greek models, his work retains a raw freshness of its own. He devised ways of adapting Greek verse metres to the Latin language, and introduced to audiences whose taste had tended towards farce and slapstick several varieties of literary comedy, such as burlesque and domestic and romantic pieces, in which verbal fireworks replaced crude banter. He also surmounted the problem of playing consecutive scenes, without any breaks between them, in front of a standard backdrop, usually a street with the entrances to two houses.

Plautus was born in Sarsina, a small village in Umbria, but left home early to go to Rome. He seems to have been stage-struck, for he first worked as a props-man and then, with the money he had earned, set himself up in the same kind of business. When that failed, he took a job turning a baker's handmill, which he was able to give up after writing his first three plays. Shakespeare's *Comedy of Errors* is based on Plautus' *The Brothers Menaechmus*; the protagonist of *The Braggart Soldier* of Plautus is the prototype of the Elizabethan stage boaster, whose appearance in *Ralph Roister Doister* by Nicolas Udall (1505–56) marks the beginning of English comedy written for public performance.

Publius Terentius Afer (c. 185–159 BC) was brought to Rome as a slave, possibly from Africa. He took his name from that of his owner, Terentius Lucanus, who educated him and gave him his freedom. The story goes that he submitted his first play, *The Girl from Andros*, to the curule aediles (one of whose functions was to act as municipal entertainments' officers); they referred him to Caecilius Statius (c. 219–c. 166 BC), the most popular playwright of the day. Caecilius was at dinner when Terence called, but immediately began to read the play aloud. He was so impressed by it that he invited Terence to join the dinner guests and to share the couch of honour with him. The play was first performed in 166 BC, and Terence wrote five more before he died in a shipwreck, or of disease, while on a trip to Greece to find further plots. He was only about 26. His plays are better plotted than those of Plautus and of some of the originals which he adapted. With him the comedy of manners effectively began. He was adept at employing the double plot, especially to illustrate different characters' responses to a situation, and at developing the situation itself. There is more purity of language and characterization than in Plautus, which may account for Terence being nothing like as popular in his own day as he was to become later. William Congreve (1670–1729), in a preface to his play *The Way of the World*, extols 'the Purity of [Terence's] Stile, the Delicacy of his Turns, and the Justness of his Characters'; the French philosopher and writer Denis Diderot (1713–84) said that of all writers of comedy only Terence and Molière (1622–73) had the gift of individualizing their characters in a timeless way.

LUCRETIUS

In the dark, confused days presaging the end of the republic, voices were abroad which questioned prevailing views about the natural and spiritual worlds. Some of these belonged to the Epicureans (see chapter 4, p. 98), whose tenets included a rudimentary theory of the atomic nature of matter. They believed, too, that every happening had a natural cause and that the ultimate aim in life was the pleasure that could be derived from the harmony of body and mind. Among the staunchest followers of Epicureanism in Italy was Titus Lucretius Carus (*c.* 99–*c.* 55 BC), about whom we know nothing else except the story that he was poisoned by an aphrodisiac, went mad, wrote poetry in his lucid spells, and committed suicide at the age of 44.

That Lucretius was mad is unlikely: that his great project ultimately proved too much for him is possible. *De Rerum Natura* (On the Nature of Things) comprises the first six books, some 7,500 hexameters, of an unfinished philosophical poem unique in Latin and with few equivalents in other literatures – the nearest in English is *Testament of Beauty* by Robert Bridges (1844–1930). It is a work of great learning and great poetry; also of considerable insight, in that while subscribing to the Epicurean objection to spiritual gods and their images, he anticipated the kind of dilemma the modern biologist has with regard, for instance, to Christianity. So Lucretius invests Venus, whom he invokes at the beginning of the poem, with an overall creative power in nature, before entering into his exposition of the composition of matter and space in atomic terms, and going on to discuss the mind, life itself, feeling, sex, thought, cosmology, anthropology, meteorology, and geology. *De Rerum Natura* is thus not so much a philosophical work as a scientific treatise; it is a mark of the skill of Lucretius that he succeeded in presenting it in the language and metre of poetry.

LYRIC POETRY: CATULLUS AND HORACE

Lyric poetry has come to mean that in which the composer presents his or her personal thoughts and feelings. Originally, it simply meant poetry or a song accompanied by the lyre, for which the Greek poets used a variety of metres. The Romans took over the metres, though not necessarily the accompaniment, and employed them in a rather more precise form to express themselves poetically.

Gaius Valerius Catullus (*c.* 84–54 BC) was born in Verona, in the north of Italy, probably of a moderately rich family. Certainly, when he arrived in Rome in about 62 BC, it was not to look for a job. He became one of the wave of 'new poets' who reacted against their elders while, from the evidence of his own poetry, boozing, whoring, and generally living it up. Catullus, at any rate, moved in high circles, especially if the woman he calls Lesbia in his poems, and with whom he had a blazing affair, was Clodia, emancipated and profligate sister of Cicero's arch-enemy Publius Clodius and the wife of Metellus Celer, consul in 60 BC. In this case she would have been rather older than her ill-starred lover. In 57 BC, Catullus was the guest, or camp-follower, of Memmius, governor of Bithynia, to whom Lucretius dedicated *De Rerum Natura*. He died soon after returning to Italy.

Catullus was not a prolific writer. We have just 116 poems, varying in length from 2 to 408 lines, and a few brief fragments, which probably represent the whole of his published work. Many of them are bitingly observant cameos of friends and enemies (among the latter was Julius Caesar), of chance meetings and alfresco sexual encounters, in which he is often coarse but always amusing. Others, including his longest (Poem LXIV), an account in hexameters of the wedding of Peleus and Thetis, have mythological themes, but still show depth of poetic emotion. And there are of course the famous love/hate poems to Lesbia/Clodia – passionate, tender, sometimes bitter.

> Sparrow, my Lesbia's darling pet,
> Her playmate whom she loves to let
> Perch in her bosom and then tease
> With tantalising fingertips,
> Provoking angry little nips
> (For my bright beauty seems to get
> A kind of pleasure from these games,
> Even relief, this being her way,
> I think, of damping down the flames
> Of passion), I wish I could play
> Silly games with you, too, to ease
> My worries and my miseries.
>
> **(Poem II, tr. James Michie)**

One cannot discount the parallels between Catullus' affair with Lesbia and Shakespeare's with his 'dark lady' of the sonnets, and especially between Catullus' denunciation of his mistress as a whore (Poems 37 and 58) and Shakespeare's of his as 'the bay where all men ride' (Sonnet 137). Of all English poets, Byron is probably nearest to Catullus in temperament, habits, and poetic genius. Byron himself may have recognized this, for while still in his teens he translated two of the poems (3 and 51) into, unfortunately, some of his lesser verse.

Whereas Catullus often wrote in the passions of the moment, his successor, Quintus Horatius Flaccus (65–8 BC), had the leisure and time to marshal his thoughts into lines which usually display more grace and artifice than those of Catullus, but less emotion. Horace was born in Venusia, Apulia, son of a freedman who made quite a living for himself, and acquired a small estate, by collecting taxes on sales at agricultural auctions. Instead of going to the local school, which was attended by sons of the rural aristocracy, Horace was taken by his father to Rome. There he was sent to the best educational establishments and was taught by the formidable pedagogue Orbilius, who was born in 113 BC and lived to be nearly 100. At 18, Horace went to Athens to continue his education, but was caught up in the civil war which followed the assassination of Julius Caesar and fought at Philippi, unfortunately on the wrong side, as a legionary commander in the army of Brutus. He was pardoned for this lapse of loyalty, but when he got back to Rome he found that his father's estate had been confiscated. He became a civil service clerk and in his spare time wrote verses which caught the eye of Virgil, who introduced him to his own patron, Gaius Maecenas (c. 70–8 BC). A few years later Maecenas set Horace up in a farm near Tibur at the foot of the mountains to the east of Rome, the remains of which still survive. Between this farm, a cottage in Tibur, and a house in Rome, Horace lived out his existence as a bachelor with, when it suited him, Epicurean tendencies.

Horace's lyric poetry comprises his 17 Epodes, and 103 Odes in four books. The former, which include some of his early work, are on a variety of political and satirical themes, with a few love poems. Most are written in an iambic metre, a longer line being followed by a shorter one, which is known as the 'epode', or 'after song'. The first three books of odes were written between 33 and 23 BC and reflect the events of the time: the opening line of the fourth verse of this one is the celebrated saying, '*dulce et decorum est pro patria mori*':

> Disciplined in the school of hard campaigning,
> Let the young Roman study how to bear
> Rigorous difficulties without complaining,
> And camp with danger in the open air.
>
> And with his horse and lance become the scourge of
> Wild Parthians. From the ramparts of the town
> Of the warring king, the princess on the verge of
> Womanhood with her mother shall look down
>
> And sigh, 'Ah, royal lover, still a stranger
> To battle, do not recklessly excite
> That lion, savage to touch, whom murderous anger
> Drives headlong through the thickest of the fight.'

> The glorious and decent way of dying
> Is for one's country. Run, and death will seize
> You no less surely. The young coward, flying,
> Gets his quietus in the back and knees . . .
>
> **(*Odes*, III. 2, 1–16, tr. James Michie)**

The fourth book was published in 15 BC. Horace's odes are regarded as his finest works and are written in a variety of Greek metres whose rules he followed strictly. His other works include *Carmen Saeculare*, a poem to various gods, commissioned by Augustus to celebrate the Saecular Games in 17 BC – a *saeculum* was an interval of 100 or 110 years; three books of *Epistles*, of which the third is generally known as the literary essay *Ars Poetica*; and two books of Satires – the Latin word from which 'satire' comes had the meaning of a medley of reflections on social conditions and events, rather than of the pointed, witty vehicle of criticism with which it was later endowed.

From remarks in his own poems and from a biography by Suetonius, Horace appears to have been short and rotund, with dark hair that turned grey early. He seems to have been a bit of a hypochondriac, while enjoying to the full his life, his work, and the position his work gave him in society. He died only a few months after his patron Maecenas.

VIRGIL

The *Aeneid*, the epic of the empire of Rome and of Roman nationalism, for its poetry and poetic sensibility arguably the most influential poem in any language, is unfinished. Its author asked his friends, just before he died, to burn it. Literary executors, faced with just this problem throughout history, have usually responded with commendable common sense and regard to posterity, as they did in this case.

Publius Vergilius, or Virgilius, Maro (70–19 BC) was born near Mantua in Cisalpine Gaul, not far from the birthplace of Catullus. He had a good education in Cremona and Milan, and went on to study higher subjects, probably in Naples and Rome. He does not appear ever to have been very fit, and this may be one reason why he then returned to the family farm to write, only to be deprived of it in 41 BC in the confiscations after the battle of Philippi. He appealed against the decision and was reinstated on the orders of Octavian, but soon afterwards he left Mantua for good, first to live in a villa owned by his former tutor and then to live in Campania. In 37 BC he published his first major work, a series of bucolic episodes (*Eclogues*) loosely based on a similar composition of the Hellenistic pastoral poet Theocritus (*fl. c.* 270 BC). Maecenas gave him the encouragement to complete four books of didactic verse about farming and the country year known as the *Georgics*, on which he spent the next seven years. Though these too show Greek influences, the agricultural activities (corn-growing, vine-culture, cattle-breeding, bee-keeping) are Italian and the message both topical and nationalistic, with its emphasis on traditional agricultural industries, on a return to the old forms of worship, and on co-operative working for a profitable future.

By this time Octavian was emperor in all but title and name. He felt that an epic poem about his own achievements – he was still only 33 – would be a suitable accompaniment to his eminence, and Maecenas (in his capacity as honorary minister of arts) approached several writers with the idea. They all turned it down, not necessarily because of any antipathy towards Augustus, to whom the Mediterranean world had much reason to be grateful, but because epic was not their style. Virgil, however, accepted the assignment, but on his own terms. He knew what he wanted to do and saw this as the means to achieve it. He worked on his epic of the mythological antecedents of Rome until his death eleven years later, by which time he had composed some 10,000 lines. Augustus frequently asked after its progress and, apparently, was not disappointed with either the pace or the product. In the year 19 BC, Virgil met the emperor in Athens and, instead of going on a tour of Greece and the east as he had intended, accompanied him back to Rome. He caught a fever on the way and died a few days after landing at Brundisium. He was unmarried and, largely thanks to his patrons, a comparatively rich man; with commendable diplomacy he left considerable legacies to Maecenas and Augustus. Virgil always wrote in hexameters, and no-one after him bettered his mastery of that medium.

The *Aeneid* is unfinished in that it awaited final revision and polishing. The story is complete and ends on a dramatic climax. Turnus, king of the Rutuli, stakes everything on single combat with Aeneas. They fight and Turnus is wounded. Aeneas is about to spare him, when he spots on his opponent's shoulder the belt of his dead ally and friend, Pallas, which Turnus has clearly stripped from the corpse in utter breach of mythological chivalry.

> . . . When the sight came home to him,
> Aeneas raged at the relic of his anguish
> Worn by the man as trophy. Blazing up
> And terrible in his anger, he called out:
> 'You in your plunder, torn from one of mine,
> Shall I be robbed of you? This wound will come
> From Pallas: Pallas makes this offering
> And from your criminal blood exacts his due.'
> He sank his blade in fury in Turnus' chest.

FIGURE 38 Though Virgil referred to the Britons as 'totally cut off from the whole world' (*Eclogues*, I. 66), Britain in Roman times was not entirely a cultural backwater. This fine fourth-century AD mosaic pavement, found at Low Ham in Somerset, illustrates incidents from the first and fourth books of the *Aeneid*. On the right Aeneas' ships arrive at the African coast. At the top a naked Venus, goddess of love, presides over the meeting between Dido, queen of Carthage, and Aeneas, with Cupid, in the guise of Aeneas' son Ascanius, between them. On the left, Aeneas and the queen go hunting, and (bottom) sheltering together from the storm engineered by Juno, they embrace. In the central panel Venus stands between cupids with raised and lowered torches, signifying that Aeneas will live and Dido die.

Source: Somerset County Museums

Then all the body slackened in death's chill,
And with a groan for that indignity
His spirit fled into the gloom below.
    (*Aeneid*, XII. 945–52, tr. Robert Fitzgerald)

The story of the *Aeneid* is a deliberate continuation of Homer's *Iliad*, to stress the connection between Rome and the heroes of Troy, with strong echoes of the wanderings of Odysseus which are described in the *Odyssey*. The gods' continuous intervention and their periodic bickering as to which of their favourite mortals shall triumph are in tune with the traditional notions to which Augustus wanted his people to return.

To modern readers Aeneas may seem a character lacking in personality: in 1914 the American poet and critic Ezra Pound described him as a 'stick'. To Virgil and his contemporaries Aeneas embodied the Stoic ideal, accepting all that fate threw at him and impassively pressing on towards his personal destiny. Literary debts to Virgil are legion. This pagan poet even became a prophet of Christianity: in the *Divine Comedy* of Dante (1265–1321), Virgil, in the personification of Human Reason, is the poet's guide to the Gates of Paradise. Among British poets who have implicitly or openly acknowledged his influence are Chaucer, Gavin Douglas, Marlowe, Shakespeare, Milton, Dryden (of course), Pope, Keats, and Tennyson. Nearer our own time, the American-born T. S. Eliot (1888–1965) wrote in his essay 'What is a Classic?' (1944):

> [Aeneas] is the symbol of Rome; and, as Aeneas is to Rome, so is ancient Rome to Europe. Thus Virgil acquires the centrality of the unique classic; he is at the centre of European civilization, in a position which no other poet can share or usurp.

ELEGIAC POETRY: PROPERTIUS AND OVID

Sextus Propertius (*c.* 50–*c.* 15 BC) was born near Assisi in Umbria, but his family, like Virgil's, was dispossessed in the proscriptions in 41 BC. His father died when he was a child, and his mother sent him to Rome to be educated for the law. Instead he turned to literature and published his first book of elegies in about 26 BC. Through this he acquired fame and an introduction to Maecenas, and though he resisted persuasion to compose patriotic verses, he was given the encouragement to write three more books before his early death from an unknown cause. Most of his poems describe his love for Cynthia, who in real life was called Hostia and appears to have been a freedwoman and a courtesan. Much of Propertius' poetry is peppered with academic allusions and pervaded with melancholy, but the emotions read as though they are sincerely expressed.

We have enough background for Publius Ovidius Naso (43 BC–AD 18), chiefly from evidence in his own poems, to form a picture of a literary philanderer, without knowing the reason why, at the height of his powers and his popularity, he was banished by Augustus, as it turned out for life, to the Roman equivalent of Siberia, a small bleak place called Tomi (modern Constanța) on the west coast of the Black Sea.

Ovid was born at Sulmo, in the mountains east of Rome, of an ancient equestrian family. Destined for a political career, he studied rhetoric and law, and was married at about 16 and divorced shortly afterwards. After doing a grand tour of Greece, Asia Minor, and Sicily, accompanied by a companion/tutor, he held minor legal and administrative posts in the civil service, but abandoned politics for poetry in about 16 BC, when he married again – his wife died two years later, having had a daughter. He combined his pursuits of poetry and pleasure in *Amores* (Love Poems) and *Ars Amatoria* (The Art of Love). These were not so much erotic as irresponsible in that they appeared to condone adultery, which under Augustan law was a public offence and on which Augustus himself was rather touchy, especially as he had in 2 BC to banish his own daughter, Julia, for just that.

Ars Amatoria was published in 1 BC; nine years later, Augustus' granddaughter Julia followed her mother into exile for the same reason. Ovid says (*Tristia*, II. 207) that the reasons for his summary removal from the scene were 'a poem' (presumably *Ars Amatoria*) and 'an error'. Since that book had appeared so many years earlier, we must look to the error for the clue to the mystery. It may have had something to do with the younger Julia – there is no reason why an impressionable and sexually voracious young woman should not have been attracted to a poet in his fifties – or possibly someone disclosed some scandal about Ovid and her mother. Whatever it was, Ovid had to go, and *Ars Amatoria* was banned from Rome's three public libraries. He was never called back, even after the death of Augustus, though he kept writing, sadly and ultimately resignedly:

> A region that neighbours the polar constellations
> 　　imprisons me now, land seared by crimping frost.
> To the north lie Bosporus, Don, the Scythian marshes, a scatter
> 　　of names in an all-but-unknown waste:
> beyond that, nothing but frozen, uninhabitable tundra –
> 　　alas, how close I stand to the world's end!
> Remote, though, from my homeland, remote from my beloved
> 　　wife, and all else I once enjoyed: I can't
> make physical contact with them, must imagine their presence,
> 　　see them all in my mind's eye,
> visions of home, the City, familiar landscapes
> 　　each with its cluster of memories. My wife's

image – visible, real, as though she were present –
both aggravates and lightens my distress:
aggravates it through her absence, lightens it by bearing
her burden with constancy, by her gift of love.
(*Tristia*, III. 4, 46–62, tr. Peter Green)

His third wife, a young widow with a daughter, whom he married in about AD 2, remained devoted to him to the last.

Ovid used elegiac couplets to amuse the reader, which he did as much by verbal effects and ingenious and delicate deployment of his verse form as by what he said.

FIGURE 39 Part of a wall painting from Pompeii of the legend of Europa and the bull, one of many stories of transformation woven into Ovid's *Metamorphoses* (II. 837–75). Europa, daughter of the king of Phoenicia, was attracted by a fine white bull while she played with her companions. It was Zeus in disguise, acting so tame that she was tempted to climb onto his back. He carried her away over the sea to Crete, where he revealed himself to her. They had three sons, who were adopted by the king of Crete, to whom Zeus married her off.

Source: C.M. Dixon

The fifteen books of *Metamorphoses* (Transformations), however, his most lasting and influential work, are written in hexameters. This vast collection of linked myths and legends was widely drawn upon by later Roman and European writers, including Chaucer and John Gower, and parts of it were translated into English by William Caxton (1480), by Dryden (1699), and recently by the late British Poet Laureate Ted Hughes. Like many writers, Ovid appears to have had a blind spot about the quality of some of his work. Seneca the Elder (*c.* 55 BC–*c.* AD 37), father of the philosopher, tells how friends of Ovid once asked the poet if he would allow them to suggest which three lines might most readily be omitted from his published work. He agreed, if he might nominate the three most deserving of immortality. It transpired that the lines were in each case the same!

EPIGRAM AND SATIRE: MARTIAL AND JUVENAL

An epigram is a Greek term meaning 'inscription', often in verse, on a tombstone or accompanying an offering. Subsequently it came to stand for almost any occasional short poem. The form was widely used in Rome, until, in the hands of Martial, it became the medium for short, pointed, witty sayings about people and the hazards of daily and social life, usually in elegiacs, but also in hendecasyllabics and other metres. Marcus Valerius Martialis (*c.* AD 40–104) was a Spaniard from Bilbilis who came to Rome in AD 64 and was taken up by his literary fellow countrymen Seneca and his nephew Lucan until in the following year they were purged by Nero. Martial lived in a third-floor flat on the slope of the Quirinal Hill, scraping a living by writing verses for anybody and any occasion, even on labels for gifts which guests took away from a party. The verses ultimately did well, for he published several books of them, and ended up owning a farm in the country as well as a house in Rome. He was a hack, a parasite, and, when it suited his interests, as it did when writing about Domitian, an unctuous flatterer. That did not prevent him, however, from being almost always witty, if often coarse, and frequently poetic, while pioneering a form of literature which has had, and still has, many exponents.

One of Martial's friends – if a man of his nature and bent can be said to have any – was Decimus Junius Juvenalis (*c.* AD 55–*c.* 140), most graphic of the Roman satirists and the last of the classical poets of Rome. As far as we can tell, he was born in Aquinum, the son of a well-to-do Spanish freedman; he may have served as commander of an auxiliary cohort in Britain and have held civic offices in his home town before trying to make a living in Rome by public speaking. At some point during the reign of Domitian, he seems to have been exiled for a while to Egypt, undoubtedly for saying or writing something offensive to the emperor, but not offensive enough to be executed for it. The sixteen *Satires* that we have, however, were published between about AD 110 and 130, in the reigns of Trajan and Hadrian. Written in hexameters, they attack various social targets, including homosexuals, living conditions in Rome, women, extravagance, human parasites, and vanity, while moralizing on such subjects as learning, guilty consciences, parental example, and the treatment of civilians by the military. There is sarcasm, invective, and broad humour, though of a kind which in modern terms would be the stocks-in-trade of a crusading journalist rather than of a satirical poet. Yet, as one reads the fourth satire, a ridiculous account of Domitian summoning a council of state to deliberate upon what should be done with a prize turbot, with which he has been presented as his due, it seems more pointed in the light of a report in 1986 of a sturgeon caught in British territorial waters. It was sold to a restaurateur, who remembered, just in time, an ancient law whereby all sturgeons belonged to the Crown. As a formality, he offered the fish to Her Majesty the Queen. The Palace replied that she would accept it.

THE NOVEL: PETRONIUS AND APULEIUS

The romance in prose was a literary form used by the Greeks in the second century AD. In the hands of two Roman writers in particular, the novel took on a very different aspect. Hovering between prose fiction and satire in its senses both of 'medley' and 'ridicule' is the *Satyricon* of Gaius Petronius (d. AD 66), known also as Petronius Arbiter from his rather inappropriate job title of *Elegantiae Arbiter* (Judge of Taste), in which capacity he organized Nero's personal revels. *Satyricon* is also the original picaresque novel, a kind of bisexual odyssey of two men and their boy round the towns of southern Italy. We only have fragments, the best-known being 'Trimalchio's Dinner-Party', which, though deliberately overdrawn, nevertheless splendidly exhibits the manners and mores of the Roman *nouveaux riches*.

> Trimalchio . . . at the top of his voice declared that now was the time for anyone who wanted a second glass of mead. Then a sudden crash from the band gave the cue and all the dishes of the first course were whisked away by a troop of singing slaves. One of the side-dishes was dropped in the flurry and a slave-boy picked it up from the floor. Trimalchio noticed him, gave orders for a clout on the ear to punish him, and made him throw the dish back where it had fallen. A litter-slave came promptly in and set to work sweeping the silver out with a broom among the other rubbish and scraps. Then two fuzzy-haired Ethiopians entered with small wine-skins, like those used for moistening sand in an amphitheatre, and squirted out wine for washing our hands. No-one offered us water.
>
> (*Cena Trimalchionis*, **XXXIV**, tr. Jack Lindsay)

Petronius, victim of one of Nero's periodic purges, died with considerable style and urbanity. According to Tacitus, he bled himself slowly to death, while conversing, eating, and even sleeping, having committed to paper a 'list of Nero's most perverted acts, classified according to the novelty of the performance, with male as well as female partners, and their names, which he dispatched to the emperor under seal' (*Annals*, XVI. 19).

Lucius Apuleius was born in about AD 125 at Madaura in north Africa. According to his own account, he married a rich widow much older than himself, and was then accused by her family of sorcery – he was certainly much interested in magic and its effects. He conducted his own defence and was acquitted. His novel *Metamorphoses*, better known as *The Golden Ass*, is a rollicking tale of the supernatural, told in the first person, of how Lucius tries to dabble in magic, is given the wrong ointment by the serving-maid who is also his bed-mate, and is turned into an ass. Several good stories are spliced into the action, including an excellent version of the legend of Cupid and Psyche. The conversion of Lucius to the cult of Isis after his re-transformation into human form gives the ending a religious significance as well as a narrative twist. Apuleius himself became a priest of Osiris and Isis, and was also a devotee of Aesculapius, god of medicine, which he seems to have found compatible with organizing gladiatorial shows for the province of Africa.

HISTORIANS: CAESAR, LIVY, TACITUS, SUETONIUS

The original Roman records, with the names of the principal officials for each year, were inscribed on white tablets in the keeping of the *pontifex maximus* and displayed to public view. The first historian who wrote in Latin was Cato the Elder, but his history of Rome is lost. The earliest surviving account of contemporary events is the seven books of Julius Caesar's own record of his campaigns in Gaul, *De Bello Gallico* (Gallic War) – an eighth book was written by Aulus Hirtius (d. 43 BC), one of Caesar's officers. Objective only in that he mentions but does not dwell on his failures, responsibility for which he tends to attribute to the weather or to his subordinates, and written in the third person, it is a distinguished general's account of his actions in war. It is written in a clear, no-nonsense style, probably as a serial publication to supplement his dispatches to the senate and promote his image to citizens of Rome and of the towns of Italy, to whom it would have been declaimed aloud by members of his publicity team. The arts of the orator and politician are more evident in what has become known as *De Bello Civili* (Civil War), in which by careful selection of facts and by linguistic legerdemain he attempts to put the blame squarely on the shoulders of his opponents.

Titus Livius (59 BC–AD 17) was born and died in Padua, lived most of his life in Rome, had two children, and was a close acquaintance of Augustus and Claudius, the latter of whom he encouraged to write history. That is just about all we know about this great writer and moderately good historian, whose reputation in his time was such that it is said that a Spaniard came all the way from Cadiz to Rome just to look at him, and, having done so, went back home satisfied. Livy's full history of Rome from Aeneas to 9 BC comprised 142 books, of which we have 35, plus synopses of the others. He was a popular historian in that he concentrated on narrative and character, and paid particular attention to the composition of the speeches he put into the mouths of his protagonists. He drew on a wide range of sources without being particularly concerned about their accuracy, though he makes up for vagueness about geographical and military details with his sense of drama and by recording traditions and legends which would otherwise have been lost. The truth he sought was that offering moral lessons from the past which would in turn reflect gloriously on the Rome of the present.

> The task of writing a history of our nation from Rome's earliest days fills me, I confess, with some misgiving . . . I am aware that for historians to make extravagant claims is, and always has been, all too common: every writer on history tends to look down his nose at his less cultivated predecessors, happily persuaded that he will better them in point of style, or bring new facts to light. But however that may be, I shall find satisfaction in contributing – not, I hope, too ignobly – to the labour of putting on record the story of the greatest nation in the world . . .
>
> My task, moreover, is an immensely laborious one. I shall have to go back more than seven hundred years, and trace my story from its small beginnings up to these recent times when its ramifications are so vast that any adequate treatment is hardly possible. I am aware, too, that most readers will take less pleasure in my account of how Rome began and in her early history; they will wish to hurry on to more modern times and read of the period, already a long one, in which the might of an imperial people is beginning to work its own ruin. My own feeling is different; I shall find antiquity a rewarding study, if only because, while I am absorbed in it, I shall be able to turn my eyes from the troubles which for so long have tormented the modern world, and to write without any of that over-anxious consideration which may well plague a writer on contemporary life, even if it does not lead him to conceal the truth.
>
> **(History of Rome, I. Preface, tr. Aubrey de Sélincourt)**

Cornelius Tacitus (*c.* AD 55–c. 117) was a public figure in his own right as well as being the son-in-law of Agricola. He was a senator, consul in AD 97, and governor of the province of Asia in AD 112. An excellent public speaker, he published a book on oratory, *Dialogus*, in about AD 101. Of two series of histories covering the reign of Tiberius to that of Domitian, we have just a few books, known respectively as the *Histories* and the *Annals*. He also wrote a short, somewhat flattering biography of Agricola, and *Germania*, a graphic report on the land and people of Germany. He was a witty writer as well as an incisive literary stylist, a shrewd, if partisan, observer and commentator, and an upholder of the ancient virtues of his nation.

> The preceding period of 820 years dating from the foundation of Rome has found many historians. So long as republican history was their theme, they wrote with equal eloquence of style and independence of outlook. But when the Battle of Actium had been fought and the interests of peace demanded the concentration of power in the hands of one man, this great line of classical historians came to an end. Truth, too, suffered in more ways than one. To an understandable ignorance of policy, which now lay outside public control, was in due course added a passion for flattery, or else a hatred of autocrats. Thus neither school bothered about posterity, for the one was bitterly alienated and the other deeply committed. But whereas the reader can easily discount the bias of the time-serving historian, detraction and spite find a ready audience. Adulation bears the ugly taint of subservience, but malice gives the false impression of being independent. My official career owed its beginnings to Vespasian, its progress to Titus, and its further advancement to Domitian. I have no wish to deny this. But partiality and hatred towards any man are equally inappropriate in a writer who claims to be honest and reliable.

> **(*Histories*, I. 1, tr. Kenneth Wellesley)**

Just over four books of the *Histories* survive, describing the years AD 69–70: the brief reigns of Galba, Otho, and Vitellius, and the beginning of that of Vespasian. Of the *Annals*, we have books covering parts of the reigns of Tiberius, Claudius, and Nero. Ammianus Marcellinus (*c.* AD 330–*c.* 395) wrote a continuation of the histories of Tacitus in thirty-one books, of which we have eighteen, covering just the years AD 353–78. Tacitus' writings were lost until the fifteenth century: thereafter his political thought influenced the Italian statesman Niccolò Machiavelli (1469–1527), and his literary style the French essayist Michel de Montaigne (1533–92), while his philosophic attitude to history is reflected in the monumental *History of the Decline and Fall of the Roman Empire* by Edward Gibbon (1737–94).

The family of Gaius Suetonius Tranquillus (*c.* AD 70–*c.* 140) probably came from Algiers. They were of equestrian class, and his father had a distinguished military career. He himself held a succession of posts in the imperial court, becoming director of the imperial libraries and then chief of Hadrian's personal secretariat, which gave him access to archive material on earlier reigns. His series of biographies of the Caesars (see chapter 3) is the only one of his many biographical and antiquarian works to have survived intact. He was, with Plutarch, the originator of the modern biography.

PHILOSOPHY AND SCIENCE: SENECA AND PLINY THE ELDER

We have already met Lucius Annaeus Seneca (4 BC–AD 65) as the tutor, and victim, of the emperor Nero, and the first patron of Martial. The second son of Seneca 'the Elder' or 'the Rhetorician', he was born in Córdoba in Spain, of a brilliant family. He was brought to Rome at an early age and was influenced by the Stoics, whose philosophy ran counter to that of the Epicureans in that its keynote was 'duty' rather than 'pleasure', and it allowed for the existence of an overall spiritual intelligence (see also chapter 4, pp. 96, 98). Seneca's pretensions to being a practising philosopher are questionable: he condoned various dynastic murders, was banished for eight years under suspicion of having an affair with one of Caligula's sisters, and, on his return, while undoubtedly but temporarily curbing the worst excesses of his pupil Nero, grew rich in the process.

In his philosophical writings, however, of which 12 dialogues and 124 'Epistles' to his friend Lucilius survive, he comes across as a moral philosopher whose aim was to live correctly through the exercise of reason. *Naturales Questiones* (Scientific Investigations) is an examination of natural phenomena from the point of view of a Stoic philosopher. *Apocolocyntosis* (Pumpkinification), by contrast, is a wicked skit on the dead Claudius. We also have ten of his verse tragedies: solid, lyrical, and bleak in their tragic vision which allows no escape from evil or defence against the brutality of fate. From his example, Elizabethan and Jacobean dramatists took the five-act structure and also the cast of secondary characters who serve to keep the action moving, to report on events off-stage, and to elicit private thoughts (especially those of the heroine through a female confidante). The violent and gruesome *Thyestes* is the archetypal revenge tragedy, such as Kyd, Tourneur, and to a certain extent Shakespeare in *Hamlet* exploited.

It was natural phenomena with which Gaius Plinius Secundus (AD 23–79), Pliny the Elder, was concerned throughout his life and at the time of his accidental death. He was born at Como of a wealthy family, practised law in Rome, and saw military service through several postings (during which he began a twenty-book history of the German wars). He probably went to ground during the reign of Nero, returning to public life in AD 70 soon after the accession of Vespasian. Between then and his death nine years later he not only held several senior government posts, including that of deputy governor of northern Spain, but wrote a further thirty books of Roman history and the thirty-seven books of his *Natural History*. This, his only surviving work, covers many subjects, including physics, geography, ethnology, physiology, zoology, botany, medicine, and metallurgy, with frequent digressions into anything else which interested him at the time. He drew his material from many written sources – when he was not actually reading something himself or writing, he had someone read aloud to him – as well as from his own observations. For example, in Book XX, on 'medicines derived from garden plants', he lists 1,606 drugs and cites the works of fifty-two writers as sources. He always carried a notebook, as he did on the expedition from the naval station at Misenum, of which he was then in command, to investigate from closer at hand the eruption of Vesuvius. He went ashore on the beach, taking notes all the time, and was either asphyxiated by the fumes or buried under falling rocks.

LETTER WRITERS: CICERO AND PLINY THE YOUNGER

Of Cicero the man, the political and forensic orator, and the statesman, something has already been said (see chapter 3, pp. 37 and 47), and a number of speeches, and also philosophical works, in which field he established a tradition of Roman writing, survive from the hand of this master of style and rhetoric. To the student of Roman life, however, the four collections of his letters, edited shortly after his death in 43 BC, are of even greater and more immediate interest: 'To his Brother Quintus', a soldier and provincial governor who also died in the proscriptions, 'To his Friends', 'To Brutus', the conspirator, and 'To Atticus', who was Cicero's closest friend and confidant. Some of these letters were undoubtedly intended for ultimate publication – what public and literary figure does not have this eventuality in mind? – but, taken as a whole, they are refreshingly revealing about himself and his day-to-day existence during the last twenty-five years of his life.

Gaius Plinius Caecilius Secundus (*c.* AD 61–*c.* 112), known as Pliny the Younger to distinguish him from his even more eminent and industrious uncle and adoptive father, certainly did intend his correspondence for publication, and in his lifetime, too. He showed early literary promise – he wrote a tragedy in Greek verse when he was 13 – and became a distinguished orator, public servant, and philanthropist. He was three times married, and though he had no children he was awarded, as Martial and Suetonius had been, honorary status as a 'three-child parent', a privilege originally bestowed by Augustus on genuine qualifiers, which brought certain privileges including exemption from taxes. Not that Pliny had any need of money. He was exceedingly rich: he endowed a library at Como, a school for children of free-born parents, and a public baths, while the interest on an even larger sum was left in his will for the benefit of 100 freedmen and for an annual public banquet. His letters range over many private and public topics; of especial interest is his first-hand account of the eruption of Vesuvius (VI. 16 and 20), the description of his villa (II. 17, see also chapter 6, p. 139), news of a haunted house in Athens (VII. 27) and of a tame dolphin (IX. 33), and his official report to Trajan (X. 97), in his capacity as governor of Bithynia in Asia Minor, on the Christians and his request for a policy decision on how to deal with them (see also chapter 9, p. 184).

FURTHER READING

Readable translations of the works of all the major authors referred to in this book are available in Penguin paperback editions. Good modem versions in English of Apuleius, Caesar, Catullus, Cicero, Horace, Juvenal, Livy, Lucan, Lucretius, Ovid, Petronius, Plautus, Propertius, and Suetonius are published in paperback by Oxford University Press. The translations in the Loeb Classical Library (Harvard University Press) tend to be more old fashioned, but the editions include the Latin texts as well.

Braund, S. Morton, *Latin Literature*, Routledge, 2001.

Harrison, S. (ed.), *A Companion to Latin Literature*, Blackwell, 2004.

Howatson, Margaret (ed.), *The Oxford Companion to Classical Literature*, Oxford University Press, new edn 1997.

Janson, T., tr. N. Vincent and M. Damsgaard Sørensen, *A Natural History of Latin*, Oxford University Press, 2004.

Kenney, E.J. and Clausen, W.V. (eds), *The Cambridge History of Classical Literature II: Latin Literature*, Cambridge University Press, 1982.

Kraus, C.S. and Woodman, A.J., *Latin Historians*, Oxford University Press, 1997.

McLeish, K., *Roman Comedy*, Bristol Classical Press, 1991.

Mellor, R., *Tacitus*, Routledge, 1994.

Poole, A. and Maule, J., *The Oxford Book of Classical Verse in Translation*, Oxford University Press, 1995.

Rutherford, R., *Classical Literature: A Concise History*, Blackwell, 2004.

Sharrock, A. and Ash, R., *Fifty Key Classical Authors*, Routledge, 2002.

8 THE ROMAN ARMY

The Roman talent for organization is nowhere better illustrated than by its army, the backbone of which was that epitome of the professional fighting man, the legionary. The civil wars pitched Romans against Romans, many of whom were conscripts. The survivors, all fighting men of experience, represented two groups of citizen soldiers: the professionals, who were looking for an extended period of service under acceptable conditions, and those anxious to be discharged and to return to civilian life. Augustus had the responsibility of deciding what kind and size of army would best suit the empire.

THE NEW MODEL ARMY

Formerly, legions had been raised as needed, and disbanded when no longer required. Maintaining peace throughout the empire and with those outside its boundaries called for permanent forces stationed a long way from Italy. After the battle of Actium, Augustus had under his notional command several armies comprising what remained of some sixty legions, many of which had fought against each other under rival commanders. He retired some 100,000 veterans, many of whom he settled in colonies. He removed, insofar as he could, potentially subversive elements, and discharged men who were surplus to his requirements. He retained twenty-eight legions as a standing army, at which strength, give or take the odd legion, it remained for 200 years. These he disposed about the provinces of the empire, with concentrations at potential trouble-spots such as Syria and along the Rhine and Danube. To maintain the loyalty of the legions to himself, provinces in which there were military units were under his control (imperial provinces), and he appointed the governors; governors of other provinces were appointed by the senate (senatorial provinces).

He nominated sixteen years as the term of service in the legions, followed by a further period of four years in reserve – to be in reserve meant staying with the legion but being excused normal duties. At the end of a man's service, he would received a set gratuity. In AD 5, the term of full-time service was raised to twenty years plus an unspecified period as a reservist, and the gratuity was fixed at 12,000 sesterces, equivalent to about fourteen years' pay for a legionary – Julius Caesar, at the beginning of the civil wars, had doubled his soldiers' pay to 225 *denarii* a year. The following year, Augustus established, with an initial gift from himself, the *aerarium militare*, a national fund for the payment of the gratuities, financed by levying taxes on inheritances and sales at auction. A soldier's pay, however, would continue to be paid out of the imperial revenues. To avoid encumbrances on the march, soldiers were forbidden to marry while on active service, though this did not prevent those on garrison duty setting up house and raising families with local women.

A legion was commanded by a legate, in republican times a senior politician assigned to the post for a limited period, after which he might proceed to a provincial governorship. Caesar used a flexible system whereby a legate might, if circumstances warranted it, command two or three legions. Augustus promoted men of ability, promise, and proven loyalty to himself, who had served in some capacity as a state official, to military appointments as legates commanding individual legions.

THE LEGION

Under the republic, new legions were assigned a serial number, numbers I to IV being reserved for those raised by consuls: those levied elsewhere were allocated higher numbers. Whatever the system, and it is still not fully understood, at any one time several legions might have the same number. To avoid confusion, each came to assume also a title or nickname, reflecting the circumstances of its formation, the name of its founder, the place where it was raised, or the front where it had served with distinction. There was a First German as well as a First Italian legion: similarly a Second Parthian and a Second Trajan's Brave. The Tenth United was formed from two original legions. The Ninth Hispana (i.e. Spanish), once thought to have disappeared in Britain, possibly in Scotland, appears now to have been transferred to Germany in about AD 115. A legion's own standard, often referred to as its 'eagle', was carried wherever it went. The eagle was the rallying point for troops in battle and a signal as to where the action was: to lose it to the enemy was both a disaster and a disgrace. The *aquilifer*, who carried the legion's standard, ranked in seniority only just below a centurion and was responsible also for the safe-keeping of the legion's pay-chest. The *imaginifer* bore a second standard, with an image or the emblem of

FIGURE 40 Scenes from Trajan's column. In the band below, legionaries are building a fortification. In the foreground above (left) a medical orderly in a field dressing station patches up a leg-wound, and (centre) a Dacian prisoner is brought before the emperor. Behind (left to right) standards are borne into battle; two musicians carry their *cornua*, circular trumpets used in battle to give orders; carts, driven by mules, transport supplies on the march.

Source: Deutsches Archäologisches Institut, Rome: Anger, Neg. D-DAI-Rom 1989.0762

the emperor, and, later in imperial times, portraits of his family, too. Both wore animal skins over their uniforms, with the heads drawn up over their helmets.

A legion was a self-contained unit which even on the march could rely on its own resources for weeks on end. The legionaries themselves did all the manual work of digging, construction, and engineering. Every man carried trenching tools and a pair of stakes which at each stop became part of the camp palisade. He also had to shoulder, or carry attached to his person, clothes, a cooking-pot, rations, and any personal possessions, as well as his weapons and armour. Marius is credited with the invention of a fork-shaped contrivance to ease the burden: the aspect of the legionaries as they marched along earned them the sobriquet 'Marius' Mules'.

Each legion had a complement of specialists and craftsmen, known collectively as *immunes*, 'exempt from normal duties': surveyors, medical and veterinary orderlies, armourers, carpenters, hunters, even soothsayers. The surveyors went ahead of the column of march to select and lay out the site of the night's camp; it was always constructed to the same pattern and surrounded by a ditch, a rampart, and a palisade, all of which had to be built afresh each time. Leather tents, each of which slept eight men, were carried separately by mules. At legionary headquarters or in the forts that defended the empire there was a wider range of non-combatant staff, including clerks to look after and process the paperwork, paymasters, and military police.

In the field, a legion consisted of ten cohorts, each divided into six centuries of eighty men, under the command of a centurion. The legionary legate was assisted by six younger officers, the military tribunes. These were short-term political appointees; the next step up for the senior tribune (*tribunus laticlavius*) was a seat in the senate. The senior professional soldier in the legion was likely to be the camp prefect (*praefectus castrorum*). He was usually a man of some thirty years' service, and was responsible for organization, training, and equipment. Day-to-day responsibility was therefore in the hands of the centurions, the most senior of whom (*centurio primi pili*) commanded the first century of the first cohort, which consisted of five double centuries. Centurions did not march; they rode on horseback, and they had powers of corporal punishment – the twisted vine-staff each carried was not just an emblem of rank.

Augustus' system was a positive encouragement to social mobility. What you did, and how you did it, mattered now more than who you were. A permanent army offered equestrians career structures as officers at the same time as the expansion of empire opened up for them military and civil posts in the provinces. Centurions could achieve equestrian rank, with the opportunities of status and wealth that it held out.

OTHER UNITS

The legions were supported by auxiliary forces, composed of inhabitants of the empire who were not citizens of Rome, and who often brought their own military skills to add bite to time-honoured Roman infantry tactics. All squadrons of cavalry were auxiliaries, each one divided into troops of thirty men. While some auxiliaries fought as infantry and were equipped like legionaries, others retained their native dress and weapons, and served as archers, slingers, spearmen, or broadswordsmen. Originally auxiliaries were led by their own chiefs, but in imperial times they were brought within an overall chain of command under Roman officers. From the reign of Claudius, an auxiliary and his immediate family qualified for Roman citizenship after twenty-five years' service, a further extension of social mobility.

Under the empire, the only armed forces in Italy were the *cohors praetoria* (the imperial guard) and the *cohortes urbanae* (city cohorts), who garrisoned Rome

FIGURE 41 Relief in the Louvre from the period of Trajan and Hadrian, showing members of the imperial guard, indicated by their rich uniforms and helmets, and oval shields. Behind is a legionary standard, with the eagle holding a thunderbolt in its claws.

Source: Deutsches Archäologisches Institut, Rome: Guidotti, Neg. D-DAI-Rom 1953.0424

itself and whose presence was to prevent unrest rather than ward off possible attack from outside, which was unthinkable, and act as a police force. The imperial guard was a crack unit whose members wore a special uniform and received double pay, in addition to the bribes which they came to be offered in the guise of bonuses for their allegiance. When the emperor went on campaign, the imperial guard went with him. In AD 6, Augustus recruited a further force, mainly from freedmen, the *vigiles*, 7,000 strong, which patrolled the streets of Rome and served as its fire brigade.

Up to the time of Augustus, mastery of the seas had been achieved by *ad hoc* measures and largely foreign naval skills and crews – no Roman citizen ever handled an oar. Augustus established a standing fleet of ships which were his own property and which he manned with free-born provincials and his own freedmen. His successors saw the wisdom of his initiative, and under the emperor's overall command there were established a number of regional flotillas: two for Italy (based at Misenum and Ravenna), and the rest to help exercise control over the provinces, centred on Mauretania, Egypt, Syria, the Black Sea, the Danube (two, upper and lower), the Rhine, and Boulogne. This last, the British flotilla, was used by Agricola in AD 84 to soften up the opposition in Scotland with lightning raids along the east coast; it also (according to Tacitus) discovered the Orkney islands and established conclusively that Britain was an island.

WEAPONS AND TACTICS

The deployment of the Roman infantry in battle depended on its mobility. Apart from his hobnailed heavy sandals, a legionary's legs were bare except in the colder climates, where tight-fitting knee-breeches were the order of the day. The most usual form of helmet was bronze, with a skull-cap inside and projections to protect the back of the neck and the ears and cheeks. A legionary carried on his left arm the cylindrical leather shield, which was shaped to fit his body and was about 1.2 metres long. It was also useful as a siege weapon; a body of men crouched underneath their locked-together shields could approach a wall undeterred by missiles from above. Not unnaturally, this formation was known as the 'tortoise'. On the march a man carried two javelins of different weights, each 2 metres long and with a metal head. One of these went into battle with him; he hurled it at the enemy when in range, before getting down to the serious business of fighting hand to hand with his short, double-edged, thrusting and stabbing sword.

Battles were largely fought with 'conventional' weapons. The artillery of the time, of which the largest and most effective weapon was known as the *onager* (wild ass) because of its kick, was used as siege batteries. Each century, however, was allocated a mechanical arrow-shooter which was deployed in battle. A Roman general's objective was to break up and, if possible, break through the enemy lines by sheer force of concerted numbers and by manipulating his infantry. Horsemen were mainly employed to head off attacks by the opposition's cavalry and to pursue stragglers. Julius Caesar's favoured tactic was to draw up his cohorts in three lines, each some eight men deep. His first victory in Gaul, at Bibracte in 58 BC, was achieved without the use of cavalry and by a manoeuvre which could only have succeeded when performed by highly trained and disciplined troops.

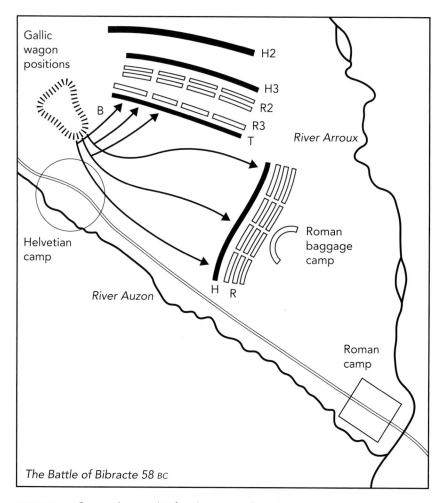

The Battle of Bibracte 58 BC

FIGURE 42 Caesar drew up his four legions in three lines (R). The Helvetii, in close-packed columns, advanced and attacked (H), but were thrown into confusion by the Roman javelins. Then Caesar advanced. The Helvetii retired to a hill to the north (H2). Caesar wheeled to face them, but was attacked in the rear by a force of Boii and Tulingi, who had then arrived on the scene (B, T). The first two Roman lines remained facing the Helvetii (R2), who returned to the attack (H3). The third Roman line faced about (R3). Both enemy forces were defeated and the Helvetii fled.

CONSOLIDATING AND PATROLLING THE EMPIRE

In republican times, the empire had been allowed to expand as opportunity, circumstances, and the senate decreed. Augustus recognized the need for a specific foreign policy and saw that to undertake random wars of aggression, and often of attrition, in pursuit of new conquests was an uneconomic and unsatisfactory method of exercising it. Military success, however, was a Roman way of life, but he would ensure that it was gained by consolidating provinces and their defences, without enabling any commander to aspire to an overwhelming personal following among his troops. The frontiers of the empire developed according to the lines to which he had withdrawn following the Varian disaster in AD 9, when Publius Quintilius Varus lost three complete legions, three cavalry regiments, and six auxiliary cohorts, after being enticed into unfamiliar territory between the rivers Weser and Ems by a chief-tain of the Cherusci, Arminius (c. 18 BC–AD 19), a Roman equestrian who had now rebelled against Rome. Varus committed suicide, the Romans retired permanently to the west bank of the Rhine, and new Germanic tribes moved into the region which they had vacated.

Tiberius was advised by Augustus not to try to extend the boundaries of the empire. His immediate successors were either too suspicious or too frightened of the army to do much else, with one notable exception, Claudius' invasion of Britain in AD 43. Three years earlier Claudius had altered the status of Mauretania from client kingdom to two provinces. Thrace, too, had been a client kingdom in the time of Augustus, and in AD 46 Claudius defused an ugly situation by making it a province. That was that, as far as the extent of the empire was concerned, for more than fifty years, until in AD 101 Trajan crossed the river Danube into Dacia, without waiting to give a chance to the treaty agreed between Domitian and Decebalus, king of Dacia. This resulted in a great victory but dubious long-term advantage (though modern Romanian is one of the Romance languages, derived from Latin), and Dacia was finally evacuated of Roman troops in AD 275. In AD 106 Trajan assumed into Roman 'protection' the area which became the province of Arabia and which controlled the main caravan route to the coast of Judaea. In AD 114 and 115 he also annexed Armenia as far as the Persian Gulf, and overran Mesopotamia, but these were tactical acts of immediate military expediency which were promptly reversed by his successor, Hadrian, in AD 117.

Some legions remained on the same station for many years; others were deployed as the situation demanded. The Second Augusta, raised by Augustus himself, and the Twentieth Valeria Victrix (Strong and Victorious) spearheaded the invasion of Britain in AD 43; they were among the last to be evacuated in AD 400, though a detachment from the Twentieth was sent to Mainz on the Rhine in AD 270 to help deal with troubles there. The Twentieth was also Agricola's strike-force in northern Britain, and it was probably his successor who constructed the fortress at Inchtuthil in Perthshire as its headquarters. This, the most northern of all Roman permanent fortifications, occupied an area 457 metres square and was to have been a purpose-built city in miniature, with streets and full administrative, residential, and leisure amenities, including separate houses for each of the officers and a hospital containing sixty five-bedded wards opening off each side of a wide corridor of the rectangular building. While still under construction, it was abandoned and systematically destroyed to prevent anything falling into the hands of the enemy.

Originally, the extent of the occupation of a region was bounded by a *limes* (plural *limites*), which just meant a 'path' or 'track'. Then it came to refer to the military road which linked the permanent forts housing units of a legion, whose task it was to discourage hostile military gatherings beyond the 'line', keep the peace and encourage Romanization within it, and allow free movement for trade across it. Thus *limes* came to mean 'boundary' or 'frontier' and the English word derived from it to signify something which 'may not be passed'. Sometimes, as in the case of Hadrian's Wall and the Antonine Wall in Britain, the *limes* was an actual wall. Hadrian was responsible, too, for reviewing the physical boundaries of the whole empire. He strengthened with a wooden palisade the defences of the Rhine which, together with those on the upper Danube, already consisted of 170 forts and fortresses. In Africa, where problems could be expected from cavalry, he devised a combination of a deep wide ditch and a low stone wall.

Prolonged periods of peace between occupying forces and the local population favoured interaction between them. Trade prospered, family roots were established, and Roman soldiers, when they where discharged, often chose to remain in the place in which they were serving at the time.

FURTHER READING

* indicates sourcebook

Bowman, A.K., *Life and Letters on the Roman Frontier: Vindolanda and its People*, British Museum, 1994.

*Campbell, B., *The Roman Army, 31 BC–AD 337: A Sourcebook*, Routledge, 1994.

Erdcamp, P. (ed.), *A Companion to the Roman Army*, Blackwell, 2007.

Goldsworthy, A., *The Complete Roman Army*, Thames and Hudson, 2003.

Keppie, L., *The Making of the Roman Army: From Republic to Empire*, Routledge, new edn 1998.

Sidebottom, H., *Ancient Warfare: A Very Short Introduction*, Oxford University Press, 2004.

Webster, G., *The Roman Imperial Army of the First and Second Centuries AD*, Constable and Robinson, new edn 1996.

9 THE EMPIRE: STABILITY, DISINTEGRATION, RECOVERY, FALL

The extinction of the Julio-Claudian and Flavian dynasties did not bring an end to a consistent policy of rule or to dynastic succession. It simply meant that the two were never again effectively combined. Able men from outside Rome were, however, now able to make their way to the very top from modest beginnings, and, if allowed to reign without internecine upheaval, could do so with as much insight and flair as any of the 'Twelve Caesars', and with more than most.

In his *Natural History*, the elder Pliny, writing between AD 70 and 79, refers to the global situation engineered by Augustus as the 'immense majesty of the Roman peace' (XXVII, 1. 3), which enabled plants to be discovered and transported to Rome from distant regions of the empire.

Of Antoninus and Marcus Aurelius, who consecutively ruled the empire from AD 138 to 180, Edward Gibbon wrote: 'Their united reigns are possibly the only period in history in which the happiness of a great people was the sole object of government' (*The History of the Decline and Fall of the Roman Empire*, I. 3). The volume in which those words first appeared was published in 1776; they still bear thinking about. By 'great people' Gibbon meant the Roman empire or commonwealth, and this was the period in which the way was being prepared for full rights for all citizens within it. Municipal governments were operating in the provinces, and where they proved moderately effective and acted within the laws and customs of Rome, they were allowed to work without much hindrance. Over a third of the senate itself came from the provinces, albeit chosen by the emperor, not the electorate.

MAKING THE EMPIRE WORK

To govern from the centre an empire of such geographical and cultural diversity, while attending to threats from outside its boundaries, required tactical understanding and favourable circumstances. Romanization did not mean trying to make everyone speak Latin and worship Roman gods. It was rather a fusion of central and local governments and of common cultural interests. It could hardly be otherwise, in that the eastern half of the empire had already been largely Hellenized, and Judaism and Christianity, with their roots in the east, as well as the eastern cults, were spreading their influence through the west.

The procedure for establishing guidelines for the administration of a province probably changed little in principle from republican to imperial times. In the light of a report from a special commission, a law, usually bearing the name of the general who had brought about the establishment of the province, was enacted. This created administrative and judicial districts, defined and regulated the status and privileges of their inhabitants, established a tax system, laid down rules for the administration of justice, with due account being taken of existing facilities, and set out arrangements for the supervision, creation, amendment, as the case might be, of local government by urban or rural authorities. None of this, however, could prevent, under the republican system, unsuitable governors being appointed and then acquitted of wrongdoing, or blameless governors being prosecuted for political or personal reasons.

What did change was the existence now of circumstances in which provincials could have more reason to trust their masters, and to benefit from this trust. One man was now at the top, with the permanent responsibility of running the machinery of empire, and to him most of the governors were personally answerable. In cases of alleged maladministration, judgement was handed down either by the emperor himself, or by judges appointed by him, or by the senate under his supervision. Governors were also, now, paid a fixed salary. An imperial civil service was established, mainly to administer the provinces. Communication was improved by road building and the imperial postal system. Roman citizenship for provincials was becoming faster and easier. Municipal institutions were founded in provincial towns, and special commissioners were appointed by the emperor to attend to the needs of impoverished or backward provinces. Provincial self-government, however, was not on the agenda. The provincial council, representing all parts of the province, met once a year at the temple of Rome and Augustus in one of its chief towns, to celebrate the worship of the emperor. It also had the right to deliberate on local affairs and make representations to the emperor or governor.

The principal functions of the provinces were to supply Rome with taxes and grain, the military with food and supplies, and the civil service and the armies of the empire with cash. Beyond this, it was up to local initiatives how far, and how far across the social scale, there was an infusion of Roman culture and mores, with the benefits of education, status, and wealth that accrued to some. The surviving remains of buildings in some former provinces of the empire testify to the prosperity that could be engendered by the 'Roman peace', even if many of these are of amphitheatres, living reminders of that unique, but fatal, Roman cultural contribution to mankind, the gladiatorial games. On many of those too far away from the centre of things, however, Rome made little impact.

THE 'FIVE GOOD EMPERORS' AD 96–180

When for the first time the senate made its own choice of emperor and appointed Nerva to succeed Domitian, its members not only chose well, but ensured that equal perspicacity would attend the selection of his four successors. There was to be a further break with tradition, for all four came from families which had long before settled out of Italy: those of Trajan, Hadrian, and Marcus Aurelius in Spain, and that of Antoninus in Gaul. Nerva was 65 when he was pitchforked into supreme power, but, like a number of stop-gap rulers in more recent times, he performed wisely and courageously. He instituted alimentary schemes to help the urban poor, and made loans available to landowners, the interest on which went to support children of needy families. He vowed publicly that he would never execute a member of the senate, and stuck to his promise, even when the senator Calpurnius Crassus was proved guilty of conspiracy against him. He not only assured himself of the support of the military by adopting as his son and joint ruler the distinguished commander in Upper Germany, Marcus Ulpius Traianus (Trajan), but set an important precedent by nominating Trajan as his successor.

Trajan, who was born at Italica near Seville in AD 52, became emperor in AD 98, and was thus of an age of considerable discretion. He demonstrated this at once by establishing that the senate would always be kept informed about what was going on, and that the sovereign right to rule was compatible with freedom for those who were ruled. That he was a brilliant general is clear from his military exploits, but he was also a good person to work for, of which there is evidence in the correspondence between him and Pliny the Younger, especially when the latter was governor of Bithynia. Pliny frequently asks for advice on matters which are outside his immediate experience, notably his uncertainty about the status of Christians.

During the second century AD Christians were being persecuted for their beliefs largely because these did not allow them to give the statutory reverence to the images of the gods and of the emperor, and because their act of worship transgressed Trajan's edict forbidding meetings of secret societies. To the government, it was civil disobedience: to the Christians themselves it was the suppression of their freedom of worship. Pliny the Younger, as governor of Bithynia in AD 111, was so exercised by the anomalies on both sides that he wrote to Trajan asking for guidance.

Trajan replied:

> The actions you have taken, my dear Pliny, in investigating the cases of those brought before you as Christians, are correct. It is impossible to lay down a general rule which can apply to particular cases. Do not go looking for Christians. If they are brought before you and the charge is proven, they must be punished; with the proviso that if someone denies they are Christian and gives proof of it, by offering reverence to our gods, they shall be acquitted on the grounds of repentance even if they have previously incurred suspicion. Anonymous written accusations shall be disregarded as evidence. They set a bad example which is contrary to the spirit of our times.
>
> **(Pliny, *Letters*, X. 97)**

Trajan perhaps exercised less discretion in his choice of military campaigns, though they brought him considerable glory. After the triumphal procession with which he celebrated his final victory over the Dacians in AD 106, and the annexation of their territory, there were 123 days of public games and gladiatorial contests. He also determined to subdue the troublesome Parthians, who occupied great tracts of rugged desert land south of the Caspian Sea. He scored some notable victories between AD 114 and 116, conquering Mesopotamia, and capturing Babylon and Ctesiphon, capital of the Parthian empire. He fell ill on his way back to Rome in AD 117, having left his 41-year-old chief-of-staff, Publius Aelius Hadrianus (Hadrian), who had been his ward since the age of 10, in charge of the inconclusive situation in the east. Later generations were so impressed by Trajan's achievements that in the late fourth century, when the empire had changed out of all recognition, new emperors were installed with the invocation, 'May he be luckier than Augustus and better than Trajan.'

Hadrian claimed that Trajan had adopted him on his deathbed; in any case he had already been acclaimed as emperor by the army in the east, and the senate had little choice but to confirm him in the post or risk civil war. In the face of widespread revolts in regions which Trajan had conquered, Hadrian abandoned the recent acquisitions in the east and settled down to restore general order throughout the empire and to consolidate the administration at home. Before he reached Rome in AD 118, four senior state officials, all Trajan's men, were executed with the acquiescence of the senate, allegedly for having plotted Hadrian's assassination. Hadrian disclaimed any responsibility for their deaths, but his relations with the senate were permanently soured.

FIGURE 43   Gold *aureus* of the time of Trajan, with the head of his wife, Plotina. Imperial consorts, and sometimes imperial daughters and nieces, as well as mothers, appear on coins of their times. It was said in some quarters that Plotina engineered Trajan's final adoption of Hadrian as his son and kept her husband's death a secret until an official bulletin about the adoption had been issued. Twice actual size.

Source: Photograph © copyright Hunterian Museum and Art Gallery, University of Glasgow

It may have been this uneasy situation at home which determined him to spend the years AD 121–5, 128–32, and 134–6, half of his rule, tirelessly travelling not just the provinces of the empire, but their outer confines as well, where he established boundary lines (see also chapter 8, p. 180). The wall in Britain which bears his name, and of which portions still survive, is a monument to and a reminder of the role he took upon himself as ruler of an empire. His energy was inexhaustible, and he was always approachable.

Hadrian was a man of exceptional ability and wide learning, who was a Greek scholar, a patron of art (especially architecture), literature (he was also himself a poet), and education, and a benefactor of the needy poor. His relationship with his wife Vibia Sabina, Trajan's great-niece, whom he married in AD 100, appears to have been difficult: they had no children, but she was said to have procured a miscarriage rather than bear a monster such as her husband. While he probably regarded his open attachment to the beautiful Bithynian youth Antinous as in the tradition of classical Greece, such relationships were regarded rather differently in ancient Rome. Antinous died mysteriously in the Nile (probably by suicide) in AD 130, while accompanying Hadrian on a triumphal tour of the province. Hadrian reacted with an extraordinary display of inconsolable emotion. The new city of Antinoopolis was founded beside the Nile near where his beloved had died, statues and obelisks were raised, and Antinous was declared a god. This act of deification, with its Graeco-Egyptian cult and attendant festivals which proliferated particularly in the east, scandalized the Roman establishment.

Hadrian's liberal-mindedness did not, however, extend to the Jews, whom he provoked into renewed revolt by forbidding circumcision, and by proposing a shrine to Jupiter on the site in Jerusalem where the ancient Jewish temple had stood before it was gutted and demolished by Titus (see chapter 3, p. 63). The rising, under Simon Bar Kochba (d. AD 135) in AD 132, was surprisingly effective, and was put down only after Hadrian had transferred Sextus Julius Severus, governor of Britain, to the Judaean front as commander. If the account of Cassius Dio is accurate, in order to

FIGURE 44 Antinous, the Bithynian youth, whom Hadrian may have first met on his tour of the region in AD 123. The statue was probably made between his death in AD 130 and Hadrian's in AD 138.

Source: Photograph © copyright Allan T. Kohl/Art Images for College Teaching (AICT)

stop the threat of further war, the Roman army destroyed 50 Jewish fortresses and 985 villages, and killed 580,000 men. The remains of Jerusalem were ploughed into the ground, and a new city, Aelia Capitolina, built on the site, which Jews were forbidden to enter on pain of death. Where the inner sanctuary of the Temple, the 'Holy of Holies', had been, now stood an idol of Jupiter and a statue of Hadrian on horseback. The province of Judaea was renamed Syria Palaestina – or Palestine.

When Hadrian died in AD 138, once again the childlessness of the emperor worked to the benefit of the state. After his first choice as successor died, Hadrian had just before his own death adopted in his place the eminent senator Antoninus, then in his early fifties. At the same time he restricted the choice of the next emperor after Antoninus to Lucius Verus (AD 130–69), son of his original nominee, or Antoninus' own nephew Marcus Aurelius Antoninus, born in AD 121. Marcus Aurelius was an active devotee of the Stoic school of philosophy (see chapter 4, p. 96), one of whose doctrines was the universal brotherhood and equality of man. When the time came, he insisted that equal imperial rights should be vested in his rival candidate, which were duly, but largely nominally, exercised by Verus until his death.

On Hadrian's death, the senate, still harbouring resentment at the executions at the beginning of his rule, and mindful no doubt of more recent killings by a man who had become obsessively jealous of anyone who was popular, refused to ratify his deification. Antoninus, however, argued so persistently and so well against the decision, that it was overturned, and in recognition of his efforts he himself was awarded the surname 'Pius'.

It was perhaps because Hadrian left the administration in such good order that the twenty-three years of the reign of Antoninus, who died in AD 161, are remarkable for lack of incident. With the reports available to him of Hadrian's globe-trotting missions, he was able to spend most of his time at the centre of government in Rome. He did, however, make two adjustments to the frontiers of the empire. The eastern boundary of Upper Germany was advanced and strengthened; in Britain, a fortified turf wall, 37 miles long, was built right across the country from the river Clyde to the Forth, some way north of Hadrian's Wall. Though the Antonine Wall, built by the Second, Sixth, and Twentieth legions, appears to have been abandoned, and perhaps dismantled, in about AD 165, Hadrian's Wall stood firm until about AD 400, when the Romans withdrew from Britain.

It appears that in his lifetime Antoninus fully justified the honorific Pius. His death, unlike that of most other emperors of Rome, was appropriately calm and dignified. It is described in a series of biographies of Roman emperors, associate emperors, and usurpers from AD 117 to 284 along the lines of Suetonius' 'Lives of the Caesars' (see chapter 3, pp. 40 ff), but in places much more fanciful, now believed to have been composed by a single author towards the end of the fourth century AD.

Though he died in his seventy-fifth year, his loss was treated as though he were still a young man. His death was said to have happened like this: having eaten rather too much Alpine cheese at dinner, he was sick in the night, and had a fever the next day. The morning after that, recognizing that he was getting worse, in the presence of the prefects he entrusted the state and responsibility for his daughter to Marcus [Aurelius], and gave instructions that the gold statue of Fortune which traditionally stood in the emperor's bedroom should be handed over to him. Then he gave the password of 'equanimity' to the officer of the watch, turned over as if going to sleep, and died . . . The senate deified him; everyone vied with everyone else in singing his praises. All, however, were agreed on his dedication, humanity, intellect, and goodness.

(Historia Augusta: Antoninus Pius, XII, XIII)

By contrast, the 'philosopher emperor' Marcus Aurelius had to spend almost all the latter part of his rule in the field at the head of his armies, fighting the dangerous Germanic tribes, the Marcomanni and Quadi. The earlier part, from AD 161 to 166, was taken up by wars against the Parthians, successfully conducted by Verus with the help of his generals, but his army brought back from the east the most virulent plague (probably smallpox) of the Roman era, which spread through the empire. In AD 169 the Marcomanni and Quadi crossed the Danube, broke through the frontier defences, and penetrated into Italy as far as Aquileia, which they subjected to a frightening siege. The two emperors rushed north with an army into which slaves had been drafted, such were the ravages of the eastern campaign and the plague. Verus died; Marcus brought his body back to Rome, then returned to resume the northern war, which would preoccupy him for the rest of his rule.

In AD 175, Avidius Cassius, governor of Syria with additional responsibility for the entire eastern region, was proclaimed emperor on a false report of Marcus' death. He was, however, murdered by staff loyal to Marcus, who had set out to challenge him in person. The emperor returned home via Alexandria and Athens, where he took the opportunity of endowing chairs of philosophy. Back in Rome, he celebrated a triumph and named his 15-year-old son Commodus joint ruler.

FIGURE 45 (opposite)   Detail from a triumphal arch: a gentle-looking, almost modest, Marcus Aurelius rides in a four-horse chariot in AD 176. This celebration of his victory over the Marcomanni had been delayed because of the insurrection in the east. Winged victory hovers above him. A trumpeter blows a *tuba*, the long horn used by the military to sound the advance and retreat. If the head and shoulders in the centre of the panel are those of Faustina, she was his late wife. Though various amours and other disloyal acts have been attributed to her, she was deified on her death in AD 175 and features frequently on coins.

Source: C.M. Dixon

There were further risings of the Marcomanni and other tribes in AD 178. Marcus returned to the northern front, taking Commodus with him. He died there on campaign at the age of 59, having impressed upon Commodus that he should continue the war, whose end seemed to be in sight. Instead, Commodus made a kind of peace of convenience, and returned to the comforts of Rome.

Marcus Aurelius left to posterity the triumphal column in Rome which bears his name and records his victories over the Marcomanni (an inferior version of that of Trajan), and, rather unusually, a book of meditations, written in Greek while he was mainly on campaign: these reflections particularly of his Stoic philosophy have influenced writers and men of action, including Sir Thomas Browne, Matthew Arnold, and Cecil Rhodes. At his death in AD 180, the empire was once again undergoing a period of general unease. As soon as one revolt was crushed or a barbarian invasion averted, another would break out, or threaten, in a different part of the empire.

GRADUAL DISINTEGRATION AD 180–284

The previous eighty-four years had seen just five emperors: during the next 104, there were no less than twenty-nine. What really started the rot was that alone of the five 'good' emperors, Marcus Aurelius had had a son whom he had nominated as his successor. Marcus Aurelius had been 40 when he assumed the imperial purple gown of an office for which he had been groomed for more than twenty years. Lucius Aurelius Commodus (AD 161–92) had a number of elder brothers who had died early: he was only 19 when he became emperor, and he proved to be a latter-day Nero. Like Nero, he showed initially some grasp of foreign and trade affairs; like Nero, he got himself into the hands of favourites and corruptible freedmen; like Nero, his private life was a disgrace and his public extravagances prodigious; like Nero, he fancied himself in the arena; like Nero, some of his actions bordered on the deranged; and like Nero, he died ignominiously – a professional athlete was suborned to strangle him in his bath.

Whatever the nature of the final conspiracy, it brought to office in his place, at the behest of the senate, a better man, Publius Helvius Pertinax, prefect of Rome and a former governor of Britain; but only temporarily, as an ominous pattern of events unfolded such as had followed the death of Nero. Pertinax, a disciplinarian, was murdered three months later by the imperial guard, who then offered the empire for sale to the highest bidder in terms of imperial hand-outs. The winner of this bizarre auction was Didius Salvius Julianus, an elderly senator, but there were out in the field three other serious contenders, each an army commander with several legions behind him. Lucius Septimius Severus (AD 146–211) in Pannonia was nearest to Rome, which he entered on 9 June AD 193, having already been recognized as emperor by the senate, which stripped Didius of office and sentenced him to death. Having disbanded the imperial guard and replaced it with three of his own legions, Severus embarked on an eastern campaign. In the course of this he defeated and killed at Issus his rival for office, Pescennius Niger, and won victories against tribes in Mesopotamia, in recognition of which he dubbed himself *Parthicus Arabicus* and *Parthicus Adiabenicus.*

He also proclaimed himself to be the son of Marcus Aurelius. His elder son was now renamed Marcus Aurelius Antoninus (AD 188–217), later nicknamed Caracalla, after a Gallic greatcoat, and appointed Caesar, or deputy emperor. The original third contender for the imperial throne, Clodius Albinus, governor of Britain, was now put in an impossible position, having also been appointed Caesar by Severus in AD 193, to secure his co-operation. He crossed into Gaul with his army, which proclaimed him emperor, but was in AD 197 defeated near Lyon by Severus, who, having purged the senate and the provinces of supporters of Clodius, departed for a second Parthian war. At the end of it the following year, Ctesiphon had been captured, and Mesopotamia, annexed by Trajan, abandoned by Hadrian, was once more a province of the empire. Severus now dubbed himself *Parthicus Maximus*, and promoted Caracalla to Augustus and his younger brother Geta (AD 189–212) to Caesar. He toured the east, including Egypt, with his family in AD 199–202, and then almost immediately set out with them for a triumphal tour of his native Africa.

Severus was born in Leptis Magna. A professional soldier, he favoured those with the greater military experience when making civil appointments. He campaigned energetically to maintain the empire's frontiers in the east in the face of the marauding Parthians, and spent the last two and a half years of his life in Britain personally leading a bid to try and bring Scotland into the empire. It was probably in his time that the prefect of Rome, whose function was primarily military, was invested also with the main jurisdiction in matters of criminal law in and within 100 miles of the city, and the commander of the imperial guard, a military office, with similar jurisdiction over the rest of Italy and the provinces. After the fall and execution in AD 205 of Fulvius Plautianus, who had performed the latter duty with rather too much authority, Severus appointed in his place a noted legal expert, Aemilius Papinianus (d. AD 212), heralding a golden age of the interpretation of Roman law. Within the army itself, the top jobs went to those with the best qualifications, not necessarily those of the highest social rank. Severus improved the lot of the legionaries by increasing their basic rate of pay to match inflation (it had been static for a hundred years), and by recognizing permanent liaisons as legal marriages. It was probably Severus, too, who improved the status of the ordinary soldier by extending the civil practice to allow veterans to style themselves *honestiores* as opposed to *humiliores* (see chapter 5, p. 104). Severus' philosophy of rule, which, according to Cassius Dio (LXXVI. 15), he impressed upon his sons shortly before his death in Britain in

FIGURE 46 The Roman tradition that women took no official part in public life was conclusively broken by the wife of Septimius Severus, Julia Domna, who came from a royal priestly family in Syria, and was granted the titles of Augusta and *Mater Castrorum* (mother of the camp). According to Cassius Dio, when Caracalla succeeded his father, she dealt with petitions and with his correspondence (in both Latin and Greek), and held soirées and receptions for philosophers and scientists (LXXXVIII. 18). Her equally formidable sister, Julia Maesa, was the grandmother of Elagabalus; Maesa's daughter was Julia Mammaea, who ran the empire with her son, Alexander Severus. Note the way a drill has been used by the sculptor to enliven the pupil and iris of the eyes.

Source: Richard Stoneman: Antikensammlungen, Munich

AD 211, was to pay the army well and to take no notice of anyone else. By 'anyone else' he meant, of course, the senate.

Severus had nominated his two unruly sons to rule jointly after him. Caracalla resolved that aspect of the arrangement by having Geta murdered in their mother's arms, before instigating a wholesale slaughter of sympathizers and innocent citizens. He kept faith with his father's advice by increasing the pay of the army by 50 per cent, thus initiating a financial crisis. Some sources suggest that it was to get more taxes to repair this crisis that he granted full citizenship to all free men in the Roman empire. Whether or not that is so, it is to him in AD 212 that is attributed this final step in the process of universal enfranchisement which had begun in the third century BC. While attempting to extend the eastern front he was murdered in Mesopotamia, in AD 217, by a band of discontented officers who preferred their own candidate, Macrinus, commander of the imperial guard since Caracalla had done away with Papinianus:

> There are many who say that Caracalla, after having had his brother killed, ordered Papinianus to play down the crime in the senate and in public. Papinianus replied that it was easier to commit fratricide than to make excuses for it.
>
> **(Historia Augusta: Caracalla, VIII)**

Macrinus, though accepted by the senate, never actually got to Rome. He continued the eastern war, only to be defeated and killed the following year by detachments of his own troops in Syria, who supported a 14-year-old supposed son, but actually a cousin, of Caracalla. This was the notoriously depraved and arrogant Elagabalus (AD 203–22), who lasted less than four years before being lynched by his own guards, having adopted as his successor his first cousin, Alexander Severus (AD 205–35). That a 16-year-old could take office as emperor and rule for thirteen years with more than moderate success was due partly to the fact that he was a sensible, likeable lad who knew his limitations and was prepared to take advice, and partly to his mother, Julia Mammaea, who recognized who would give the soundest advice. His rule thus qualifies as the only imperial matriarchy in the history of the Roman empire. Indeed, having successfully restored order in the east, where the Sasanid dynasty, successors to the Parthians, had threatened to overrun all the former Persian territories, Alexander took his mother with him on a campaign against the Alamanni in AD 234. The following year they were both set upon and murdered by mutinous soldiers at the fortress town of Mainz.

This was certainly the work of Maximinus (AD 173–238), a giant of a Thracian peasant who had risen through the ranks to become commander of the imperial guard. He now nominated himself as emperor, doubled the pay of the army, and continued the German campaign at its head. In AD 238 no fewer than five emperors died by various means and hands. The senate tired of Maximinus and put up its own candidate,

Gordian, the 80-year-old governor of Africa, who extended the invitation to include also his son, Gordian II. They had hardly had time to pack their bags before the governor of Numidia, who was a supporter of Maximinus, attacked and defeated their soldiers. Gordian II was killed in the battle; his father committed suicide. Shortly afterwards, Maximinus invaded Italy, but was murdered by members of his own army. The senate had in the meantime deified the Gordians and replaced them with two further candidates of its own, who were in turn killed by the imperial guard in favour of Gordian III, nephew of Gordian II. Though he was only 13, this Gordian, with the help of a capable pair of hands in Furius Timesitheus, enjoyed civil and military success until Timesitheus died of an illness while leading an eastern campaign. Gordian himself was murdered in Mesopotamia in AD 244 while innocently collecting wild animals to take part in his triumphal procession in Rome for the victories in Persia.

While during the ensuing twenty-six years, thirty-four emperors, pretenders, and usurpers, came and, usually violently, went, the hostile peoples outside the frontiers gathered themselves for the kill. In Germany, the Goths, Franks, and Alamanni established the permanent threat to the Roman empire which ultimately led to its annihilation. In AD 259 the Persians even managed by treachery to capture the emperor, Valerian, who spent the rest of his life very uncomfortably in their hands. He was used as a human mounting-block to assist the Persian king onto his horse, and, when he died, his skin was stripped off to serve as a permanent symbol of Roman submission. His son Gallienus, who had been joint ruler, carried on alone until in AD 268 he too fell to the more usual method, murder by his staff. Some Christian writers suggested that Valerian's fate was punishment for his edicts against Christianity; certainly these were reversed by Gallienus, who appears to have made a peace with the Christians which lasted some years.

The threat of the empire being overrun from several directions at once was temporarily averted by Aurelian (AD 214–75), commander-in-chief of all Roman cavalry, who was in AD 270 proclaimed emperor by his troops while campaigning against the Goths. In addition to evacuating the Roman garrisons in Dacia north of the Danube, which he abandoned as a province, he defeated the Alamanni, who on this, their fourth invasion of Italy, had got as far as Ariminum. He also dealt with two dangerous outbreaks of separatism. At the time of Gallienus, numerous petty emperors had surfaced in various parts of the empire. Some were readily disposed of; others were simply murdered by their own troops. In Gaul, however, Gaius Latinius Postumus had established an independent state, with its own senate. In AD 268 the local soldiery murdered Postumus, and then his three successors. The senate of Gaul now appointed Gaius Pius Tetricus as ruler, in which capacity he remained for three years until he surrendered to Aurelian's army.

The dominion of Gaul was at an end, but in the meantime the influential city of Palmyra, under its formidable regent, Zenobia, was threatening Roman rule throughout the east. Attacks into Egypt and Asia Minor as far as the Bosporus were repelled, and Aurelian, after negotiating 100 miles of desert with his troops, destroyed Palmyra itself. Zenobia was brought back to Rome to walk, with Tetricus, in Aurelian's triumph. Both were allowed to live: Zenobia with a generous pension, and Tetricus with a responsible job in local government in Italy. It was also Aurelian who built the great defensive wall round Rome itself. Murdered by his own staff, he earned the epitaph, 'He was loved by the people of Rome, and feared by the senate' (*Historia Augusta: Aurelian*, L). The dreadful game of musical thrones continued after him, until AD 284, when yet another commander of the imperial guard, Diocles (AD 245–313), a Dalmatian of obscure and humble origin, emerged from the crush of contenders to be proclaimed emperor by the troops.

PARTIAL RECOVERY: DIOCLETIAN AND CONSTANTINE AD 284–337

One aspect of the problem was not so much that the empire was falling apart, but that it had always consisted of two parts. Much of the region which comprised Macedonia and Cyrenaica and the lands to the east was Greek, or had been Hellenized before being occupied by Rome. The western part of the empire had received from Rome its first taste of a common culture and language overlaid on a society which was predominantly Celtic in origin. Diocles, who now called himself Gaius Aurelius Valerius Diocletianus (Diocletian), was an organizer. In AD 286 he split the empire into east and west, and appointed a Dalmatian colleague, Maximian (d. AD 310), to rule the west and Africa. A further division of responsibilities followed in AD 293. Diocletian and Maximian remained senior emperors, with the title of Augustus, but Galerius, Diocletian's son-in-law, and Constantius (surnamed Chlorus, the 'Pale') were made deputy emperors with the title of Caesar. Galerius was given authority over the Danube provinces and Dalmatia, while Constantius took over Britain, Gaul, and Spain. Significantly, Diocletian retained all his eastern provinces and set up his regional headquarters at Nicomedia in Bithynia, where he held court with all the outward show of an eastern potentate, complete with regal trappings and elaborate ceremonial. The establishment of an imperial executive team had less to do with delegation than with the need to exercise closer supervision over all parts of the empire, and thus to lessen the chances of rebellion. There had already been trouble in the north, where in AD 286 the commander of the combined naval and military forces at Boulogne, Aurelius Carausius, to avoid execution for embezzling stolen property, proclaimed himself an emperor, set himself up as ruler of Britain, and even issued his own coins. This outbreak of *lèse-majesté* was not finally obliterated until AD 296.

FIGURE 47   The tetrarchs: (left) Diocletian and Maximian, (behind) Constantius and Galerius. Porphyry sculpture of AD 305, Piazza san Marco, Venice.

Source: Photograph © copyright Allan T. Kohl/Art Images for College Teaching (AICT)

Diocletian ruled for twenty-one years, during which he only visited Rome once, in AD 303, the year of his formal edict against Christianity. On 1 May AD 305, after a health failure, he took the unprecedented step of announcing from Nicomedia that he had abdicated, and offered Maximian no choice but to do the same. While his reign had been outwardly peaceful, the years of turmoil had left their mark on the administration of the empire and on its financial situation. Diocletian reorganized the provinces and Italy into 116 smaller units, each governed by a *rector* or *praeses*, which were then grouped into twelve *dioceses* under a *vicarius* responsible to the appropriate emperor. He strengthened the army (while at the same time purging it of Christians), and introduced new policies for the supply of arms and provisions.

Diocletian's monetary reforms were equally wide-ranging, but though the new tax system he introduced was workable, if not always equitable, his bill in AD 301 to curb inflation by establishing maximum prices, wages, and freight charges fell into disuse, its effect having been that goods simply disappeared from the market. Its interest today lies in its comparisons, even though or because these are much as one would expect. Ordinary wine was twice the price of beer, while named vintages were almost four times as much as *vin ordinaire*. Pork mince cost half as much again as beef mince, and about the same as prime sea fish. River fish were cheaper. A pint of fresh quality olive oil was more expensive than the same amount of vintage wine; there was a cheaper oil as well. Fattened goose was prohibitive; ten dormice cost about as much as one chicken. A carpenter could expect twice the wages of a farm labourer or a sewer cleaner, all with meals included. A teacher of shorthand or arithmetic might earn half as much again per pupil as a primary-school teacher; grammar-school teachers earned four times as much as primary-school teachers, and teachers of rhetoric five times as much. Baths' attendants, who guarded the clothes of bathers, and barbers were all paid the same rate per customer.

Somehow assured or confident of his own safety, Diocletian had built for his retirement a palace near Salona, on the coast of his native Dalmatia, round the ruins of which stands the modern town of Split. Here he lived on until his death in AD 313, doing nothing more active than gardening and studying philosophy, while refusing to take sides when the system of government he had devised almost immediately foundered. When he retired, Diocletian had promoted Galerius and Constantius to the posts of Augustus, and appointed two new Caesars. The troubles broke out when Constantius, while campaigning against the Picts, died at York in AD 306, and his troops proclaimed his son Constantine as their leader. Encouraged by this development, Maxentius, son of Maximian, had himself set up as emperor and took control of Italy and Africa, whereupon his father came out of his involuntary retirement and insisted on having back his former imperial command. The situation degenerated into chaos. At one point in AD 308 there seem to have been six men styling themselves Augustus, whereas Diocletian's system allowed for only two. Galerius died in AD 311,

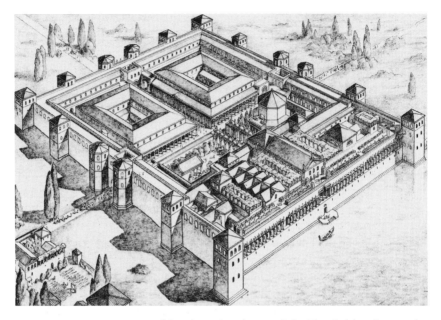

FIGURE 48 Reconstruction of Diocletian's palace at Split. The Golden Gate in the north wall (top left) opened onto a colonnaded street, on one side of which was accommodation for the staff, and on the other quarters for the imperial guard. Across the transverse street linking the west and east gates was a further colonnade leading to the domed entrance to the palace, with its throne room and private apartments. On either side of the colonnade was an elaborate courtyard, containing to the west the temple of Aesculapius, and to the east the great domed mausoleum of Diocletian. It has been estimated that the palace, which covered an area of nearly 8 acres, housed about 3,200 people.

Source: Richard Leacroft

having on his deathbed revoked Diocletian's anti-Christian edicts. Matters were not fully resolved until AD 324, when Constantine defeated and executed his last surviving rival. The empire once again had a single ruler, and against all the odds he lasted some years yet.

Constantine was born in Naissus in Upper Moesia in about AD 272, his father subsequently being forced to divorce his mother (a former barmaid) and marry Maximian's daughter. His appellation the 'Great' is justified on two counts. Under Diocletian especially, Christians had had a terrible time. In AD 313, while the struggle for imperial power was at its height, Constantine initiated the Edict of Milan – Milan, not Rome, was now the administrative centre of the government of Italy – which gave Christians (and others) freedom of worship and exemption from any religious ceremonial. It is said that before the battle of the Milvian Bridge in AD 312, at which he enticed Maxentius to abandon his safe position behind the Aurelian Wall and then drove most of his army into the Tiber, Constantine had dreamed of the sign of Christ. Thereafter, though he was not actually baptized until just before his death in AD 337, he regarded himself as a man of the god of the Christians, and can therefore claim to be the first Christian emperor or king. In AD 325 he assembled at Nicaea in Bithynia 318 bishops, each elected by his community, to debate and affirm some principles of their faith. The outcome, known as the Nicene Creed, is now part of the Roman Catholic mass and the Anglican service of communion, and is commonly used by many Protestant denominations. And, in AD 330, he established the seat of government of the Roman empire at Byzantium (which he renamed Constantinople, 'City of Constantine'), thus ensuring that a Roman (but Hellenized and predominantly Christian) empire would survive the inevitable loss of its western part. Its capital stood, until the middle of the fifteenth century, as a barrier between the forces of the east and the as yet ill-organized tribes and peoples of Europe, each struggling to find a permanent identity and culture.

To the Jews Constantine was ambivalent: while the Edict of Milan is also known as the Edict of Toleration, Judaism was seen as a rival to Christianity, and among other measures he forbade the conversion of pagans to its practices. In time he became even more uncompromising towards the pagans themselves, enacting a law against divination. He also destroyed temples and confiscated temple lands and treasures, which gave him much-needed funds to fuel his personal extravagances. His reign constituted, however, a series of field days for architects, whom he encouraged to celebrate the religious revolution by reinventing the basilica as a dramatic ecclesiastical edifice.

Constantine was a dynamic military commander. He had a great victory in AD 332 over the Goths, 40,000 of whom enlisted in the Roman army as allies. Two years later he defeated the Sarmatians, 300,000 of whom now settled within the empire. He also developed Diocletian's reforms, and completed the division of the military into two arms: frontier forces, and permanent reserves, who could be sent anywhere at short notice. He changed the system of command so that normally the posts of civil governor and military commander were separate. He disbanded the imperial guard, and established a chief of staff to assume control of all military operations and army discipline; the praetorian prefects (commanders of the imperial guard), who had hitherto held military ranks while also being involved in civil affairs, under him became supreme appeal judges and chief ministers of finance.

FIGURE 49 Constantine, the head from a colossal statue, c. AD 313–15, on display in the courtyard of the Palazzo dei Conservatori, Rome.

Source: Photograph © copyright Allan T. Kohl/Art Images for College Teaching (AICT)

THE FALL OF ROME

Constantine had intended that on his death the rule of the empire should devolve to a team of four: his three sons, Constantine II (*c.* AD 316–40), Constantius II (AD 317–61), and Constans (c. AD 322–50), and his nephew Dalmatius. To form a tetrarchy on a dynastic principle was, however, more than the system could stand. Dalmatius was murdered, the brothers bickered, their armies fought, and the empire was in splinters once again.

The pieces were retrieved after Valentinian (AD 321–75) was nominated as emperor by the troops at Nicaea, on condition that he appoint a joint ruler. What happened next is described by the historian Ammianus Marcellinus, a former soldier, writing some twenty-five years after the event, in his continuation of the histories of Tacitus.

> Now, after Valentinian had been acclaimed emperor in Bithynia, he gave orders that the army should march in two days' time, and called a meeting of his senior officers, as though he intended to seek sound advice rather than follow his own inclinations. When he enquired who would be the best person to be his partner in running the empire, everyone was silent, except Dagalaifus, the master of the cavalry, who answered confidently: 'If you love your family, great emperor, you have a brother; if you love the state, choose someone else to invest with this office.'
>
> Valentinian was not pleased, but made no comment, hiding his thoughts. By a forced march, the army reached Nicomedia on 1 March [AD 364], where he appointed his brother Valens as chief of his personal staff, with the rank of tribune. Then, after arriving at Constantinople, he gave considerable thought to the matter. Having concluded that he was already overwhelmed by the amount of urgent business and that there should be no further delay, on 28 March he publicly presented Valens on the outskirts of the city and proclaimed him Augustus. There was universal acceptance of the appointment – no-one dared oppose it.
>
> **(*History*, XXVI. 4)**

Valentinian and Valens (*c.* AD 328–78) made an amicable east–west division. The empire was briefly, if only technically, united again in AD 394 under Theodosius I (*c.* AD 346–95), the 'Great'. He was a Christian who had been baptized in AD 380, and it was he who effectively made Christianity the official religion of the empire by sanctioning the destruction of the great cult temple of Serapis in Alexandria, and by passing measures prohibiting pagan practices. It was also he who revenged the lynching of one of his army commanders by inviting the citizens of Thessalonica to a show at the circus and then massacring them in their seats, a lapse for which the archbishop of Milan persuaded him to do public penance. Under his sons, Arcadius (*c.* AD 378–408) and Honorius (AD 384–423), the eastern and western parts of the Roman empire finally each went its own way.

At some point in the fourth century AD a fierce nomadic people known as the Huns set out inexorably westwards from their homelands on the plains of central Asia, triggering off similar and equally destructive movements on the part of the tribes in their way. They displaced the Alani who lived mainly between the rivers Dnieper and Dniester, and who then displaced the Vandals from their territories between the Vistula and the Rhine, who in turn swept right through Gaul and Spain, and down into north Africa. Also displaced in the orgy of migration were the Ostrogoths (Bright Goths) and Visigoths (Wise Goths), who bordered on the Roman empire immediately on the other side of the lower Danube, and had in various guises fought implacably with Rome before. Britain was now abandoned to the determined waves of Picts, Scots, and Saxons who had threatened to overwhelm the land, and its legions were rushed to the final defence, no longer of the empire, but of Rome itself.

In AD 410 Rome was captured and sacked by Alaric the Visigoth (d. AD 411), after he had only the previous year accepted a bribe to go away. Though Pope Leo I, who reigned AD 440–61, managed in AD 452 to negotiate terms with Attila the Hun (c. AD 406–53) to leave Italy after he had ravaged much of it, in AD 455 it was the turn of the Vandals: Rome was sacked once more, this time from the sea.

The final act of the ongoing drama was played out in AD 475–6. The Roman empire in the west was to all intents and purposes now Italy, and its proud armies reduced to a mixed bag of Germanic mercenaries. Orestes, formerly secretary to Attila the Hun, was appointed military commander-in-chief by Julius Nepos, who, at the instigation of Leo I, emperor of the east AD 457–74, had been sent to Italy to take up the vacant position of emperor of the west. Orestes responded by marching his troops on Ravenna, to which Honorius had transferred the imperial court in AD 404. Nepos fled, and Orestes, having apparently waited in vain for some official authorization from the east, nominated his 14-year-old son Romulus emperor in the west, with himself as supreme head of internal and external affairs. The crunch came when he refused to honour requests for land grants from the mercenaries, such as had been granted to their predecessors in the service of the empire. They turned to their commander, Odoacer (d. AD 493), who agreed to meet their demands if they would recognize him as their king.

In AD 476, Odoacer, feeling that an emperor was now surplus to requirements, captured and killed Orestes, and deposed Romulus, who was now known as Romulus Augustulus. Odoacer then informed Zeno, emperor in the east AD 474–91, that he would be happy to rule as king of Italy under Zeno's jurisdiction. Effectively, the Roman empire in the west was at an end. The Roman Catholic Church now assumed the role of unifying the lands and peoples which had formerly been Roman, organizing its sphere of influence along Roman lines.

For truly catastrophic disasters, there is rarely a single cause. Civilizations less stable or well organized than Rome have survived inert autocracy, economic failure, political and administrative incompetence, chronic internal disunities, plague, class barriers, corruption in high places, decline of moral standards, and the necessity of radically changing the structure and status of the workforce. Ultimately, what hastened the end was the failure of the very instrument by which the empire had been founded, the Roman army. The policy of dividing it into frontier forces and mobile field forces which could be dispatched to trouble spots had its disadvantages. However effective communications might be, the infantry had to march to its destination – in training, recruits were required to march 20 miles in five hours, but that would be about the most that an army could travel on foot in a day. The creation of more mobile armies simply meant that each one was weaker, at a time when heavy losses had been incurred in the civil wars in which prospective emperors engaged and in fighting off the invasions of Italy and of Gaul.

The eastern Roman empire, largely by reason of its geographical situation, was bypassed by the ant-like hordes of invaders. It was, in any case, less vulnerable to outside attack than the west, and its internal political stability was greater. Between AD 364 and 476, there were sixteen emperors in the west, and only eight in the east, and those figures do not take into account usurpers who did not make it to the top, of which there were only two in the east during that time.

Byzantium, capital of the eastern empire, had first been reconstructed in the time of Septimius Severus not just as a Roman city, but modelled on Rome itself, on and around seven hills. The building of a racecourse on the lines of the Circus Maximus where there was insufficient space for it, was not beyond the skill and ingenuity of the architects. It was constructed on the flattened summit of a hill, with one end of the stadium suspended over the edge on massive vaulted supports. Eastern influence led to the development of a distinctive style of Byzantine architecture, with the dome the predominant feature, and interiors richly decorated. In AD 532, during the rule of Justinian, much of the city was destroyed during what is known as the Nika rebellion, which began as a riot between two sets of fans, the Blues and Greens, in the stadium, and developed into a full-scale revolt against his authority. The rebellion was, with difficulty, quelled, but the damage caused enabled Justinian to exploit his own hobby of building, at a time when the golden age of Byzantine architecture had just been reached. Among four major new churches was the sensational Hagia Sophia, designed by Anthemius, the main dome of which was built, unusually, on a square base and was replaced in AD 555 by one with forty arched windows around its circumference. Hagia Sophia survives; it became a mosque in 1453, but since 1935 has been a museum.

Justinian ruled from AD 527 to 565, and is said to have been 83 when he died. He was born in Illyricum, the son of a Slavonic peasant, and was appointed joint emperor in AD 527 by his uncle Justin, who died a few months later, having risen through the ranks of the army to be emperor, still, it was alleged, unable to read or write. He had not, however, spared the education of his nephew, whose ambitious aims included stamping out corruption in government, refining and upholding the law, uniting the churches in the east, and taking Christianity forcibly to the barbarians in the west, thus recovering for the empire territories that it had lost. In pursuit of this last aim, his skilled generals Narses, formerly employed as an imperial eunuch, and Belisarius tore into the barbarian kingdoms and restored to the empire, though only temporarily, its former African provinces and northern Italy, including the city of Rome itself. At the same time Justinian himself recaptured southern Spain while that region was in the throes of a civil war.

Before becoming emperor, Justinian had committed the solecism of marrying an actress called Theodora. Until her death in AD 548, however, she proved an admirable foil and a supportive wife, on the one hand standing up for persecuted members of the heretical Monophysite sect whose views she supported, and on the other comforting and encouraging her husband at times of stress, notably during the Nika rebellion. While the eastern empire was largely Greek in its mores, it still upheld Roman law. The Justinian Code (AD 528–9) brought together all valid imperial laws. In addition he issued a revised and up-to-date 'Digest' (AD 530–3) of the works of the classical jurists, and a textbook on Roman law (AD 533). He is also credited with introducing into Europe the culture of the silk-worm.

After Justinian, the eastern empire was Roman only in name. In 1053 the Church of the east split with the Church of Rome and in due course begat the Church of Russia. On 29 May 1453, Constantinople and its emperor Constantine XI fell to the Turks and the forces of Islam, who had already overrun what remained of the empire's narrow footholds along the coast of the Sea of Marmara.

THE LEGACY OF ROME

The remarkable thing about the civilization of Rome is not that it ultimately collapsed, but that from such minute beginnings it survived for so long under so many external and internal pressures. It lasted long enough and the pressures were resisted firmly enough for so many of what were Roman practices or traditions, even before the Christian era, to become entrenched in modern life.

Except for the addition of three letters, the alphabet used today for the English language, as well as for the Romance languages (French, Italian, Spanish, Portuguese, and Romanian), German, Scandinavian, and other European languages, is that which the Romans developed and refined for their own language. Further, the Romance languages themselves are firmly based on Latin, as is one-third of the English

FIGURE 50 The inscription on this first-century or early second-century AD sepulchral chest in the form of a house reads: 'Marcus Junius Hamillus, freedman of Marcus, for himself and his dearest wife, Junia Pieris'. The lettering is of an informal kind, reflecting the style of advertisements or public announcements painted on walls with a brush. The basic Latin alphabet consisted of twenty-one characters: Y and Z were added in later times for the spelling of words borrowed from the Greek; J, U, and W were introduced in the Middle Ages.

Source: British Museum

language. The success of Latin as the foundation of so much of modern language is not just due to the fact that it was possible to use it eloquently for the expression of literary forms – and without a close acquaintance with Latin literature on the part of writers in other languages, there would be virtually no English or European literature before about 1800 – but that it could be employed so precisely to express points of law, science, theology, philosophy, architecture, agriculture, and medicine.

As such it was the language of scholarship, and prose, in western Europe during the Middle Ages and the Renaissance; it is the language of the Roman Catholic Church; and it survives intact within the English language in the form of many tags, phrases, and abbreviations. While it was not in the Romans' nature, or necessarily in their interest, to invent startling labour-saving devices, their systematic attitude to measurement enabled them to establish the basis of a calendar which has never been improved upon (see Appendix 1, p. 207), and to devise methods to assess distances with great accuracy. They turned building into a science and gave a new impetus to hydraulics. The contribution of Roman law to European law is incalculable, and from the Romans come the traditions of impartial justice and trial by jury. Banking, insurance, public hospitals, the postal system, the daily newspaper, the fire service, motorways (and motorway hotels), public libraries, central heating, glass windows, apartment blocks, sanitation, drainage and sewers, social benefits, and public education are all Roman institutions. So is that universal common bond and basis of social life throughout the modern world, which they called *familia*, and we recognize as the family, the extended family, or the family unit.

FURTHER READING

Bennett, J., *Trajan: Optimus Princeps*, Routledge, 1997.

Birley, A.R., *Hadrian: The Restless Emperor*, Routledge, new edn 2000.

Birley, A.R., *Marcus Aurelius: A Biography*, Routledge, new edn 2000.

Birley, A.R., *Septimius Severus: The African Emperor*, Routledge, 1999.

Jenkyns, R. (ed.), *The Legacy of Rome: A New Appraisal*, Oxford University Press, 1992.

Meijer, F., *Emperors Don't Die in Bed*, Routledge, 2004.

Pohlsander, H.A., *Emperor Constantine*, Routledge, 2004.

Rousseau, P. (ed.), *A Companion to Late Antiquity*, Blackwell, 2008.

Ward-Perkins, B., *The Fall of Rome: And the End of Civilization*, Oxford University Press, 2005.

Appendix 1

THE ROMAN CALENDAR

The reformed calendar which Julius Caesar instituted in 46 BC, on the advice of the Peripatetic Alexandrian philosopher and astronomer Sosigenes, enabled the traditional agricultural year, based on the circuit of the earth round the sun, to be reconciled with the duration of a complete revolution of the moon round the earth. His year of 365 days (366 every fourth year) consisted of seven months of 31 days, four of 30 days, and one of 28 days (29 every fourth year). A slight, and temporary, adjustment had to be made in the time of Augustus when it was discovered that the *pontifices* had misinterpreted the instructions and had decreed a leap year every three years instead of four. The year was still actually 11 minutes 14 seconds too long, which it remained until Pope Gregory XIII in the sixteenth century corrected the error and adjusted the incidence of the leap year so that it does not fall on the opening year of a new century unless that year is divisible by 400. Thus the year 2000 was a leap year; 2100 will not be.

Each month was divided into three parts by three special days: *kalendae* (the calends) always fell on the first day of the month; *idus* (the ides) signified the notional day of the full moon, and was the 15th day of March, May, July, and October – the months of 31 days – and the 13th of all the rest; *nonae* (the nones) occurred on the 9th day before the ides in each case, including in the calculation the day at each end of the period. Thus the nones of March was 7 March, that is the 9th day before the ides. A date was always reckoned according to the number of days it fell before the next special day, both that day and the special day being included in the calculation. Thus 16 March was known as the 'the 17th day before the calends of April'.

Certain days were given over to religious and other festivals and celebrations, almost all of which took place on dates of an uneven number, which were regarded as being lucky. Other days were designated *fasti*, indicating that civil and judicial business could be conducted; *comitiales*, on which a meeting of an assembly could be held; and *nefasti*, on which neither could take place. The Romans worked an eight-day week, the eighth day by our reckoning, the ninth by theirs, being known as *nundinae*; it was the day on which traditionally the farmers downed tools and went to market.

The Roman day was divided into twelve hours of equal length, from sunrise to sunset, and likewise during the night. Thus the length of an hour, and the hour itself, varied according to the season of the year. The ninth hour of the day gave its name to Nones, a church service held at about 1500 hours; at some point in the Middle Ages this was brought forward to the sixth hour, that is about 1200. The name Nones persisted, however, and gave the word 'noon' its meaning of the middle of the day. So when we speak of a.m., we mean *ante meridiem* (before the middle of the day); p.m. is *post meridiem* (after the middle of the day). Sundials or water-clocks, or a combination of both, were employed to tell the hour.

Appendix 2

ROMAN NUMERALS

The basic symbols by which all Roman numerals were and still are expressed are:

I = 1   (a single digit)

V = 5   (a graphic possibly representing five fingers or four upright strokes crossed by a diagonal line)

X = 10   (the fingers of two hands joined)

L = 50   (adapted from a Chalcidic sign)

C = 100   (adapted from a Chalcidic sign; it is also the first letter of the word for a hundred, *centum*)

D = 500   (half the Chalcidic sign ⋒, which represented a thousand)

M = 1,000   (the first letter of the word for a thousand, *mille* – not used separately as a numeral before the second century AD)

Numbers other than these were expressed by adding symbols after the higher numeral, e.g. VI = 6, XII = 12, CLXI = 161; or by subtracting those that preceded the higher numeral, e.g. IV = 4, XL = 40; or by a combination of both processes, e.g. XLI = 41, CDXIII = 413. In medieval times and beyond, dates were represented by Roman numerals, e.g. MCCCLXII = 1362. The year 1998 was MCMXCVIII, 2008 is MMVIII.

Towards the end of the republic, thousands were denoted by a line above the numeral, e.g. $\overline{V}$ = 5,000, $\overline{IX}$ = 9,000. Hundreds of thousands were denoted by additional lines on each side, e.g. $|\overline{V}|$ = 500,000, $|\overline{X}|$ = 1,000,000.

Calculating was done with the help of an abacus, or by a complex counting system involving the use of the fingers, finger-joints, and thumbs of both hands.

Appendix 3

HISTORICAL TIMELINE

The origins of Rome

(Most of these dates are approximate)
3100–2686   Early dynastic period in Egypt.
3000–1400   Minoan civilization in Crete.
1400–1200   Mycenean civilization in Greece.
1250   Israelite settlements in Canaan.
1220   Destruction of Troy.
1152   Traditional date of founding of Alba Longa.
1000–750   Phoenician expansion overseas.
1000   Latins settle in Latium.
814   Traditional date of founding of Carthage.
775   Euboean Greeks establish trading post in Bay of Naples.
753   Traditional date of founding of Rome.
753–510   Period of the kings in Rome.
750   Greek alphabet, based on a Phoenician version of the Canaanite alphabet, begins to be used.
650   Etruscans occupy Latium.
616–578   Tarquinius Priscus.
578–534   Servius Tullius.
534–510   Tarquinius Superbus.
510   Ejection of kings.
505   Final defeat of Etruscans.

The republic

509 Establishment of the republic. First consuls.

496 Romans defeat Latins at Lake Regillus.

451/450 The Twelve Tables.

390 Gauls sack Rome, but withdraw in return for ransom.

338 Latin league of states dissolved.

335–323 Campaigns of Alexander the Great, king of Macedon.

327–290 Samnite wars.

321 Disaster at Caudine Forks.

283 Final capitulation of Etruscans.

280–275 Pyrrhus leads Greek cities in south of Italy against Rome.

265 Rome now holds all Italy south of river Arno.

264–241 First Punic War.

241 Western Sicily becomes first Roman province.

239–237 Rome annexes Corsica and Sardinia.

227 All Sicily and Sardinia with Corsica become provinces.

218–202 Second Punic War.

218 Hannibal invades Italy.

216 Hannibal defeats Romans at Cannae.

202 Battle of Zama.

197 Spain annexed and divided into two provinces.

191 Rome completes conquest of Cisalpine Gaul.

184 Cato elected censor, having been consul in 195. Death of the playwright
      Plautus.

169 Death of Ennius, father of Latin poetry.

167 End of third war against Macedonia, which is divided into four self-governing
      regions.

167–160 Maccabaean revolt in Judaea.

153 Roman year begins on 1 January.

149–146 Third Punic War.

146 Destruction of Carthage. Province of Africa established.

133 Tiberius Gracchus is tribune of the people. Pergamum bequeathed to Rome and
      in 129 becomes the province of Asia.

123–122 Gaius Gracchus is tribune of the people.

121 Transalpine Gaul becomes a province.

107 First consulship of Marius.

102–101 Marius defeats Teutones and Cimbri.

100 Sixth consulship of Marius.

91–88 Social War between Rome and Italian allies.

88 First consulship of Sulla. Having marched on Rome, he departs for the east, where Mithridates has massacred Roman citizens.

87 Marius and Cinna capture Rome.

86 Seventh consulship of Marius, who dies 13 January.

83 Sulla lands in Italy, and is joined by Crassus and Pompey.

82–80 Sulla is dictator. Proscriptions and constitutional reforms.

78 Death of Sulla. The beginning of the end of the republic.

Transition

74 Bithynia and Cyrenaica become provinces.

73–71 Slave revolt of Spartacus.

70 First consulship of Pompey and Crassus.

67 Pompey crushes the pirates.

66–63 Pompey defeats Mithridates and reorganizes the region.

63 Consulship of Cicero. Conspiracy of Catiline. Caesar is elected *pontifex maximus*.

60 'First Triumvirate' of Caesar, Crassus, Pompey.

59 First consulship of Caesar.

58–50 Caesar's Gallic wars. The whole of Gaul becomes part of the empire.

c. 55 Death of the poet Lucretius.

55–54 Caesar's invasions of Britain.

52 Pompey appointed sole consul.

49 Pompey authorized to deal with Caesar, who crosses the Rubicon, signifying that he comes as an invader. Pompey leaves for Greece. Caesar is dictator for eleven days.

48 Caesar defeats Pompey at Pharsalus.

48–47 Caesar in Egypt. Local war in Alexandria.

47 Caesar defeats Pharnaces at Zela.

46 Caesar is appointed dictator for ten years. His wide-ranging legislation includes reform of the calendar.

45 Final defeat of Pompeians in Spain. Caesar returns to Rome.

44 Assassination of Caesar.

43 First consulship of Octavian. Formation of second triumvirate: Octavian, Antony, Lepidus. Proscriptions, in which Cicero dies.

42 Caesar is officially deified. Brutus and Cassius are defeated at Philippi. Cisalpine Gaul incorporated into Italy.

31–23 Successive consulships of Octavian/Augustus.

31 Battle of Actium.

30 Antony and Cleopatra commit suicide. Egypt is annexed.

28 Octavian awarded the title of *princeps*.
27 Octavian renounces his special powers; he accepts the provinces of Spain, Gaul, and Syria for ten years, and assumes the name of Augustus. Agrippa builds the original Pantheon.

The empire: Julio-Claudians and Flavians

23 Augustus is awarded full tribunician powers for life, with extended *imperium*.
19 Death of Virgil.
 9 Dedication of *Ara Pacis*.
 8 Death of the poet Horace.

AD

 4 Augustus adopts Tiberius, who is granted tribunician powers for ten years.
 9 Varian disaster.
13 Augustus' control of his provinces renewed for a further ten years.
14 Census enumerates 5 million Roman citizens. Death and deification of Augustus.
17 Death of the historian Livy.
18 Death, in banishment, of the poet Ovid.
31 From Capri, Tiberius denounces Sejanus, on whom the senate pronounces the death sentence.
33 Probable date of the crucifixion of Jesus of Nazareth under Roman law.
41 Assassination of Caligula. Claudius becomes emperor.
43 Invasion of Britain, part of which becomes a province.
44 Achaea and Macedonia become subject to the senate. Judaea reverts to being a province.
46 Achaea is annexed.
47 Aulus Plautius celebrates a triumph for his success in Britain, the last time a subject is so honoured.
48 Claudius registers about 7 million citizens of Rome, and opens the way for more provincials to be senators.
61 Revolt in Britain of Boudica.
64 Great fire of Rome.
66–74 First Jewish War.
69 Year of the four emperors.
74 Vespasian confers Latin rights on all parts of Spain.
78–84 Agricola is governor of Britain.

79 Eruption of Vesuvius.
80 Fire in Rome. Opening of Colosseum.
96 Assassination of Domitian. Nerva is elected by the senate to succeed him.

The 'Five Good Emperors'

97 Nerva adopts Trajan as co-ruler and successor.
101 Trajan invades Dacia, which is finally annexed in 106.
104 Death of the poet Martial.
113 Dedication of Trajan's column.
114–16 Trajan conquers Mesopotamia.
c. 117 Death of the historian Tacitus.
117 Accession of Hadrian. Roman empire is at its greatest extent.
122 Hadrian in Britain.
c. 126 Rebuilding of Pantheon in its present form.
132–5 Second Jewish War.
139 Accession of Antoninus.
c. 140 Death of the poet Juvenal.
142–3 Building of Antonine Wall in northern Britain.
161 Accession of Marcus Aurelius.
161–6 Parthian wars, followed by plague.
167 Barbarian invasions across the Danube.
178 Further risings of Marcomanni and other tribes.
180 Accession of Commodus.

Gradual disintegration

192 Murder of Commodus brings the Antonine dynasty to an end.
193 Septimius Severus proclaimed emperor and marches on Rome.
194 Severus defeats Pescennius Niger and campaigns in Mesopotamia.
195 Severus defeats Clodius Albinus and departs for a second Parthian war.
203 Erection of Arch of Severus in the Forum.
208 The imperial family leaves for Britain.
211 Severus dies at York.
212 Caracalla has his brother Geta murdered. All free inhabitants of the empire are now entitled to Roman citizenship.
224 The Sasanid dynasty succeeds the Parthians.
226 The *Aqua Alexandrina*, the last of Rome's eleven significant aqueducts, is operative.

235 Assassination of Alexander Severus and his mother.

238 Year of six emperors.

242–3 Roman victories over Goths and Persians.

250 Widespread persecution of Christians by Decius.

251 Gothic invasions of the empire.

257 Edict of Valerian against the Christians.

259–74 *Imperium Galliarum*, breakaway state of Gaul.

260 First edict of toleration for Christians.

270 Aurelian proclaimed emperor while campaigning against the Goths.

270–3 Revolt of Zenobia.

271 Aurelian defeats Vandals and Alamanni, and begins Aurelian wall and defences of other cities.

275 Assassination of Aurelian while on his way to fight the Persians.

283 Carus, having been proclaimed emperor the previous year, subdues the Quadi and Sarmatians, but dies suddenly on his way to fight the Persians.

Diocletian and Constantine

284 On the death of Carus' son, Diocles, cavalry commander of the imperial guard and suffect consul 283, is proclaimed emperor and changes his name to Diocletian.

286 Maximian is promoted to Augustus, with responsibility for the west. Carausius declares himself ruler of Britain and part of northern Gaul.

287–90 Diocletian campaigns on the Danube and in the east.

293 Galerius and Constantius appointed Caesars. Murder of Carausius by Allectus.

296 Constantius defeats and kills Allectus.

c. 297 Diocletian begins dividing the provinces into smaller units.

303 Edict against the Christians. Diocletian visits Rome for the only time.

305 Abdication of Diocletian and Maximian. Galerius and Constantius are Augusti.

306 Death of Constantius at York.

308 Galerius appoints Licinius as Augustus.

309/10 Constantine and Maximinus, who is Galerius' nephew and adopted son, are recognized by Galerius as Augusti.

312 Vision of Constantine. He becomes sole ruler of the western empire.

313 Death of Diocletian. Edict of Milan, ending persecution of Christians.

315 Erection of Arch of Constantine.

322–3 Victories of Constantine over Sarmatians and Goths.

324 Victory over, and execution of, Licinius makes Constantine sole ruler of the empire.

325 Council of Nicaea; formation of Nicene Creed.
330 Dedication of new capital city, Constantinople.
332 Great victory over Goths.
334 Victories over Sarmatians.
337 Baptism and death of Constantine. Constantine II, Constantius II, and Constans recognized as Augusti.

The fall of Rome

340 Constans defeats and kills Constantine II.
350 Constans is replaced in a coup by Magnentius, and then murdered.
353 Suicide of Magnentius, who was defeated by Constantius in 351, sparks off official reprisals in Britain against his supporters.
c. 356 Alliance between Picts and Celtic Dál Riata (later known as Scots).
361 Constantius dies in Cilicia while marching to oppose Julian, who has been declared Augustus by his troops. Julian enters Constantinople as emperor, having publicly declared his paganism.
363 Julian dies of wounds. Jovian is declared emperor.
364 Death of Jovian. Valentinian elected emperor. He chooses his brother Valens to rule the east.
368–74 German wars.
375 Death of Valentinian.
378 Death of Valens.
379 Theodosius I, supreme commander against the Goths, succeeds Valens.
388 Maximus, who has had to be recognized by Theodosius as Augustus over Britain, Gaul, Spain, and Africa, is defeated and executed. The ruler of the western empire is once again Valentinian II (d. 392), son of Valentinian.
391 Theodosius passes measures banning paganism.
395 Death of Theodosius. His elder son Arcadius is emperor in the east, and his younger son Honorius emperor in the west. The division of the empire is now permanent.
396 Augustine becomes bishop of Hippo.
401 Alaric the Visigoth invades Italy.
404 Honorius transfers his court to Ravenna.
406 Germanic tribes cross the frozen Rhine.
408 Death of Arcadius, who is succeeded by his son Theodosius II.
410 Alaric sacks Rome. Rescript of Honorius, allegedly informing the inhabitants of Britain that they must organize their own defence against the Saxons.
418 Honorius grants Visigoths federate status in Gaul.

423   Death of Honorius.

429–38   Publication of Theodosian Code of laws.

439   Vandals now occupy most of north Africa, Suevi north-west Spain, and Visigoths, Burgundians, Alans, and Franks almost all of Gaul.

440–61   Leo I is pope.

450   Death of Theodosius II.

451   Attila the Hun invades Gaul, but is defeated for the only time.

452   Attila invades Italy, but withdraws under persuasion from Pope Leo.

455   Vandals sack Rome from the sea.

476   Romulus Augustulus (aged 14), is deposed by Odoacer, his Germanic mercenary commander, who informs Zeno, emperor in the east, that he will rule under his sovereignty. Establishment of a Gothic kingdom in Italy, and the end of the Roman empire in the west.

527   Justinian succeeds his uncle as emperor in the east.

528–9   Code of Justinian.

530–3   Digest of Justinian.

532   Nika revolt in Constantinople.

532–7   Building of Hagia Sophia.

559   Justinian's retired general Belisarius delivers Constantinople from the Huns.

565   Death of Justinian.

622   Traditional date for the founding of Islam.

760   Foundation of Turkish empire.

1053   Split between Church of Rome and the Church in the east.

1453   Fall of Constantinople to Mehmed II and the Turks. End of the eastern Roman empire.

Appendix 4

LITERATURE TIMELINE

BC

753   Traditional date of founding of Rome.

c. 750–c. 725   Iliad and *Odyssey* of Homer, Greek epic poet.

c. 700   Works and Days of Greek epic poet Hesiod.

c. 630   Birth of Greek lyric poet Sappho.

c. 620   Birth of Greek lyric poet Alcaeus.

c. 580   Birth of Greek philosopher and mathematician Pythagoras.

c. 560   Final editing, in Babylon, of the Pentateuch and the books of Joshua, Judges, Samuel, and Kings of the Hebrew Bible.

525/4–456/5   Aeschylus, Greek writer of tragedies.

c. 518   Birth of Greek lyric poet Pindar.

496/5–406   Sophocles, Greek writer of tragedies.

c. 485–406   Euripides, Greek writer of tragedies.

c. 480–*c.* 425   Herodotus, Greek historian.

469–399   Socrates, Greek philosopher.

c. 465–*c.* 386   Aristophanes, Greek writer of comedies.

c. 460–*c.* 400   Thucydides, Greek historian.

c. 430–*c.* 355   Xenophon, Greek historian.

c. 429–347   Plato, Greek philosopher.

384–322   Aristotle, Greek philosopher and critic.

342–*c.* 292   Menander, Greek writer of comedies.

341–270   Epicurus, Greek philosopher.

c. 300   *Elements*, by Euclid, Greek mathematician.

c. 287–212/11   Archimedes, Greek mathematician and inventor.

c. 285–*c.* 215   Apollonius Rhodius, Greek epic poet.

c. 270   Theocritus, Greek pastoral poet, writing.

c. 260   In Alexandria, the Septuagint, first translation into Greek of the Biblical
          Pentateuch.

254–184   Plautus, writer of comedies.

240–207   Livius Andronicus writing plays and verse in Latin.

239–169   Ennius, writer of tragedies in verse.

234–149   Cato the 'Censor', historian and general writer.

c. 215   Fabius Pictor, first Roman historian, writing in Greek.

c. 200–*c.* 118   Polybius, Roman historian who wrote in Greek.

c. 185–159   Terence, writer of comedies.

116–27   Varro, scholar and critic.

106–43   Cicero, orator and letter writer.

100–44   Julius Caesar, military historian.

c. 99–*c.* 55   Lucretius, poet and philosopher.

86–35   Sallust, historian.

c. 84–54   Catullus, lyric poet.

c. 70–8   Maecenas, patron of literature.

70–19   Virgil, epic and pastoral poet.

65–8   Horace, lyric poet.

59–AD 17   Livy, historian.

c. 50–*c.* 15   Propertius, elegiac poet.

43–AD 18   Ovid, elegiac and narrative poet.

c. 40   Vitruvius writing treatise on architecture.

4–AD 65   Seneca the 'Younger', philosopher and scientist.

AD

23–79   Pliny the 'Elder', historian and scientist.

37–*c.* 100   Josephus, Jewish historian who wrote in Aramaic and Greek.

39–65   Lucan, epic poet.

c. 40–*c.* 104   Martial, writer of verse epigrams and satire.

c. 46–*c.* 120   Plutarch, Roman historian and biographer who wrote in Greek.

c. 55–*c.* 140   Juvenal, writer of verse satire.

c. 56–after 117   Tacitus, historian and biographer.

c. 61– *c.* 112   Pliny the 'Younger', letter writer.

66   Death of Petronius, author of *Satyricon*.

c. 70–*c.* 140   Suetonius, biographer.

c. 125   Birth of Apuleius, novelist.

c. 160   Appian, Roman historian, writing in Greek.

c. 165–*c.* 235   Cassius Dio, Roman historian who wrote in Greek.

c. 330–*c.* 395   Ammianus Marcellinus, Roman historian.

Appendix 5

GLOSSARY OF LATIN TERMS IN THE TEXT

aerarium militare: military fund.
amicus (plural *amici*): friend.
aquilifer: (literally eagle-bearer) bearer of the chief standard of a legion.
atrium: hall.

caesura: (literally cutting) break in a line of verse.
candidatus (plural *candidati*): (literally clothed in glittering white) one standing for election to office.
cena: dinner.
centurio primi pili: commander of the first century of the first cohort.
cliens (plural *clientes*): (literally listener) client, follower.
coemptio: form of marriage by pretended purchase.
cohors praetoria: praetorian guard, imperial guard.
cohors urbana: city cohort, city guard.
comitia centuriata: assembly by centuries.
comitia curiata: assembly by wards.
comitia tributa: assembly by tribes.
concilium plebis: meeting of the people.
confarreatio: form of marriage incorporating an offering of bread.
consul suffectus: deputy (or 'substitute') consul.
curia (plural *curiae*): senate house; a tenth part of one of the three original tribes of Rome.
cursus honorum: (literally course (race) of honours) the steps by which a politician moved upwards in seniority from post to post.

decemvir (plural *decemviri*): one of a committee of ten.

devotio: act of self-sacrifice.
dilectus: (literally choosing) an army recruitment operation.
diocesis: division.
divi filius: son of a god.
domus: house, home.

eques (plural *equites*): horseman, knight.

familia: family, household.
fasces: bundle (of rods and an axe), carried before officers of state; it was the badge of Mussolini's party in Italy, hence the name fascists.
flamen (plural *flamines*): priest of a particular god.
flamen dialis: priest of Jupiter.
frumentum: grain, military rations.

genius: birth-giving spirit.
gens: tribe, clan.
gravitas: dignity, integrity.

honestiores: citizens of honourable circumstances.
humiliores: citizens of humble circumstances.

imaginifer: image-bearer.
immunis (plural *immunes*): exempt (from normal duties).
imperator: commander (the title conferred by his troops on a victorious general); emperor.
imperium: command, power.
impluvium: basin for collecting rain.
indigitamenta: spirits attendant on a deity.
in flagrante delicto or *flagrante delicto*: (literally with the crime blazing) redhanded.

jentaculum: breakfast.

lar (plural *lares*): spirit of the household.
lar familiaris: special household spirit.
larvae: see *lemures*.
latus clavus: broad stripe (on a toga, indicating senatorial rank).
lemures: mischievous spirits of the dead.
levitas: lightness, inconstancy.
liber: written work or division of a work.

libra: Roman pound weight (= 327 g).

limes (plural *limites*): path, line, frontier.

ludi circenses: events in the arena.

ludi scaenici: theatrical events (at the games).

magister (plural *magistri*): magistrate, officer of state.

maiestas: treason.

manes: spirits of the dead.

manus: (literally hand) husband's legal power over his wife.

mille passus or *mille passuum*: 1,000 paces (= 1 Roman mile).

mos maiorum: custom of our ancestors.

municipium (plural *municipia*): town possessing the right of Roman citizenship.

naumachia: sea-fight.

nemus: grove.

nobilitas: nobility, fame, recognition.

novus homo: (literally 'new man') first of his family to achieve high office; upstart.

numen (plural *numina*): divine will, divine power.

omen (plural *omina*): sign, omen.

palla: robe of a woman.

passus: pace (= 5 Roman feet). See also *mille passus*.

pater (plural *patres*): father, senator.

patria potestas: authority of the head of the household, authority of the father.

pecunia: money.

pecus: head of cattle (the original Roman monetary unit).

penates: spirits of the larder.

peristylum: colonnade.

pietas: duty, devotion, loyalty.

plebiscita: decree of the people.

plebs urbana: city plebs.

pontifex (plural *pontifices*): priest.

pontifex maximus: chief priest.

praefectus castrorum: camp prefect, camp commander.

praeses: chairman.

prandium: lunch.

princeps: first, chief.

pro consule: proconsul; provincial governor after his term of office as consul.

pro praetore: propraetor; provincial governor after his term of office as praetor.

prorogatio: prorogation, extension of a period of office.
provocatio: challenge, appeal.

quindecimvir: member of a committee of fifteen.

rector: supervisor.
respublica: state, commonwealth.
retiarius: gladiator armed with a trident and net.
rex sacrorum: king of religious rites.
rumor: unauthenticated report.

senatus consultum: decree of the senate.
senatus consultum ultimum: extreme decree of the senate.
socius (plural *socii*): ally.
spina: (literally spine) wall dividing the race-track.

tablinum: multi-purpose room.
terminus: boundary stone.
toga praetexta: robe of a child.
toga virilis: robe of a man. See also *latus clavus*.
tribunus laticlavius: senior military tribune, entitled to wear a broad purple stripe on
    his tunic. See *latus clavus*.
tribunus plebis: tribune of the people.

usus: (literally use) practice, custom.

vestibulum: entrance-hall.
vicarius: deputy (to an emperor).
victimarius: attendant at a sacrifice, slaughterer.
vigiles: watchmen, night-guards.
villa: country house.
virtus: manliness, strength, worth.
volumen: roll, volume.

Further reading

GENERAL INTRODUCTIONS

Alföldy, G., *A Social History of Rome*, Routledge, 1988.

Beard, M. and Henderson, J., *Classics: A Very Short Introduction*, Oxford University Press, 2000.

Boardman, J., Griffin, J. and Murray, O. (eds), *The Oxford History of the Roman World*, Oxford University Press, new edn 2001.

Boatwright, M.T., Gargola, D.J. and Talbert, R.J.A., *A Brief History of the Romans*, Oxford University Press, 2006.

Garnsey, P. and Saller, R., *The Roman Empire: Economy, Society and Culture*, University of California Press, 1987.

Goodman, M., *The Roman World, 44 BC–AD 180*, Routledge, 1997.

Huskinson, J. (ed.), *Experiencing Rome: Culture, Identity and Power in the Roman Empire*, Routledge, 2000.

Jones, P. and Sidwell, K. (eds), *The World of Rome: An Introduction to Roman Culture*, Cambridge University Press, 1997.

Kelly, C., *The Roman Empire: A Very Short Introduction*, Oxford University Press, 2006.

Lane Fox, R., *The Classical World: An Epic History from Homer to Hadrian*, Penguin, 2005.

Le Glay, M., *A History of Rome*, Blackwell, 3rd edn 2004.

Mackay, C.S., *Ancient Rome: A Military and Political History*, Cambridge University Press, 2005.

Wacher, J. (ed.), *The Roman World*, Routledge, reissue 2001.

Wells, C., *The Roman Empire*, Fontana, 2nd edn 1992; Harvard University Press, 2nd edn 1995.

Woolf, G., *The Cambridge Illustrated History of the Roman World*, Cambridge University Press, 2003.

USEFUL WORKS OF REFERENCE

Bispham, E., Harrison, T. and Sparkes, B. (eds), *The Edinburgh Companion to Ancient Greece and Rome*, Edinburgh University Press, 2006.

Erskine, A. (ed.), *A Companion to Ancient History*, Blackwell, 2009.

Hazel, J., *Who's Who in the Roman World*, Routledge, new edn 2002.

Hornblower, S. and Spawforth, A. (eds), *The Oxford Classical Dictionary*, Oxford University Press, 3rd edn revised 2003.

Scarre, C., *The Penguin Historical Atlas of Ancient Rome*, Penguin, 1995.

Shipley, G. et al., *The Cambridge Dictionary of Classical Civilization*, Cambridge University Press, 2006.

INDEX

All Latin words are indexed. Names are listed in their most usually recognizable form. *Indicates a quotation. Italic figures refer to the caption to an illustration. Bold figures indicate a main item.